The New York State Soldiers Home

By Robert E. Yott

Copyright © 2006 Robert E. Yott

Copies of this work are strictly prohibited without the written consent of the author.

ISBN: 9798866982806

For my daughter, Marissa

CONTENTS

1) 1863-1879: Bath Carries Off the Prize...............2
2) 1879-1889: The Making of a Home...............46
3) 1890-1899: Such a Lovely Place...............104
4) 1900-1909: The Population Peaks...............140
5) 1910-1919: The Decline...............170
6) 1920-1929: The End of an Era...............199
7) 1930-1954: The VA Takes Control...............217
8) 1955-1979: Another Crisis Averted...............230
9) 1979-Present: The Legacy Continues...............242
10) Investigations...............256
11) Profiles...............171
12) Superintendents - Directors...............281

ACKNOWLEDGMENTS

Countless hours of research were spent in an attempt to bring the history of the New York State Soldiers' and Sailors' Home to light. Missing annual reports, conflicting newspaper articles, and indifference were but a few challenges to overcome.

Today, the Bath VAMC places high on the list of caregiving facilities in the nation. However, had not been for our predecessors' determination and fortitude, we would not be here today. This was a story which needed to be told. But it could not be told without the help of others.

Ed Presley shared with me his vast historical and architectural knowledge. Danny Wheeler of Ithaca allowed me access to his private library. The dedicated volunteers Steuben County Historical Society (Magee House) were very supportive of this endeavor. Sharing the Magee House is the County Historian, Twila O'Dell, a most pleasant person who enjoyed surprising me with rare finds.

The photo of Captain James T. Brady was courtesy of the Brady family, the photo of Robert F. Kennedy was provided by the Hoffman. Jim Desrosiers offered his collection of Centerpieces. The photo of Warren Oxx was courtesy of Helen Brink. Rick Small offered some amazing photos and Mona Lawton-Yott lent her high-speed keyboarding skills. Thanks to Al "Ski" Yezarski for opening doors.

To Denis Oliver, thank you. And my very dear friend, Sis Conrad has been very supported of my work from the very start. Thanks Sis, you're the best! To the Grand Army of the Republic, we owe a debt which we can never repay.

BATH CARRIES OFF THE PRIZE
1863 - 1879

As the Civil War entered its third year, it became apparent that no end was in the immediate future. By early April of 1863, the casualty list of the northern army had risen to over 101,000 dead, wounded and missing. Obviously, the war was not going well for the North and no immediate end was in sight. It was during this time that ex-Governor Edwin Morgan, whose term as governor just expired, observed many veterans returning to New York disabled, unemployable, and homeless.

Morgan, a veteran himself, had seen the need to establish a refuge for the victims of this American tragedy. With the aid of eighty co-incorporators, Morgan pushed the issue until the State Legislators passed an act to incorporate a State Soldiers' Home on April 24, 1863. This was a full two years before one of the last acts signed by Abraham Lincoln incorporating a National Asylum for disabled volunteer soldiers and sailors of the Civil War.

Large contributions and pledges were made by ex-Governor Morgan and others. However, after a State Board of Trustees canvassed the area, they found that patriotism was running so high in the North that the very thought of returning veterans being turned out into the street or housed in asylums and poorhouses was absurd.

Families and friends of the veterans were reluctant to having them committed to an asylum, a stigma that was not befitting to the returning soldiers. So, due to the lack of public interest, the idea of a soldiers' home was abandoned.

It was not until 1872 that the issue was brought up again. Through the personal effort of Major-General Henry A. Barnum, Commander of the Grand Army of the Republic, Department of New York (G.A.R.) the Legislature passed an act incorporating The New York State Soldiers' Home. Ironically, no funds were appropriated for the project.

Throughout 1873 and 1874 more attempts made by the G.A.R. for appropriations had failed. It had repeatedly sent committees to the Legislature asking for funding. Finally, in one last effort, Captain Edward C. Parkinson of Brooklyn, Department Inspector, made the recommendation to appeal directly to the public. Captain Parkinson called on leading citizens from Brooklyn, procuring $100 subscriptions, to be paid only when the goal of $10,000 had been reached.

On January 4, 1875, The Honorable John F. Henry, brevetted "Comrade" of the G.A.R., was one of the first to subscribe, along with John B. Norris, A. S. Barnes, B. B. Hagerty, C. P. Dixon, Wm B. Kingsley, J. S. T. Stranahan and Philip S. Crooke.

At the ninth annual G.A.R. encampment held in Rochester on January 20 and 21, 1875, Captain Parkinson recommended that a committee of 15 members be chosen to consider the feasibility of a soldiers' home. The appointed members were Captain Parkinson, General Henry W. Slocum of Brooklyn, General William Findlay Rogers of Buffalo, John Palmer of Albany, L. W. Fiske of Boonesville, Edmund L. Cole of Troy, John B. Murray, General Stewart L. Woodford, George H. Sharpe, E. Jardine, T. J. Quinn, M. S. Hicks, E. J. Loomis, B. A. Willis, and James E. Curtis. These men were to report their findings at the next semi-annual encampment.

The New York State Soldiers Home

When the committee reconvened at the following meeting, they reported that the citizens of Penn Yan and vicinity had made an offer of 188 acres of land lying on Lake Keuka. However, for reasons unknown, no positive action was taken and the offer was not accepted. (This land would be offered again a year later.)

The G.A.R. was not discouraged however and on November 29, 1875, another meeting was held in Sawyer's Hall in Brooklyn regarding the matter. Ex-soldiers and sailors of Kings County sat in while Captain A.H. Doty, Secretary of the Committee of Organization, read the minutes of the previous meeting. (Captain S.H. Mildenberg, upon a motion by Captain Parkinson, had been appointed chairman of the committee.)

After considering that appropriate steps were not being taken, the committee adopted the following resolution that at the next annual encampment, the G.A.R. should "...appoint a suitable committee, with the full power to organize a corporation, under the general laws of New York, to be called the Soldiers' Home, whose duty it shall be to immediately organize, adopt and pursue all necessary measures for the establishment of a Soldiers' Home, for the relief of indigent and invalid soldiers and sailors of the State of New York."

Once adopted, it was resolved to have statement prepared and presented to the encampment in Albany in January of 1876. The contents of the address were for all being in favor of the soldiers' home. Tasked with drafting the letter were James (Corporal) Tanner, of Brooklyn, Captain Parkinson, Colonel E.B Fowler, Captain R.H. Chittenden, Captain F.R. Jaschke, Captain Doty, Captain Judson A. Lewis of Brooklyn, Captain Mildenberg, Colonel James McLeer, Brevet Lieutenant Colonel James L. Farley, Captain L.H. Rowan and General Stewart L. Woodford of New York City.

By December, the draft was complete. Not only did it endorse a soldiers' home, but it also suggested that the encampment "...provide for an active committee-one fully alive to the necessities of the case-composed not only of representative soldiers and sailors, but also of some of those charitable and large hearted friends who were not active in the late struggle, but whose sentiments and sympathies are and have in the past been responsive to the wants of our comrades, and concludes with the assurance that in case proper action is taken, friends in Brooklyn will contribute $10,000 as their share towards the liquidation of the debt owing to the men who risked their all in defense of their country."

The article continued on stating that it was a painful fact that the veterans who had earned the privilege of a "Home" had to leave the boundaries of New York to do so. The draft concluded by bringing to light that "...it is with a view of righting this wrong, and providing an asylum which shall be non-political and non-sectarian that this action is urged."

The tenth annual encampment was held in Albany on January 25 and 26, 1876. After routine business, Corporal Tanner, acting on behalf of the delegation from Brooklyn, pleaded their case. He then pledged $10,000 which would be Brooklyn's share toward the building of the Soldiers' Home.

A motion was then made to form another fifteen-member committee, known as the State Committee on Soldiers' Home. Only four of the original fifteen members, Captain Parkinson, General Rogers, L. W. Fiske and Edmund L. Cole would remain on the list. They were joined by The Honorable Seymour Dexter of Elmira, Frank H. Shepard of Utica, Major Judson A. Lewis, M. F. Sheppard of Penn Yan, R. L. Fox of Oneonta, Captain Albert H. Nash of Geneva, J. H. Curtis, E. B. Green, General Benjamin F. Finley of New York City, William Bullard, and C. R. Becker. This committee was given the power to add six additional members and had full power to act as they deemed necessary in establishing the soldiers' home.

The committee convened at once with Captain Parkinson as chairman. The Honorable Seymour Dexter, Willard Bullard and R.L. Fox were appointed to a subcommittee on organization and planning, while a locating committee consisting of Corporal Tanner, (newly elected department commander and chairman of the committee), Captain E. C. Parkinson, Frank H. Shepard of Utica, General Wm. F. Rogers, Captain Eugene B. Gere of Owego and Benjamin F. Finley. The Honorable Seymour Dexter drafted the bill of incorporation. Next, it was presented in Assembly by The Honorable Eugene Gere and then taken charge of in the Senate by The Honorable Bradford L. Prince of Queens County.

The act was duly passed on May 15, 1876, and signed by Governor Samuel L. Tilden. Thus, in the ninety-ninth Session, under Chapter 270, the Grand Army of the Republic Soldiers' Home of the State of New York was incorporated. By the terms of the bill, the committee, along with the Governor and Comptroller of the State, the Commander of the Dept. of N.Y., G.A.R., and the six additional members appointed would form the first Board of Trustees.

During this time, no time had been wasted securing funds for the enormous project which lay ahead. An invitation had been made out to the Reverend Henry Ward Beecher of Plymouth Church in Brooklyn. Endorse by Commander Tanner and Captains Parkinson and Lewis, a detailed plan for the proposed soldiers' home, what had been done and a heartfelt plea for his assistance was forwarded to the Reverend Beecher. The committee was asking for one night of the famous orator's time and skills in which he may appeal to the public.

The response dated April 15, 1876, was a resounding yes. The reverend would "cheerfully comply" to any of their wishes, leaving the arrangements to the committee. The event was to be held at the Academy of Music in Brooklyn. Presided over by Commander Tanner, the Reverend Beecher delivered a powerful speech to a sold-out audience; the hall filled to its capacity of 2,200. Over $14,000 had been raised in just 35 minutes. New York City soon followed suit, donating an additional $10,000, while large amounts flowed in from other parts of the state. The word was getting out and grateful, patriotic citizens began answering the call, generously donating to the cause. After a four-year struggle, the New York State Soldiers' Home was becoming a reality.

At a meeting at Department Headquarters, located at Room 139 of the Trinity Building, 111 Broadway, New York, on June 1, 1876, six additional members were appointed as follows: Major Judson A. Lewis, John F. Henry and Henry W. Sage, both of Brooklyn, Henry W. Bellows of New York City, Chas. G. Craft of Albany, Farley Holmes of Penn Yan and Frederick Davis Jr. of Watkins. The board was then duly organized by the election of Captain Parkinson, President; Major Lewis, Secretary; and John F. Henry, Treasurer.

The first order of business was to recognize and assign duties of the Organization and Planning Committee and the Location Committee. The location committee's charge was to give notice to all places in the state that were interested in offering inducements for the site of the home. All proposals were to be received no later than July 10, 1876, and then reviewed by the committee at a special meeting held at Elmira on that same day.

On June 9, 1876, a notice appeared in the *Farmers' Advocate* that a Soldiers' Home would be located in the upstate region of the New York. Penn Yan proposed Lake Keuka as the best possible location for the soldiers' home. Roat's Point, located on the eastern shore of the lake, was 8.5 miles north of Hammondsport and favored by Hammondsport, Wayne and Pulteney. Brandy Bay was located 3 miles south of Penn Yan and favored by that town. The exact site would be determined later if and when the soldiers' home was located on the lake.

The article appealed to the villages of Bath and Hammondsport for support, as Elmira and Watkins had already made proposals for the location of the soldiers' home. On June 21, an article appeared in the *Steuben Courier* stating that Bath had no interest in a soldiers' home and heartily endorsed the location of Lake Keuka.

One month later, on Friday, July 7, 1876 Hanford Struble, Esq., of Penn Yan, spoke at the Nichols House in Bath, asking the citizens for support of Penn Yan's endeavor to secure the soldiers' home on Lake Keuka. The crowd reacted enthusiastically and promised to contribute to such a noble cause.

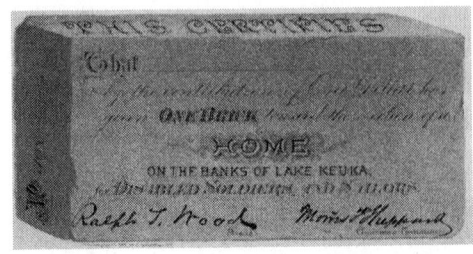

A committee was formed at once, consisting of Messrs. Ira Davenport, William Rumsey, John F. Little, Abram Beekeman, and H. B. Williams to solicit contributions for the soldiers' home on the lake. By Saturday, nearly $2,000 was raised; however, while talking to the citizens, the fund-raisers discovered that many more would be willing to contribute to the cause if the soldiers' home should be built in Bath.

A second meeting was called for that night and a proposal was made to offer Bath as a proposed site. Another committee was formed, consisting of Messrs. Wm. B. Ruggles, Joseph S. Dolson, Jonathon Robie, Colonel Archie E. Baxter, and J. F. Parkhurst. These men canvassed the immediate area and received in a short time an incredible $20,000 in pledges. Bath was now in the game.

On Wednesday, July 12, 1876, the day was reported as warm and calm. The lake was placid as The Yates, a steamer owned and operated by Captain Allen Wood, arrived with the Locating Committee at Grove Spring. Committee members were met by delegates and prominent citizens of Penn Yan, Bath and Hammondsport. Because Roat's Point had no docking facilities, the party traveled by land to inspect the site. After inspecting every feature of the proposed sites, the committee expressed a very positive view of the locale as being suitable for the soldiers' home.

The Steamer Yates

Upon returning to Grove Spring, the party partook of a delicious meal, followed by toasts and speeches. The context of the speeches was said to be all favoring the site most recently visited.

Around 3 p.m., the party boarded the steamer again and embarked for the Urbana Wine vaults. Here they spent time sightseeing and wine tasting until they departed for Hammondsport, arriving at 5 p.m. The party loaded onto Captain Wood's narrow-gauge railcars and after a brief stop at the Pleasant Valley Wine Co., they headed for Bath. Arriving at the depot, the committee was met by a large crowd. Several handsome carriages were there, waiting to escort them to the proposed location of the Soldiers' Home.

So elegant was the entourage that, as they made their way down Liberty Street through the excited crowd, little Davey Wiley of Bath was heard to exclaim "Jim ...who's dead?" The committee was put up in the Nichols House where throughout the evening many residents stopped in to pay their respect.

The following day, the committee left for Elmira. There they would meet with the Board of Trustees at the Rathbun House to disclose their findings. After briefing the seventeen members present, the board adjourned the meeting until the following morning at 9 o'clock. All proposed bids were to be submitted by 10 o'clock, no later.

Thursday night in Bath was a festive evening. Bands were parading about the streets, bringing folks to the park. An impromptu meeting was organized and ex-mayor Reuben Robie appeared on the balcony of the Bath National Bank and gave a short but direct speech, firing up the crowd. Other village notables made other speeches and the crowd, seized by the moment, pledged an additional $2,013.

On Friday morning, the large parlor room of the Rathbun House held the local Locating Committees from the prospective towns, which were anxiously waiting to give their proposals. Other interested parties were also present when, at 10 o'clock, the sealed bids were opened and read by Commander Tanner.

Elmira was the first to be announced. Its inducement was 50 acres of land and $25,000 in cash. Penn Yan offered 188 acres on Lake Keuka and $5,000, Watkins offered 200 acres and $5,000 and Bath offered 220 acres and $6,000 in cash.

Beginning in alphabetical order, Bath, Elmira, Penn Yan and Lake Keuka, and Watkins would all have fifteen minutes to make their proposals. Colonel William Rumsey, representing Bath, spoke on the virtues of that village. He also made mention of the Davenport Institute for Orphaned Girls, where the daughters of soldiers would be well cared for until the age of eighteen, or until they could go to friends or be placed in reliable families.

Seymour Dexter spoke on behalf of Elmira, stressing the contributions Elmira had made during the war effort, its central location and easy access by rail. Captain Allen Wood and Mr. Farley Holmes gave argument for Penn Yan and Lake Keuka. Watkins, situated on Seneca Lake, was represented by Mr. D. J. Sunderland and supported by Mr. Frederick Davis Jr.

After hearing the presentations, Commander Tanner gave to the board the report of the locating committee. In his report, the young corporal told the committee that all personal feelings were put aside in the matter and that after four days of hard and patient labor all locations had been visited. He went on to say that, while the claims made by Elmira and Watkins were munificent, they would be put aside; however, the committee was divided on Lake Keuka and Bath. The majority in favor of Bath included Commander Tanner, Rogers, Parkinson and Shepard. In favor of Lake Keuka were Gere and Finley.

Upon receiving the report the board, adopted by unanimous decision a resolution to visit the sites one last time before the final vote should be taken. Agreeing to reconvene in Watkins the following day at 2 p.m., the board proceeded at once to Bath.

Upon arriving at Bath, the board climbed into waiting carriages, which drove them out to the Rider Farm. There the grounds underwent another full and thorough investigation. Next, Captain Wood again provided a special train of cars that took the board to Hammondsport. Farley Holmes provided a steamer, which took the delegation to the Grove Spring. Due to the hour, board members stayed at the Grove Spring House and departed early the next morning for Roat's Point. After a careful examination of this location, they again boarded the steamer and headed for Brandy Bay to examine that site.

From Penn Yan the Board headed by rail for Watkins, accompanied by a large delegation of representatives. There, they clambered aboard yet another steamer and, in full view of the site of the Watkins location, sailed past. Arriving at the Lake View House, the Board took a hurried dinner and immediately went into session.

Beginning the session was an informal ballot with the following results: Bath, 8; Roat's Point, 3; Lake Keuka, 3; Brandy Bay, 2; Watkins, 1

The formal ballot resulted in: Bath, 8; Lake Keuka, 8; Blank, 1.

A second formal ballot was taken to break the tie, resulting as: Bath, 9; Lake Keuka, 6; Watkins, 1; Elmira, 1.

Bath, having received the majority, was declared the location for the soldiers' home. The Honorable Seymour Dexter, as Counsel of the Board, drew up a contract binding the People of Bath to the Board of Trustees and vice versa. The contract, which located the proposed soldiers' home on the Rider Farm in Bath, also stated "...the title to said farm shall be transferred by September 1, 1876, and when erection of proposed buildings shall commence, the sum of $6,000 shall be paid."

The contract having been accepted, it was then signed by Wm. B. Ruggles, Jonathon Robie, A. E. Baxter, L. D. Hodgman, William Rumsey, and Ira Davenport and dated July 15, 1876. The meeting was then adjourned.

Businessmen and locals gathered at the Bath telegraph office awaiting the decision. At 4:00 p.m., the following message was received: To W. E. Howell and Committee:

"We have had a devil of a fight, and won. Vote-Bath 9, Keuka 7, Watkins 1. Will be home by 10 P. M., overland. Hold down the Fort, for we are coming. JONATHON ROBIE, A. E. BAXTER"

A second telegram followed, stating that Commander Tanner, Captain Parkinson, L. W. Fiske, and Major Lewis would also accompany the returning committee to Bath.

Postmaster Joseph S. Dolson rode down Liberty Street announcing the good news. It was reported that the entire population of Bath and the surrounding communities turned out en masse for a celebration to be held that night. Pulteney Square was illuminated. Lookouts had been placed on the roads of their expected arrivals, waiting to give notice. A large bonfire had been prepared, artillery placed in position and a number of bands alerted to perform. The park and streets were packed but still no arrival. The celebration continued until 12:30 a.m. when crowd began to thin lightly but many would still "hold the fort."

At a little past one in the morning, the committee members arrived in town. Cheer after cheer went up, and church bells began ringing. The bonfire was stoked anew and the crowd quickly swelled to its former size. The committee was awed by such a reception. The crowd called for Commander Tanner to make a speech. Even after five hours of travel from

Watkins, the ever-popular corporal rose to the occasion. He gave an "earnest and thrilling" speech, which was interrupted several times by loud applause and cheers.

Next came Rumsey's turn to speak, followed by Baxter, Parkinson, Little, Fiske, Lewis, Ira Davenport and others. It had been a long and busy week and by three in the morning, the crowd began dispersing. The heroes of the evening were driven to various residences for the sleep that they so desperately needed. It was said to be the largest celebration in Bath since General Lee's surrender eleven years earlier.

On July 18, 1876, Major Lewis, Secretary of the Board of Trustees, took the opportunity to express in the *Elmira Advertiser* their heartfelt thanks to the generous and patriotic citizens of Elmira, Watkins, Penn Yan and Bath for the openhearted manner in which they treated the board from the beginning of the campaign to the end. He also disclosed that a resolution was unanimously adopted at the July 14th session in Watkins, stating that the Board of Trustees tendered to Mr. Farley Holmes and the good people of Penn Yan their grateful acknowledgement for the zeal and enthusiasm shown the Board of Trustees on behalf of the Soldiers' Home.

An article in an Elmira paper dated July 21, 1876, was captioned "Bath Carries Off the Prize" and it was not long before Bath began receiving criticism. Articles by the *Penn Yan Democrat* and *Yates County Chronicle* criticized Bath as a "... side show of frog ponds, mosquitoes and fogs," isolated by hills where the rattlesnakes live. The *Steuben Courier* rebutted, mentioning that the beautiful lake that the *Democrat* boasted of would not be as inviting to the amputees who would enjoy their swims and skating.

The *Brooklyn Daily Argus* gave the following description of the soldiers' home's new location. The site purchased for the home was the former W.W. McKay farm, now owned by the Rider family. The 220 acre farm, about evenly divided between fine fertile farmland and rolling wooded upland, cost the town

$16,000. The farm, nestled between the Conhocton River and steep hills to the southwest, and the Rochester Branch of the Erie railroad to the north, was an exceptional choice because of proximity to transportation and an unlimited supply of water from springs on the property.

View of Bath West to East A. Russell 1859

The Locating Committee probably took into account the crops they saw growing during their visit there. Grass, wheat, barley, oats and corn and an apple orchard were said to be of a superior quality. An ever-flowing spring, located about one hundred and fifty yards above the site of the proposed buildings was capable enough to sustain a 3' pipe.

Because the farm was on a gentle slope, drainage would be optimal. A private drive, running parallel to the river was shaded by 400 young sugar maples. Two good houses and numerous outbuildings in good repair existed on the grounds. Everything taken into account, the soldiers' home was assured of being self-supporting.

On August 18, 1876, the Town of Bath purchased the Rider Farm for $16,000 and in turn deeded it to the G.A.R. on September 1, 1876.

At 1 p.m. on Tuesday, September 25, 1876, Captain Parkinson, President of the Board of Trustees, called a meeting to order at the Nichols House. After transacting routine business, the board and committee members worked together as a whole, drafting the by-laws and clearly defining the duties of president, secretary, treasurer and counsel of the board.

The Committee on Organization and Planning then

made their report. They informed the board that they had enlisted the aid of Mr. John Y. Cuyler, the Superintendent of the Brooklyn Parks. Mr. Cuyler was hired as chief engineer and landscape architect. Cuyler had met with the committee previously at the Rider Farm and critically examined the entire area with reference to the location of the buildings and lay out of the grounds. Taking advantage of the wooded hillside and private drive lined with large maple trees, Mr. Cuyler came up with a plan for the proposed home.

Mr. Cuyler then drew up a lengthy report, given in great detail, and submitted it to the committee. He gave in his report the pros and cons of the grounds and reasons for his recommendations. Supplied with a colored sketch made by Cuyler, the committee presented their recommendations to the Board. Mr. Cuyler thought in all practicability that three large buildings of Lombard architecture should be built side by side on the northern plateau of the grounds. This would place the buildings between the wooded sloping hill to the west and the shaded lane to the east, offering protection from the elements. Another advantage was it would not disturb the fields, which would be used to support the home.

The two outer buildings would be the east and west barracks. The center or main building would be set back half the distance of the two others and contain the dining hall, kitchen and other necessary rooms connected with such an establishment. The "superstructures" would be three stories tall and built of brick with stone trimming. The barracks would be 125' in length by 30' wide, and the dining hall would be 125' long by 60' wide. A bakery, engine and boiler house would be built in close proximity to the dining hall.

It was also recommended that the dining room proper would be two stories in height and have a more complete architectural finish than the barracks. Mr. Cuyler suspected that these plans would be sufficient to house 500 men. The board accepted the recommendations proposed.

The committee then resolved that work on one or more of the foundations should begin as soon as plans were approved and accepted. This would give the project a head start come the following spring.

The committee also recommended that a Building Committee should be appointed; consisting of the Executive Committee and a local Building Committee made up of three residents of the village of Bath. The board appointed Captain Parkinson, Chairman and Major Lewis, Secretary. Others appointed were L. W. Fiske, Seymour Dexter, General Rogers, John Palmer, and Frederick Davis, Jr. The three residents appointed to the Local Building Committee were David Rumsey, Ira Davenport and Jonathan Robie, Esq. These three men would work hand in hand with the Executive Building Committee and together have full power of the board to go ahead with proposals and the work to follow.

The board next appointed Commander Tanner, Major Lewis, Benjamin F. Finley, Frank H. Shepard, Captain Nash and Captain Parkinson as a Committee on Ways and Means.

On October 9, 1876, the Building Committee met with various architects at the Nichols House to examine submitted plans for the soldiers' home. Among those who submitted plans were I. G. Perry of Binghamton, M. E. Beebe of Buffalo, John Y. Cuyler of Brooklyn, L. J. O'Conner of New York City, W.H. Hamilton of Utica, and A. J. Warner and Cutler of Rochester.

Since none of the plans submitted were entirely satisfactory, further consideration of the plans was postponed until October 26, 1876. At that time, modified plans by Messrs. Warner & Cutler, Cuyler, Beebe and Perry were re-submitted. On November 1, 1876, the plans of Warner & Cutler were unanimously accepted and Mr. Warner was duly employed as architect of the buildings.

No time was wasted. A stone quarry had been opened on the farm in the second week of October. The quarry, said to be far superior to any other quarry in the Conhocton Valley, supplied sufficient stone for all foundations. All the cut stone, excepting the window sills, could be obtained right on the grounds. Sand was also obtainable on the farm.

Teams became busy drawing stones for the foundation and by November, thirty men were at work. The cutting of stone would continue as long as the weather permitted. A course, half a mile in length, was laid out for the water pipe, leading from the reservoir to the buildings. (This ditch probably led to the spring located on Chas. Lang's property, on a hill west of the grounds.)

The local building committee soon put an ad in the local paper for bids on the lumber contract for the three buildings. Dimensions, quantity, and type of lumber to be used were given. The contract was awarded to Mr. Ed J. Armstrong, of Campbell and by January of 1877, large quantities of lumber were being delivered to the Soldiers' Home. Snow on the ground made hauling the lumber much easier for the teams.

In December of 1876, the Board of Trustees bought the Brothers' Mill, consisting of a little over 20 acres located just east of the bridge. This was to insure that businesses involved in liquor sales could not build in too close a proximity to the Home. The cost of the piece was $4,000, bringing the acreage of the Home up to about 241.

At the eleventh department encampment held in New York City on January 25-26, 1877, Commander Tanner spoke once again on behalf of the Soldiers' Home. In his speech, the commander stated that the department would devote most of its time to the project. Thirty-six thousand dollars had thus far been raised by subscription, mainly through the city of Brooklyn and the town of Bath. The material for the three buildings had been contracted for and he presumed that work would begin as soon as spring arrived.

He further stated that $60,000 was needed to complete the buildings and another $100,000 to have them furnished and in running order. Commander Tanner also predicted that the cornerstone would be laid at the semi-annual encampment held in Bath.

Colonel William Rumsey of Bath was elected to the Board of Trustees of the Soldiers' Home. The encampment then passed a resolution instructing the board to send a circular to every member of the clergy in the state, regardless of creed, requesting them to, on a stated Sabbath, preach a sermon on, and take up a collection for the soldiers' home.

The annual meeting of the Board of Trustees of the Soldiers' Home followed. The preliminary study of the Rider Farm, the layout of the home, and colored drawings provided by Mr. Cuyler were on display and attracted the men's attention. Many began reminiscing about their travel to Bath and the sites they visited. After some discussion, the report of the Building Committee was accepted, and the election of officers for the ensuing year took place. Captain Parkinson was nominated for president and was unanimously elected. Major Lewis was unanimously elected to the position of secretary and the Honorable John F. Henry was re-elected treasurer. The Honorable Dexter was re-appointed counsel. President Parkinson then appointed Major Lewis to supervise the erection of the soldiers' home at a salary of $1,500 a year.

On April 2, 1877, Mr. Fred Arnd, who owned a business just off the grounds of the proposed site, moved onto the grounds to keep a boarding house for the workers. The El Dorado House just east of the river was to be used for that purpose. Mr. Arnd also began preparing and filling a large icehouse in which to make ice cream in the summer. There were also six houses on the grounds for let with sixty applicants anxiously waiting to be chosen.

By the end of April 1877, the ground had been broken and the dining hall cellar had a four-foot wall up around all four sides. The work was done under the supervision of Mr. Albert Clark. Mr. Clark had rebuilt the Bath Presbyterian Church, which was dedicated in February of 1877.

The payroll for April was approximately $2,000 for the 100 men employed and veterans enjoyed a preferred status in the hiring process; all of whom took great pride in their work. A layout of the buildings and grounds could be seen at the Bath Bookstore for all who had an interest, which were many.

Work continued at an amazing pace as the money came in. By June 10, 1877, the stone basement had risen to 9' and was ready for brick. The Erie Railroad Company had constructed a spur behind the buildings to save on cartage and the bricks were now being delivered.

As the work progressed, Governor Tilden approved a resolution passed by the Legislature basically stating, that if the completion of the soldiers' home, as well as the cost of the land, did not exceed $100,000, and if it was transferred to the state, free of encumbrances, then the state would make adequate provisions for its maintenance as one of the state's charities.

In May of 1877, Commander Tanner, along with Major Lewis, continued to lead the drive for funds. Circulars were sent to 5,000 clergy of New York State explaining the purpose of building the soldiers' home. In his letter, Commander Tanner explained that 1,561 veterans were fortunate enough to reside in National Homes in Virginia, Maine, Ohio and Wisconsin. Unfortunately, he added, this meant banishment of New York veterans from their home state and their loved ones.

He further stated that, in rewarding these fellow veterans, who had served honorably, by bringing them back to New York, "...their more favored surviving comrades are building a New York Soldiers' Home." Among the signatures endorsing Tanner's letter was Henry Ward Beecher's. The many churches responded selflessly and many donations were made.

On Monday morning, June 11, 1877, the village of Bath began to bustle with activity. The foundation of the main building (dining hall) had been completed and was ready for the cornerstone laying ceremony. The event promised to be no minor affair. At least 300 members of the G.A.R. were expected to attend and the townsfolk opened their doors to honored guests expected for the celebration.

Notices appeared in the *Brooklyn Eagle* advertising the event. A general invitation had been made and arrangements were made with the Erie Railroad to reduce their rates dramatically. A round-trip ticket from New York City to Bath would cost a nominal nine dollars. This included leaving Monday night at 7 o'clock and arriving in Bath at 7:30 the following morning. The train would leave Wednesday evening after the event and arrive back to the city the next morning. A sleeping car would cost extra.

As bands warmed up, the entire village was transformed with patriotic sentiments. Ropes had been stretched across Liberty Street in all direction, from which hung banners, streamers and buntings of all colors. American, English, French and Irish flags were proudly displayed. Nearly every public building and private home was affected by the spirit of the occasion. As one local paper put it "...the whole community gave the event an air of a general holiday."

On Tuesday morning, June 12, 1877, the G.A.R. began their semi-annual encampment. Led by Greisinger's Band, members of the Grand Army of the Republic formed a procession at the Nichols House and marched to Purdy's Opera House, where their opening meeting would be held. There they were met by Captain John F. Little, who called the meeting to order. They were then introduced to John Davenport, Esq., President (Mayor) of the village and brother of Ira Davenport. President Davenport welcomed the members to Bath and extended the hospitality of the community.

After thanking President Davenport, Commander Tanner paid a high compliment to the hospitality of Bath. He went on to say that "...the G.A.R. assembled at this time...as the height of their ambition...were about to be attained...a temple was to be reared which should perpetuate the memory of those who saved the State and Nation from destruction."

After further remarks, Commander Tanner proposed the singing of "Marching Through Georgia," a familiar song of the old comrades in arms. Greisinger's Band played accompaniment. The band then played their medley, which was energetically received. General Wm. F. Rogers, ex-Lieutenant Governor General John C. Robinson of Binghamton, and Colonel Baxter of Bath, were then called upon to make speeches.

When Colonel Baxter's turn came, he proceeded to deliver a stirring and reflective speech of old army life, and the present condition of the disabled and needy soldiers and what this home would mean to them. Colonel Baxter was interrupted continually throughout his speech by applause. In conclusion, he wrapped up his speech with reference to Commander Tanner and how he almost lost his Deputy-Collectorship (tax collector) through his disability but was vindicated. He likened Corporal Tanner's triumph to "...that of General Sheridan in the Shenandoah Valley, how he turned defeat into a glorious triumph." (Tanner had been wounded and both legs amputated in the field during the second Battle of Bull Run.)

Commander Tanner next came forward, visibly shaken by the reception of the remarks and good will of the members. He repeated what an old comrade had told him that previous Sunday, "Let it be distinctly understood that while I am President of the United States, no worthy, competent, disabled soldier shall be removed from office." Three cheers were then given for President Rutherford B. Hayes, author of those words.

The general public then withdrew and the encampment went into executive session at 12:15 p.m. The roll was called with 150 delegates answering the call. Seventy-five posts out of the 106 were represented. Routine business was conducted during the session and it was adjourned at 2:00 p.m.

Later that evening, a brisk thunderstorm passed over, cooling the air and, as quickly as it had appeared, the storm passed. A banquet had been planned for the visiting G.A.R. members and by 9 p.m., the men of the Grand Army and delegates formed up in front of the Nichols House and, led by Greisinger's Band, marched to the agricultural hall at the fairgrounds. (The Opera House was originally chosen for the meal but could not provide adequate space.)

An experienced decorator from New York City had charge of trimming the hall and had hung lines of bunting from the center of the ceiling to the top of the galleries, from which flags had been draped. The ladies of Bath had supplied the flowers, which were placed throughout the hall at the most proper places.

Six long tables were laid out on the ground floor and over 400 places were set for the guests while the ladies and residents looked down from the galleries. The air was lively as the guests feasted on the meal provided by John Messerschmitt.

When the men were fully sated, the toasting began. Coffee was the beverage of the evening, as no liquors or wines had been served. (The Murphy Movement had come to Bath three weeks prior and the town had passed through a rigorous temperance revival. A blue ribbon upon your breast meant you had taken the pledge.) The delegates would give at least seventeen toasts, speeches, and recitals by the time the assembly finally broke up at 1 a.m.

Wednesday, June 13, 1877, began clear and with a gentle breeze. A bugle was heard playing reveille at an early hour, waking those who might still have been stirring in bed. The rain the night before had settled the dust on the roads, making traveling a pleasant experience for visitors to Bath. By 8 a.m. vehicles of all conveyances brought visitors from the countryside into town, gathering at Pulteney Square.

Soon the streets became crowded as trains arrived, bringing in people by the thousands. The Erie and Bath and Hammondsport Railroads were crowded to capacity, even with the extra coaches provided. A special train arrived from Buffalo, carrying a detachment of the famous Linderman Battery and a crowd of people, while another special train came from Corning, carrying even more passengers. The upcoming ceremony drew such a crowd that many streets and area roads were nearly impassable. By noon, the crowd had swelled to well over 11,000 people.

Many of the delegates and distinguished guests went to Hammondsport to visit the wine cellars of the Pleasant Valley Wine Company; returning about noon. It was noted that not one of the guest had removed their blue ribbon which they had donned since arriving at Bath.

A procession was planned to form in Pulteney Square and at 2:00 p.m. head to the soldiers' home. However, due to the crowd it was nearly 3:00 p.m. before the procession was underway. Leading off the procession was Greisinger's Band, Custer Post, No. 81, G.A.R., under command of Comrade Wm. Rumsey. Next in line were white and black veterans, a Detachment of Battery A, 31st Brigade, National Guard New York State, under command of Captain H. W. Linderman, delegates to the department encampment, and other board members, visiting guests and dignitaries, which included Parade Marshall General Sherman S. Rogers and Aide de Camp Colonel John K. Perley.

The cortege proceeded down the highly decorated Liberty Street and then onto Washington Street, which was also adorned in proper decor. The crowd had hindered the procession as it made its way to the soldiers' home. Reverend Henry Ward Beecher and Commander Tanner had advanced to the grounds to await their arrival.

The early arrivals had a chance to tour, inspect and critique the grounds, the foundations for the buildings and other improvements and alterations made. What they saw was the outline of three main buildings, all parallel to one another, the foundations slightly higher than ground level. A temporary floor had been laid across the center foundation, to be used as the speaker's platform. A roof had been constructed and covered with a colorful canopy decorated with bunting, offering protection for the speakers and dignitaries. The cornerstone, which contained a time capsule, had been made ready and conspicuously placed, waiting to be set at the proper moment.

Main Entrance circa 1883

The Erie Railroad accommodated the crowd with a special train made up of five coaches, making trips to the brickyard every 30 minutes. (The brickyard was located where the spur veered off the main line.) Hacks and wagons brought more folks to the grounds while others merely strolled to the site. When the entourage had arrived at the grounds, a detachment of artillery stationed on the rise just west of the platform greeted them with a cannon salute. (This rise would later be the site of the home's cemetery.) The report of the guns excited the crowd almost to frenzy, causing people to rush forward, hoping for a chance to glimpse the men of the hour who had made this moment possible.

Seats had been erected in the front for the crowd and all around the grounds vehicles of all sorts could be seen, containing spectators waiting for the ceremony to begin. The roofs of the various buildings on the grounds gave the curious onlookers a vantage point from which to view the ceremony. The crowd in front of the platform began to press and struggle

The New York State Soldiers Home

under the human weight. It was said that no fewer than 20,000 people had been present at that time.

At least twenty reporters were present representing the press. They came from as far away as New York City, Rochester, Buffalo, Owego and Binghamton. Some of the papers, which ran features, were the *New York Times and Sun*, the *Brooklyn Argus* and the *Brooklyn Eagle*; the *Buffalo Courier*, the *Rochester Democrat*, the *Corning Journal* and the *Corning Independent*, the *Elmira Advertiser* and the *Horseheads Free Press*. Furnished reports of the proceedings by the *Steuben Courier* were also sent to the *New York Tribune* and the *New York Post*. *Leslie's Weekly* also sent a reporter and photographer to cover this momentous event.

Seated upon the northeast corner of the platform were the guest speaker Henry Ward Beecher, Commander Tanner, General Slocum, a Mr. Grady, of New York City, Reverend Henry Hyland Garnett, a "colored divine" of "pure African descent" from New York City, and General John C. Robinson, among other notable dignitaries. At 3:40 p.m., the program began. Captain Parkinson, President of the Board of Trustees, called the immense assemblage to order. The Reverend Thomas Farrell, pastor of St. Joseph's Catholic Church of New York, gave the invocation. Their congregation had donated $217 with an additional $100 from the Rev. Thomas Farrell himself.

Captain Parkinson then introduced the Honorable Sherman S. Rogers, of Buffalo. Rogers made a few remarks, referring to their reasons for assembling that day. He then spoke of the obligation of the State and its responsibility to provide for its disabled soldiers. Rogers also alluded to the fact that the State had thus far neglected its duty in that respect.

In introducing the Reverend Beecher, General Rogers reminded the audience that not only did the North need fighting men carrying muskets during the war; orators and reasoners were needed as well. Beecher, whose half-brother was Thomas K. Beecher (the first clergyman allowed inside the notorious Elmira Civil War prison camp during the war), had convinced the North that the war was a just and necessary war. His efforts at home and abroad aided the war effort and his powerful speeches to a hostile audience in England had helped to keep England out of the war.

Beecher began his speech by telling what the "Great War" achieved. He stated that in other wars of their time nothing had been gained, that things remained the same, as in the Crimean War and the Prusso-Austrian War.

Beecher then explained that principles were won by the North during the late war. He told of how slavery had been allowed to exist when the constitution was formed. He likened this to a tapeworm. He then remarked that by the end of the war, the tapeworm was removed and the Constitution was redeemed when slavery had been abolished.

He concluded his speech by stating that the disabled soldiers laid claim to a home provided by the State for the remainder of their lives.

Next to speak was Commander Tanner. In his brief speech, Corporal Tanner spoke of how difficult it was to follow such a grand speaker but he said, speaking of Beecher, "...as that grand old man has gone to dinner, I will tell you what he has done for the Soldiers' Home." The young corporal then told the crowd of Reverend Beecher's speech at the Academy of Music.

James Tanner

Commander Tanner then spoke of what a great undertaking it had been but he had trusted in the generosity of the public. As for the soldiers' home, he said that those living in poorhouses or in destitution would be asked only three questions before admission: "Were you in the Army or Navy? Were you honorably discharged? Are you needy?"

Always the patriot, Commander Tanner also mentioned in his speech the housing of the colors that had represented the various troops who fought. He exclaimed, "We want an honorable housing to the flags of New York troops, now stored in an engine house in Albany."

At the end of his speech, Albert Smith, the Superintendent of Construction, spread the mortar and Commander Tanner formally laid the cornerstone into place. The Reverend Garnet then offered the benediction, thus ending the ceremony. As a side note, over $1,000 was raised for the soldiers' home fund during the two-day event.

By the second week of September of 1877, the large maples that grew over the private drive were deemed in need of pruning. Visitors felt as if they were walking through a long corridor; the leaf-covered limbs allowed no sunlight to shine through. The committee felt that this subtle change would only enhance the beauty of the grounds. Many of the curious visitors agreed with the change.

The brickwork by now was complete on the three main buildings. The carpenters were busy installing roofing timber and boards for the slaters, who would begin enclosing the structures with slate roofs the following week. The verandahs and outside woodwork were ready to be put up and the carpenters waited for their opportunity to install these. The brickwork on the boiler-house had yet to be completed but it was scheduled to be enclosed by the first of November.

The *Brooklyn Eagle* printed a story on January 13, 1878 relating to the work done by the police force of that city for the benefit of the soldiers' home. Over $3,400 worth of tickets were sold by the men in the precincts for the entertainment given at the Academy of Music to be held the 15th of that month. As an incentive, Captain Parkinson offered $50, $20, and $10 gold pieces to the men who sold the largest number of tickets. The winners of these gold pieces were Officers Miles O'Reilly, Detective Riggs and Officers Reeves, respectively. Out of the 7,800 tickets sold, nearly a third of the purchasers came to hear the lecture, comfortably filling the Academy.

The entertainment planned was a lecture given by General Woodford and Corporal Tanner. Remarks were also made by the Honorable John F. Henry. (General Woodford alluded in his speech that Mr. Henry had, when funds were diminishing, "put his name to his check.")

On January 24, 1878, Senator Davenport introduced a bill into Legislature recommending that the soldiers' home, under the direction of nine trustees appointed by the governor and senate, be transferred as property to the state. This was passed unanimously on February 15, 1878, and was forwarded to the Assembly, where it was approved.

On March 11, 1878, Governor Lucius Robinson signed the bill into law and on April 8, 1878, the Grand Army of the Republic Soldiers' Home of the State of New York was, by deed of conveyance and bill of sale, transferred over to the State and renamed the New York State Soldiers' and Sailors' Home. This, according to the Soldiers' Home report of January 9, 1879, included 241.5 acres of land, two large brick buildings to be used as barracks, and one large brick building for the dining hall, all three storied. There also were a boiler-house, bathhouse and laundry (also built of brick), a good frame dwelling house, four smaller frame houses and some personal property, all at a value of $70,000. The cash turned over was in the amount of $2,406.72.

These figures varied from the formal notification Governor Robinson received from Comptroller Olcott on May 15, 1878, upon the completion of the transfer. According to the *Albany Argus*, the state assumed a mortgage of $12, 409.76 on the property. Cash received amounted to $51,663.26 (according to a letter dated September 1, 1877, Major Lewis, Secretary, recorded $52,272.28 being taken in) and disbursement amounted to $50, 981.42. The total current liabilities, including contracts, came to $12,558.40.

Because of a constant stream of receipts and disbursements and the enormity of the task, the bookkeeping was an arduous and tedious job. However, every examination of the books showed no discrepancies

There was much rejoicing in Steuben County when the transfer was complete and a great amount of credit was given to Senator Davenport for his role in the matter.

The act of transferring the soldiers' home to State control enabled the governor to appoint nine men to form a Board of Trustees to manage the soldiers' home. A piece appeared in the *Brooklyn Eagle* calling for at least one man from that city to be placed on the board. It was a movement, after all which originated in Brooklyn and it only seemed fair that Corporal Tanner or Captain Parkinson should be chosen for such a position. Neither man was chosen however, but both would continue to play a large roll advocating the veteran soldier.

In early May 1878, Governor Robinson nominated nine

men for the trustees' positions to make up the new Board of Trustees. Their task was to complete, manage and care for all matters regarding the soldiers' home. The governor and attorney-general would also act as ex-officio trustees. The first nine nominations were Generals Henry F. Slocum, James McQuade, Isaac F. Quimby, Wm F. Rogers, Nirom M. Crane, Major John F. Little, Byron B. Taggert, Ansel J. McCall and Jonathon Robie.

Although Senator Davenport approved the nominations in the executive session, he also criticized the governor's appointment, alleging that the governor ignored all the men who took an active interest in the soldiers' home when it was falling behind. Davenport claimed that these men were passed over by six Democrats and three Republicans who had no claim to their appointments because of their past service to the soldiers' home.

After the nominations were approved by the Senate, the new Board of Trustees met on May 31, 1878, at the Office of the Secretary of State in Albany. Here, the term of office for each trustee was determined by lot. The selected trustee would hold one-, two- and three-year terms as follows:
One year: General Isaac F. Quimby, General Wm. F. Rogers, Ansel J. McCall.
Two years: General Nirom M. Crane, Major John F. Little, Jonathon Robie.
Three years: General Henry F. Slocum, General McQuade, Byron B. Taggert.

The election of officers followed, resulting in General Slocum's being elected as president. General McQuade was voted in as vice-president, secretary went to Captain Little, and General Crane was made treasurer.

During the winter of '77-'78 construction work slowed due to waning funds. The Board of Trustees turned to the Legislature for aid and on May 18, 1878, Governor Robinson appropriated $82,361 to be used solely for the soldiers' home.

Of this, $13,316 would pay off existing debts, $54,045 would complete and furnish the buildings and the remaining $15,000 would be for support and maintenance for the fiscal year beginning October 1, 1878.

Originally, the board had asked for $30,000 for support but the Senate Committee cut it down to $10,000. Through the efforts of Senator Davenport, however, the appropriation was raised to $15,000. This amount was thought sufficient, considering that it was believed the soldiers' home would not be ready for occupancy by October.

The work was promptly resumed but the workers could not make up for the lost time. The projected completion date would not fall before December; rather, it would fall nearer the date of the annual encampment in January of 1879. General Slocum decided that the encampment should coincide with the official opening. Letters were sent to the various posts and the replies were in favor of the change.

On June 7, 1878, the trustees held another meeting, this time at the soldiers' home. At this meeting, an Auditing Committee and a Grounds Committee had been appointed. Captain Parkinson was appointed General Superintendent of Construction at a rate of $150 a month until the completion of the buildings or the pleasure of the board. He was to report directly to the executive committee.

General Slocum appointed a committee to draft the by-laws governing the board of trustees and fixing the terms of admission to the home.

On July 25, 1878, General Quimby, accompanied by Engineer Thomas J. Rogers, Esq., of Buffalo, set out to locate a site for an upper, or feeder, reservoir. The place they had chosen was in near direct line between a main spring (located on the property of Chas Lang) and the building site. A perpetual lease had to be settled with Mr. Lang and the spring and right of way to it were purchased from him. Lang would be hired to run the farm until October of 1883.

Thomas Rogers, who happened to be the son of General Sherman S. Rogers, was hired to supervise the construction. Civilian and veteran laborers employed by the soldiers' home under Rogers' supervision did the prep work on the reservoir and digging the ditch.

By September 5, 1878, the reservoir was ready for construction and the water pipes installed. James and R. H. Walker, of Elmira were awarded the contract for the laying of the water mains and the setting of fire hydrants, for the sum of $1,860.00. They began to work immediately and on Friday, October 18, 1878, the water lines were tested. With only three inches of water in the reservoir on the hill, the water line to the building site was gradually reduced down to a one inch opening; allowing a stream of water to be directed over the top of the three story buildings.

At the November 13, 1878, meeting of the Board of Trustees, after some debate, Captain Parkinson was appointed Superintendent of the Soldiers' Home. He was to be paid $2,000 annually and given a home upon the grounds with fuel and lights. Superintendent Parkinson and his family took up residence at the Rider mansion on July 11, 1878.

Additionally, Doctor Farand Wylie had been appointed the first surgeon, at a cost of $500 annually, to be paid quarterly.

By Christmas Day, 1878, construction had finally reached a stage of completion to accommodate the first Civil War veterans at a banquet. It is not certain how many were actually at the first meal on Christmas Day. According to one local paper, nineteen veterans from the county home were admitted to the Soldiers' Home on December 23, 1878. The same article states that twenty-four admissions had been approved. A research project written by Eloise Morgan in the latter part of the 20th century gives these names as the 25 Civil War veterans present for the Christmas dinner:

John Collins, Pvt Co A, 99 NYI; Mathew Dooley, Pvt Co

G, 2 NYSA; George Hedrick, Pvt Co D, 119 NYI; James Harris, Pvt 15 NY Ind. Batty; John J. Icklin, Pvt Co C, 18 NYI; Joseph J. Johnson, Pvt Co H, 24 NY Cav; Thomas Naylor, Pvt Co H, 67 NYI; Matthew Smith, Cpl Co H, 88 NYI; Frederick W. Drake, Pvt Co G, 151 NYI; John W. Adams, Pvt Batty F, 2 NYHA; Michael Kelly, Pvt Co I, 105 NYI; Frank Gallagher, Pvt Co A, 161 NYI; David S. Jamison, Pvt Co C, 98 NYI; Edward Hayes, Pvt Co E, 100 NYI; George Davis, Sgt Co E, 100 NY Cav; Cornelius Cook, Pvt Co F, 125 NYI; Edward Clynes, Pvt Co M, 1 NY Vet Cav; Edward Blaney, Pvt Batty B, 16 NY Cav; Patrick Hughes, Pvt Co I, 102 NYI; Patrick Kenny, Pvt Co E, 13 NY CAV; John D. Lent, Pvt Batty E, 16 NYHA; Patrick O'Brien, Pvt Co D, 1 NY Lincoln Cav; William McCrea, Pvt Co H, 13 NYI; Thomas Quinn, Pvt Co A, 1 NY Eng; John Phifer, Pvt Batty B, 14 NYHA.

The *Farmers' Advocate* ran an article telling of thirty-two uniformed soldiers who assembled in the West Barracks at 1 p.m. in the charge of Major O'Driscoll, the Adjutant. After the rules and regulations were read to them the inmates were assigned to their quarters. Dinner was then announced and the men marched over to the main building which contained the dining hall. The tables had been set and laden with a bountiful feast fitting for such an occasion.

Original Dining Hall

Superintendent Parkinson then addressed the boys, once again donning the Union blue uniforms, with appropriate endearments and the meal commenced. The men supped on roasted turkey, giblet dressing, cranberry sauce, baked potatoes, bread and butter, apple pie and coffee. When dinner had ended, the informal opening of the soldiers' home was complete.

As if the flood doors had been opened, soldiers were beginning to come in at a steady rate. By December 31, 1878, there would be forty inmates on the roll.

The first "delegate" of the Home, as it will be referred to from here on out, made his appearance in town on December 30, 1878. Of the man garbed in semi-military dress and regulation beaver, the local papers wrote "...he looked like a Brigadier-General-at-large."

After months of delays and exhausted funds, the date was finally chosen for the moment so many people were waiting for. Billed as the greatest event of the year 1879 in the Conhocton Valley, the formal opening of the New York State Soldiers' and Sailors' Home took place on January 23, 1879.

The thirteenth annual encampment, originally planned to take place in Auburn, changed its location to Bath to coincide with the opening. This plan had been unofficially decided at the June 1877 encampment.

Many of the guests and distinguished notables arrived in Bath as early as Tuesday, January 21, 1879. Among them were the Letchworth Rifles, 50 members strong, under the command of Captain Abram B. Lawrence, of Warsaw. Having arrived that evening, they were quartered at the Home, where they were assigned guard duty.

Letchworth Rifles Circa 1880

They were accompanied by a 20-piece band, under the same name, and handsomely uniformed. During the dedication, they gave the home a martial appearance for which they received much praise and many compliments. L. L. Thayer, Esq., B. H. Randolph of the *Warsaw Democrat* and S. Wilson Wade of the *Warsaw Times* accompanied them.

On Wednesday, in the main hall, Department Commander Wm. F. Rogers, called the encampment to order. In following with proper encampment proceedings, Commander Rogers gave the opening address, relating once again the story behind establishing the Soldiers' Home. He remarked that no other public building was ever erected for the same number of men at such a small cost. For this, Commander Rogers recommended that Superintendent Parkinson should be praised.

The commander also correctly predicted that the buildings would not, in another year's time, be sufficient to accommodate all that would seek shelter here. He then pointed out that completion of the home was the incentive needed to bolster the membership of the G.A.R., proving how essential the G.A.R. was to their comrades in need.

When Commander Rogers had finished, the officers of the department began to read their reports. At the end of their reading, as if on cue, General Slocum, as Chairman of the Board of Trustees, entered the main hall and was greeted with large cheers.

Among other items on the agenda was a telegram to be sent to President Hayes, requesting he sign the bill for the payment of arrears of pensions, which had already been passed by Congress. President Hayes signed the bill on January 25, 1878.

The election of the new department commander came next. General James McQuade of Utica and the Honorable L. Coe Young of Binghamton were the nominees. The election was close and on a motion by Young, McQuade was voted in unanimously. McQuade then made a short speech in which he promised to do his utmost to advance the interests of the home of which he was a trustee.

General McQuade assumed command of the department on February 10, 1879, and on February 21, 1879, he issued General Order No.1 establishing the Soldiers' Home as his headquarters. He would later move to Bath temporarily.

After a one-hour adjournment for dinner, the encampment resumed with the elections of the remaining officers. Other business pertaining to the organization then took place and the encampment was formally closed. The delegates then took to their quarters at the home and it was reported that little sleep was had by the members until late into the night.

On Thursday, January 23, 1879, at 11:00 a.m., the buildings were all thoroughly inspected by the Board of Trustees and members of the G.A.R. Although not yet completed, all were well pleased with the neatness and comfort the home so far afforded.

By noon, the halls of the main building were teeming with people. Among the speakers were Commander-elect General James McQuade, General Wm. F. Rogers, and the Honorable William Pryor Letchworth who was President of the

State Board of Charities; past Commanders Corporal Tanner, John C. Robinson, and Henry A. Barnum. A. J. Warner, Esq., the architect of the Home was also present.

Again, the out-of-town press represented was the *New Times and Sun*, the *Brooklyn Eagle*, the *Brooklyn Argus*, the *Buffalo Courier*, the *Rochester Democrat*, the *Wellsboro Agitator*, and various local newspapers. Furnished reports were also sent to the *New York Tribune* and the *New York Post*.

The citizens of Bath and the surrounding communities were again true to form in their attendance. According to one source, "Bath was never before so highly honored in the number of distinguished gentlemen present." Over 3,000 people were present for the ceremony, including 76 inmates of the Home. Access to the front door required great effort. Within a week, there would be 96 members in the barracks and seven in the hospital.

A platform had been erected at the end of the great hall on the second floor where the ceremony was to take place. Here, military dignitaries, guests and representatives of the press filled the seats. Among others who occupied the seats were, on the left of the platform, Greisinger's Orchestra of Bath and the Letchworth Rifles Band. On the right sat the Apollo Glee Club.

At around 2 o'clock, General Slocum, President of the Board of Trustees, called the assemblage to order. He invited Department Chaplain John H. Barnard, to give the invocation; followed by the reading of some of the letters of those unable to attend.

General Slocum then opened with his address. In his speech, he shared that New York State had contributed 445,758 men, or 1/6 of the 2,690,401 soldiers that answered the call to defend our country. (Forty states and territories had provided soldiers for the Union Army.) More than 1,500 New Yorkers who had resided in Almshouses, or poorhouses, before the war answered the call to proudly serve their country.

There were now more than 9000 veterans, many of them New Yorkers, residing in four National Homes established shortly after the war. These four National Homes were located in Togus, Maine; Dayton, Ohio; Milwaukee, Wisconsin, and Hampton, Virginia.

One Soldiers' Home, established in 1851, was located in Washington, D.C. This was a Home for Regular Soldiers who were disabled, crippled or well advanced in years and could only house 400 men. Using these numbers, General Slocum explained the reason why the need was so great for a Soldiers' Home here in New York.

General Slocum continued with the contributions made by the public and the cost of the Home. In his closing remarks, he stated "Although this is now a State institution, and must be hereafter supported by the State, it bears the name of 'The Soldiers' and Sailors' Home of the Grand Army of the Republic.'" With that, he then introduced General Wm. F. Rogers and the band broke into "The Star Spangled Banner."

General Rogers began his speech by telling how honored he was for the position he held; to be department commander on such a colossal day was very humbling. He, too, spoke on what the State of New York had done for the Soldiers' Home.

He also explained the purpose of the Grand Army of the Republic and its objectives: first, to preserve and strengthen those kind and fraternal feelings which bind together the soldiers, sailors and marines; second, to assist former comrades in need of protection and extend willful aid to widows and orphans of those who had fallen; and third, to maintain true allegiance to the United States of America. That, General Rogers proclaimed, was the platform of the Grand Army of the Republic.

General Rogers then concluded his speech by stating that this day was the proudest day in the State of New York. Of the Home he stated, "Here is erected a monument which will perpetuate the Grand Army, whose comrades can appreciate the services of the humble heroes who will be gathered within these walls."

General Slocum returned to introduce the next speaker, the Honorable William Pryor Letchworth. General Slocum expressed that, while this is not a charitable institution, the State Board of Charities had been invited to examine the work and expenditures of the board. He explained that while the Board was not compensated in their work, they wanted the advice and assistance of such an organization as the State Board of Charities.

Mr. Letchworth then addressed the crowd. His was a very lengthy speech and covered many areas, from the cost of the Soldiers' Home as compared to the cost of public buildings with useless ornamentations, to the cost and maintenance of state and county poor-houses. He dazzled the crowd with facts and figures and expounded the wasteful spending of the government.

Letchworth then expressed amazement at the results of the Board of Trustees, the work done at such a small cost and the degree of efficiency at which the Home would appear to operate.

This led to Mr. Letchworth's reiterating the need for such an institution for our soldiers. He stated that they do not have an accurate statistical number of those soldiers housed in the poorhouses but assured the crowd that it was a very large number. (In March of 1877 a survey was made of the 60 poor-houses in New York State; only 28 responded, stating that over 400 veterans were residents of said homes.) Letchworth then requested that these men be transferred to the Soldiers' Home and ". . . thus lift the stigma of pauperism."

Wm. Pryor Letchworth

Further along in his speech, Letchworth spoke of temperance. He stated that he was led to believe that by the exalted character of the gentlemen who made up the board, an elevated moral tone would be maintained at the Home.

He then ventured to suggest the prohibiting of sales of intoxicating drinks within a five-mile radius of the Home. The audience responded with such a large applause that Letchworth repeated the request. Letchworth also requested healthful occupations, recreation, literary entertainment, and the solace of music to help while away the remaining days of the brave soldiers.

In closing, Letchworth remarked that the farm was a fitting site for the Home for the war-worn veteran. Three cheers were then given to Mr. Letchworth.

General Slocum then read a dispatch from Edwin F. Brown, Governor of the National Home in Dayton, Ohio, saying 800 New York veterans of the Dayton Home are "...united with him in sending greeting and congratulations." (Governor Brown was unable to attend the ceremony due to delay of the train.) A dispatch was also read from John Mueller, Dept. of N.J., G.A.R., sending forth fraternal greetings and congratulations of the New Jersey Encampment. Three cheers were given to both dispatches.

Senator J. H. Loomis of Attica, was next to speak. In his short speech, the senator promised to return to Albany and vote in the affirmative on any and all requests made by the board for the good of the Home.

After some music, the Honorable W. D. Brennan, of the Assembly, was called forward. He, too, delivered a short speech which he began by expressing that "...I am proud to be here as a representative of the great State of New York . . . I am more proud to call you fellow soldiers." As he continued he spoke of the comforts of the Home and how glad he was that the word Home was used. He spoke of how sweet it was and "...how it brings comfort to the heart of every civilized man."

After the glee club and audience sang "Marching Through Georgia" Corporal Tanner was introduced amid cheers of the crowd. The past commander began by stating that although he had never broken down in front of an audience, he thought he might today, merely because the Home was finished. He reminisced about some of the events leading up to the completion of the Soldiers' Home. He spoke of how Senator Ira Davenport, E. C. Parkinson and he reported to the Senate Committee on Finance and after presenting the proposal, Senator Robinson, Chairman of the Committee, gave his approval.

He recalled the first subscriptions secured in Brooklyn and the mass meeting led by Henry Ward Beecher at the Academy of Music. Tanner told the audience that Beecher told him "...when the work got heavy and we needed help...he would go to every city, town and village and lecture for us."

Corporal Tanner then announced that they would not be content with just three buildings, not while there were wounded and disabled soldiers in the poor-houses and the National Homes. He also reiterated the need for a building here in which to hang in a prominent place every tattered battle-flag of the state.

Corporal Tanner then spoke of his visit with Governor Brown of the National Home in Dayton, Ohio. He remarked that hundreds of New York veterans had asked him for the opportunity to return to New York and how he had promised them that a Soldiers' and Sailors' Home would soon be built. The young corporal then spoke of how those men are "...gazing eastward with longing eyes, hoping we will send for them."

Corporal Tanner concluded his speech by stating, "In the name of those who suffered and died for the Union we ask the help of the people of the State for these men."

More music and speeches followed before the Reverend O. R. Howard, D. D., of Bath, pronounced the benediction; however, repeated calls for Commander-elect McQuade finally resulted in a short speech. In his brief remarks, General McQuade spoke of the newly erected buildings as a monument, in "...honor of the valor of the heroic living, and the heroic dead." He also hoped aloud that this monument would not "...keep alive any animosities, rancor, or jealousies of the war."

Commander McQuade then speculated that "...there was not a Union veteran in the Home that would not stretch out his hand to a weary Confederate soldier who might find his way there." This was answered by a loud applause.

General Barnum came next. He too recalled briefly the history of how the Soldiers' Home was established. He then offered the following, "...thanks to A.B. Lawrence...his Command and splendid band, for their attendance...and that we rejoice to see that the exact teachings of military service have not become obsolete...as attested by their superior discipline and superb military bearing."

The Home was now officially opened. The officers in charge of the facility were Captain E. C. Parkinson, Superintendent; Major Daniel O'Driscoll, Post-Adjutant; and Captain Albert H. Nash, Secretary.

The following day, an editorial appeared in the *Brooklyn Eagle* lamenting the fact that so much was done to erect such a fine institution but no thought was given to transporting the unfortunates from the almshouses to their new Home. A letter from a prominent New York physician to the Charities Commissioners of Kings County complained of several "broken down inmates" in the almshouse in Flatbush. While the commissioners were aware of this, they answered that nothing could be done as no funds were available to send these men to Bath. The earliest sign of transportation being provided is mentioned in 1882.

Since word of the Soldiers' Home first became public in 1876, veterans began to inquire of the reality of such a place. Letters were received mostly from the National Home in Dayton, Ohio, where nearly 800 fellow New Yorkers resided.

The New York State Soldiers Home

On August 30, 1876, the *Nunda News* reported that 1,400-1,600 soldiers would come to Bath from various homes when the Soldiers' Home was complete. That was a fair estimate as to the number in the various National Homes at that time.

Interestingly enough, some veterans actually took their leave from the National Home or traveled from other parts of the country to see for themselves if the rumors were true. Men were anxious to see what, if any, progress was being made. More than once Captain Parkinson had replied by mail or placed ads in papers throughout the state, notifying soldiers that an announcement would be made when the Home would be ready to receive the eligible soldiers.

Applications began being accepted and processed by November of 1878 and it was determined to admit soldiers who were currently housed in the poorhouses, asylums and institutions throughout the state first. Reports varied as to how many veterans were actual residents of such places but it was thought that 800 was a safe number. It was unsure how many of these would want to leave the local poorhouses and relocate farther from their families.

It was also considered that a great influx would come from those soldiers whose pride had kept them out of the county homes. With an institution designated especially for the veterans, it was thought that these soldiers might be induced to come here, with pride.

When the decision was made as to who would be considered first, some offered their opinions on this idea. The *Farmers' Advocate* had received a letter dated September 17, 1878, from the National Military Home in Ohio. Here the writer, who signed his letter "Inmate," stated that he believed that nearly one-half of those soldiers who resided in the poorhouses were there of their own device.

The writer continued, explaining that these men were probably denied admission to the National Homes because of their bad conduct, or because they received a dishonorable discharge from the army. He further wrote that the homeless soldier would probably gain admission to the "State Home" but in time would be dishonorably discharged due to bad behavior, thus making room for others more deserving.

While this writer does not mention outright overcrowding as an issue, something must have compelled him to write to the Bath paper. Perhaps he felt that this might better his own chance of admission to the new Soldiers' Home.

Two years prior to this letter, Postmaster Dolson received a letter from Robt. F. Cones of the Military Asylum, Dayton, Ohio, on July 28, 1876. This fellow requested verification of a Soldiers' Home being built. He stated that nearly 3,000 men were assembled in the Dayton Home and room was so limited that the men had taken to sleeping on the floor for lack of bed space. The letter also mentioned that the Home contained men from New York who "...have not seen our friends since we left them, before we were wounded."

Note the following letter refers to the National Home in Dayton as The Military Asylum whereas the previous letter refers to it as The National Military Home. Both letters also allude to the fact that the Home was full and there were New York veterans waiting to come back to their native state.

By November 15, 1878, these rules for admission were as follows, applicants must be: a resident of New York State for one year prior to application; that he served the United States in a New York Regiment, Battalion, Company or Battery; or in the US Navy with one prior residence; be disabled from wound(s) or sickness while serving; that he is indigent; if receiving a pension, the applicant must file his pension certificate; inmates who received a pension would pay to the Home a nominal fee. Those receiving $8-10 a month paid $2 a month and so on using a progressive scale.

Applicant agrees to conduct himself according to the rules of conduct which included no profanity, vulgarity, or quarrels. No liquors or spirits were to be brought onto and consumed on the grounds, or in the buildings. Smoking allowed in designated areas only. No defacing of walls, buildings or fences.

Inmates were not allowed to leave the grounds without permission of the superintendent. All inmates were to rise at reveille, wash and have quarters cleaned by breakfast. They were to attend all roll calls at reveille and tattoo. Offenders were subject to punishment.

THE MAKING OF A HOME
1879 - 1889

The New York State Soldiers' and Sailors' Home was now opened, becoming the second oldest State Soldiers' Home; the first being located in Kearny, New Jersey. As the newest attraction to the community, the Soldiers' Home held a great fascination for the area. It became the center of attention and visits to the Home were frequent as people were curious about what went on there and improvements being made.

On March 4, 1879, correspondents of the *Steuben Courier* made an early tour of the Home. They met with Superintendent Parkinson and his assistants in his office. (This was probably located in the left-hand pavilion of the main building.) Here the officers were found deeply immersed in the paperwork necessary for admitting applicants. The Home now contained 188 inmates and there were over 100 new applications to be acted upon.

It was explained to the visitors that upon arrival, the newly accepted applicants reported to the superintendent's office where they signed for receipt of the clothing they would be issued. Civilian clothing was examined and if salvageable, were taken to the storehouse and held until the member took his discharge or passed away. The remainder of the clothing was burned. The applicants were then supplied with a pair of pantaloons, a blouse, an overcoat (all blue), two over-shirts, two undershirts, two pairs of drawers, two pairs of socks and one pair of army shoes. The inmates were then assigned to quarters.

Under the guidance of Captain Nash, the visitors made their way through the spacious dining hall. One-third of the tables were now being used. The smell of the next meal being prepared led them to the kitchen where they encountered the chief baker and cook, Edwin S. Smead, a popular baker of Bath. Four inmates under his charge were quietly engaged in preparing dinner. Smead produced for them a list of ingredients, provided by Quartermaster Leavens, for Sunday's meals. Two hundred and forty pounds of mutton, 90 pounds of potatoes, 180 pounds of bread (only quality white wheat flour is used), 14 pounds of coffee, 13 pounds of cheese, 30 pounds of sugar, 3 pounds of tea, 21 pounds of butter, and 15 pounds of English currants, to be used for pudding. (The meat, potatoes, wheat and other produce were bought on the open market until the farm and garden began operation. Ads were run for *Wicks Wheat*, potatoes and other produce and meat for the Home.)

Coffee Kettles

The kitchen was considered state-of-the-art. A twelve foot long cooking range held three fires and contained three ovens. Also included were three 75 gallon copper coffee-pots, soup kettles capable of holding 265 gallons of soup and four giant jacket kettles used for cooking meats and vegetables. A 15 horse-powered boiler provided the steam for the cooking.

On the other side of the kitchen was a 15 foot long sink used for dish washing. The water would then run outside where the grease could be skimmed off and used for soap. On the east side of the kitchen, as in all the rooms, a hose attachment would be provided. Here a stream of water could be reduced into a one-inch hose in case of fire.

In the rear of the kitchen was an addition where the bakery and ovens were housed. The ovens were 11x7 ½ feet and set in a brick arch. A steam table would be added to the kitchen on October 23, 1883, making it possible to serve meat hot.

One item the reporters neglected to mention was the repairs made in the kitchen after an explosion of one of three 75 gallon coffee boilers on January 12, 1879. The force had blown out several windows, and a large hole was smashed through the ceiling directly over the area. The partition wall separating the kitchen and bakery had not received much damage however; the rear wall of the bakery was blown out to the point that it needed repairs.

The cause of the accident was a build-up of lime on the self-acting escape valve, which prevented the steam from escaping. The two other boilers on either side received no damages and Superintendent Parkinson ordered the necessary changes to prevent a recurrence. Only one man was in the kitchen and it was fortunate that he received no injuries.

They next visited the West Barracks, or Company A. The first two floors of the barracks were used as dormitories. Here, the reporters described the ease and comforts provided comparable to any "...high-priced water-cures." Each soldier was supplied with an iron bedstead, a spring bed of woven wire and a hair mattress.

The third floor was being utilized as a reading and lounging room. The reporters had remarked that the dense atmosphere of tobacco smoke made by the old soldiers forced them to make a hasty retreat without making many observations. (Included in the cost of maintenance is a monthly allowance of one pound of tobacco for the inmates.) The library may have had its start here as on February 6, 1879, General

Crane, as Treasurer, received from G.A.R. Chapin Post No. 2 and Bidwell-Wilkeson Post No. 87, both of Buffalo, New York, $106.74.

The lecture committee of these posts found this surplus and voted unanimously to forward the funds to the Home for the purpose of instituting a new library. However, by the end of the fiscal year, there would be no room to spare for a library. It would not be until the beginning of 1880 that room for a library would be provided.

They next found themselves entering the East Barracks, or Company C. The first two floors were identical to the West Barracks so they made their way to the third floor where the hospital was located. (Why the hospital was located on the third floor was a mystery however; as the population grew, the hospital was moved down to the first floor of the West Barracks.)

Dr. Farand Wylie of Bath had been appointed the first surgeon of the Soldiers' Home. Assisted by Robert H. Gansevoort, the hospital steward, Dr. Wylie visited the Home daily and performed his duties with the utmost satisfaction of all involved. On this particular day, he had 18 patients in his care, most suffering from rheumatism and consumption. (By the end of September, seventy-seven different disabilities would be listed.)

Dr. Wylie's medicine closet was described as a "marvel of order and beauty." The bottles were described as "clean and shapely, and ornamented with handsome labels." The reporters also made note of the many amputees about the grounds (there were thirty-two amputees listed on the rolls by September 30, 1879.)

The last stop for the day was the boiler-house and gas-works. They commented that the buildings were pleasantly and sufficiently heated. The daily coal consumption for the heating, kitchen and laundry was three and one-half tons. The gas-works was also said to be a perfect success and a superior quality of gas was furnished at less than one dollar per thousand feet.

At the end of the tour, the reporters remarked that everything appeared in a state of good order. The floors of all buildings were scrubbed daily and cleanliness prevailed.

The reporters returned the following day to witness the monthly review and inspection. At 3:00 p.m., 200 men, in ranks of four, were formed and assembled on the third floor of the West Barracks. (It is possible that twelve men were admitted since the tour the previous day.) As if still in the military, the ranks were opened. Adjutant O'Driscoll, then thoroughly inspected the men. Upon closing the ranks, the adjutant read to the men General Order No. 1, defining the duties of the inmates and rules for their government. Major O'Driscoll then saluted Superintendent Parkinson, who took charge of the men.

Superintendent Parkinson addressed the men, complimenting them on their appearance and conduct. He stated that, in the coming spring, he hoped he could increase their happiness by finding suitable employment on the grounds at a fair rate of pay. He further reminded them of their pledge they signed and the rules that applied. Some men had been caught imbibing on and off the grounds and he would not tolerate such actions. He brought to their attention that when they signed their pledges for furlough no spirituous liquors were to be brought on the grounds.

He further stated that he did not want them thinking that this was just a "mere winter retreat" or that they could find outside employment at higher wages and remain here for a nominal fee. He told the men that this was their home and that they would work on making it a happy, comfortable and beautiful one."

At the end of his remarks, Superintendent Parkinson was enthusiastically applauded. Calls were then made for Trustee A. J. McCall to speak. McCall was a favorite of the men for his small acts of kindness he had shown them since their arrival. In addressing the men now, McCall reiterated what Superintendent Parkinson had spoken of. He also requested that the men live a harmonious life with one another, which would make life at the Soldiers' Home much more smooth and agreeable to all. (Seventy soldiers had taken the Murphy Pledge and donned the "blue ribbon.")

On Thursday, March 27, 1879, General Order No. 4, was issued giving a dishonorable discharge to Moses M. Crants, of Company G, 107 N.Y. Infantry, for "willful and persistent violations of the Rules and Regulations of the Home" given by Order of the Commander, Captain Parkinson.

On April 8, 1879, the Board of Trustees met for the first time since the official opening. Among the items addressed was a petition received from a large number of inmates. They asked that those who had dependent relatives be allowed to send all their pensions to their families as opposed to transferring it to the Home.

By a vote of 7-2, the request was denied. One reason given was that a pension was given to a soldier to aid in his support and maintenance. It was felt that since the veterans of the Soldiers' Home were now supported by the State, they should forfeit a portion of their pension.

General McQuade then proposed the following resolutions, which were adopted:

Resolved, Inmates, who knowingly violate the code of conduct, such as habitual intoxication, disobedience to orders, or refusing any duties or tasks assigned them, shall be summarily dismissed.

Resolved, a written report by the Treasurer must be presented to the Board at each quarterly meeting. Said report should reflect the condition of each fund appropriated for the Home.

Resolved, in answer to the large quantity of applications asking for appointment for a resident chaplain it was decided to forego any appointment for the current year. As to avoid charges of sectarianism, ministers of different denominations in town took turns officiating services.

Resolved, the committee on Building and Grounds begin drawing plans for the construction of a hospital, headquarters building, quartermaster's store and an icehouse. (Superintendent Parkinson was authorized to invite Mr. John Y. Cuyler to again visit the Home for the purpose of locating the site for the hospital and headquarters building.)

Resolved: that repairs be made on existing buildings as needed and the erection of new buildings as deemed necessary by the officers.

Resolved: the committee was to also address the matter of cultivating the farm and further instructed to select a site for the home's cemetery. (On February 14, 1879, Private William O. Terrell died of consumption at the Home. He was the first to be buried in the home cemetery. On March 31, 1879, Patrick Murphy was the second inmate to die at the Home.)

Major O'Driscoll departed for New York City on April 11, 1879, and was superseded by Captain Nash, who was promoted from secretary to adjutant. The men rejoiced at Captain Nash's promotion as he was also well liked and respected.

By April 24, 1879, there were 326 inmates at the Home; sixty-eight of whom were in the hospital. Warmer weather began bringing the men outside, strolling up the hills and taking in the sights. Superintendent Parkinson had instituted a provost guard upon the post. Known as the Home Police Guard, this new force, furnished with dress coats and badges, were to discourage inmates from heading to town without passes from the adjutant. A strict dress code was also to be followed when going into town.

Fishing was becoming a popular pastime amongst the inmates and one article in the local papers noted an old veteran catching an eel. While in the process of being skinned, the eel slipped out of the fisherman's hands and back into the river. Ironically, the man caught the same eel again three days later.

At the beginning of May, work at the Home began in earnest. A team of mules that was purchased for the fieldwork had plowed eight to ten acres. Stones were removed and piled for roads, and potatoes were prepared for planting. The garden and farm work was supervised by Sergeant Prosser (probably an inmate) and members of the Home did the work.

Five teams of horses and several inmates were employed doing grade work, drawing dirt and doing prep work for construction of the new buildings. A bridge, probably heading to the site of the home cemetery, was also being built and old sheds were being torn down. The numerous outbuildings of the original farm that were in good shape would be used for housing farm animals and storage.

In the Corner of the Garden

A large number of carpenter, blacksmith and farming implements, had also been purchased. Many of the inmates had the experience in these trades and the tools would help insure that the home would become more self-supporting. (As the years passed, surplus from the farm and garden were sold outside the home to help defray the cost of maintenance.)

On April 26, 1879, the Building Committee again met with the architect, A.J. Warner at the Home to discuss the proposed buildings. Mr. Warner was authorized to draw up plans for the three new buildings. At the board's quarterly meeting held on May 2, 1879, Mr. Warner supplied the Building Committee with their proposed plans. Thomas J. Rogers was also present. The first building shown was the headquarters building. The first floor of this three-story structure would contain offices for the superintendent, officers and clerks of the Home. A library would be located on the second floor and a chapel on the third. An addition would be added on in 1888 and used for more barrack space.

The second proposed building would be the hospital, built in two phases. This two-story structure would be built on the northwestern elevation of Company A. The main floor would consist of the dining rooms, sergeant and surgeon's rooms, bathroom and kitchen. The upper floor would be the hospital proper, with accommodations for seventy patients.

The third building, a combination quartermaster, commissary and icehouse (Bldg. 32) would be located between the West Barracks and the proposed site of the hospital. A two-story frame cottage for the accommodation of officers would also be built.

These buildings would all be built of brick and would be of corresponding style with those recently built by the same architect.

The announcements for bids went out immediately and on June 1, 1879, the bids were opened. Mr. Cooley S. Chapin of Buffalo was awarded the contract for the three buildings, which ran about $24,000 for the first phase. The ground for the hospital was broken on June 26, 1879.

May 30, 1879, brought the first Decoration Day at the Soldiers' Home. Custer Post No. 81 conducted the services and "...excelled in interest and impressiveness those of any former year, and reflected the greatest credit upon the Post, and the many others who took an active interest in them."

Accompanied by 16 members of Greisinger's Band, 45 comrades of Custer Post turned out on the perimeter of the Soldiers' Home. There, at 11:00 a.m. they formed up and proceeded to march to the Home. With 175 inmates waiting in formation, the band and post members took their place ahead of the line. From there the cortege preceded four abreast to the grassy knoll just north of the buildings where the first five soldiers of the home were buried.

Maimed and badly disabled veterans followed slowly behind the entourage while those hospitalized crawled to the windows to observe the services. The invocation was offered by the Reverend I. W. Emery, followed by music and benediction. After the services, the procession marched back to the Home, where dinner was to be served.

After dinner, members of Custer Post and 180 veterans returned to town. Another procession was formed at the park. Under command of Captain Conrad Gansevoort, the procession went on to the Grove Cemetery. Marching along on the sidewalks were 48 little girls, possibly from the Davenport Girls Home, dressed in white, carrying bouquets of flowers, accompanied by 20 little boys. Many of the citizens of Bath and the surrounding towns, close to five thousand, accompanied the procession, which was the "most credible and imposing we have ever seen here on Decoration Day." Upon arrival at the cemetery, the children and members of Custer Post began to decorate the graves of "Bath's fallen heroes."

Thursday, June 12, 1879, was "pension day." The *Steuben Courier* reported that 100 drunken soldiers had been on the street during the past week and several arrests had been made. A rebuttal was written by the Reverend John Cowan protesting the report as being a "...slander upon us and calculated to mislead the public." The editor commented after printing his letter that since the story was printed they had not seen a single drunken soldier on the street.

In the third week of June, 1879, the Board of Trustees met. It was resolved that, to save on spending, the buildings and grounds committee halt all construction on such projects that did not fall below 25% of the appropriated funding, or that could not be performed by inmates. However, the board felt it essential to erect a temporary blacksmith shop and carpentry shop.

It was also resolved that the pay rate of the Home Police Guard would be fixed at $3 a month, effective January 1, 1879. The contractor, Mr. Chapin, would continue with the buildings provided however, he accepts vouchers of indebtedness. (Appropriations came in a three-month interval at this time.)

General Slocum proposed the sale of the mill acquired from the purchase of the Brothers property to the highest bidder and that a suitable fountain be purchased and placed in front of the main building. (Even while trying to save money, the board felt work on cosmetics of the Home should continue.)

On Thursday, June 5, 1879, Harry Lee Post No. 21 of Brooklyn donated a costly 8-stop cottage cabinet organ. Also donated by Mr. R.M. Tuttle, of Hornellsville, was a valuable collection of books for the Home library. Acknowledgement also went to the U.S. Express Company for the free transportation of the books.

By the end of June there were, on the average, 352 inmates on the rolls. In July of 1879, the Board of Trustees directed Superintendent Parkinson to inform all applicants that, due to insufficient accommodations, any inmates from the National Homes or anyone who had been discharged from one within three months prior would be denied readmission.

On Sunday, July 27, 1879, General Slocum paid a visit to the Home. The purpose of his visit was to lecture the inmates on their behavior and let it be known to them that drunkenness was giving the "...institution a bad reputation as evil." He concluded his lecture by stating that this conduct would not be tolerated and a prompt discharge would be the result of such infractions.

The first week of September brought another visit to the Home from reporters of the *Steuben Courier*. In their report, they first mentioned the road leading from the bridge up to the Home. Great effort and money were spent in the crushed stone, which was described as level as a "trotting course." The road, which led up past the superintendent's residence, was now met just below the house by a swath cut into the ground for a new road.

The new roadway led off in the direction of the new headquarters and hospital buildings and around the back of the three main barracks before joining with the main drives beyond (Longwell Lane). Another road is planned, leading up to the woods for a pleasure drive. (This was probably up near the cemetery.) All the stones used for these roads are picked up from the Home farm. Approximately 60 men were engaged in this work during the time of the visit.

Besides the stone-pickers, other men were actively engaged in various jobs. Carpenters, masons, pavers, blacksmiths, and shoemakers were among those listed. Two men employed at the blacksmith shop were busy mending tools and shoeing horses, among other duties their jobs called for. Three men worked at the shoe shop repairing old shoes or making new pairs for any veteran who might have a deformity due to wounds from the war.

Commandant's Residence

The carpenters and masons were scurrying around, engaged in all sorts of activities on the buildings, while the pavers were busy laying bottoms for the drains.

The visitors noted that the brickwork on the quartermasters and commissary building was nearly finished. The hospital brickwork was also near completion. Pipes were being laid from the main sewer to the hospital and headquarters building, where the foundation was finished and ready for brick.

The temporary carpentry and blacksmith shops, which had been called for in June, were nearly completed as well. They were small wooden structures, modestly built and thought sufficient until such time as when more permanent structures could be constructed.

The oat crop, they noted, had been harvested and thrashed and was up to average. The potatoes were also of good crop in both quality and quantity. The first growing season at the Home produced a great harvest of crops. Ezra M. Peters, book-keeper of the Home, listed the following crops for the year: 80 bushels of spinach, 106.5 bushels of beet greens, 125 bushels of green peas, 9 bushels of string beans, 139.5 bushels of tomatoes, 190 bushels of green corn, 3,015 bushels of potatoes, 375 bushels of onions, 500 bushels of flat turnips, 350 bushels of beets, 125 bushels of carrots, 100 bushels of parsnips, 50 bushels of white beans, 775 bushels of oats, 20 tons of hay, 15 tons of oat straw, 25 loads of pumpkins, 1,400 heads of cauliflower, 10 barrels of cucumber pickles (3,000 in each barrel), 1,500 bushels of celery, 16,595 bushels of young onions, 380 bushels of parsley, 1,725 bunches of radishes, 6,697 pounds of squash, 3,437 green cucumbers, nearly 4,000 gallons of milk, 7,000 heads of cabbage (good).

The return on said crops was a low estimate of $3,881.04, with a total investment of about $200. All the work had been performed by the veterans except the oat crop, which was more economically done by machines with experienced men operating them. The Home would remain self-supporting until 1929.

The Cortland Iron Bridge Company was awarded the contract for a new bridge at the main entrance, at a cost to the town of $1,600. Work began on September 5, 1879, and by

Main Entrance Circa 1885

December 26, 1879, after a delay on behalf of the contractor, the iron bridge was completed. Three hundred inmates gathered on the structure to see if it would sway. The bridge did not budge, thus passing the test.

The *Steuben Courier* reported on September 8, 1879 that Messrs. Martin and Shell, "Managers of the Home Menagerie", had recently constructed an commodious quarters for the "coon brigade", a family of raccoons who took to visiting the Home. It was said that, looking at the new headquarters building being erected and then looking at the raccoons' dwelling, a person would think that the headquarters was designed after that of the raccoons' lodging. The animals were quite an attraction to the men.

New road to Hospital (San Juan Ave.) Circa 1885

Although funds were running low, Superintendent Parkinson placed an ad in the *Steuben Courier* in September 1879, seeking 30 more laborers. This was probably to complete construction on the new buildings before winter set in.

On October 23, 1879, the *Steuben Courier* printed a letter written by A. Schoonmaker Jr., Attorney-General. His letter, dated September 26, was in response to inquiries sent to him by inmate Ezra M. Peters. The crux of the two letters was asking the position of the state on inmate's right to vote. In his lengthy response, the attorney-general stated that it was his opinion that "...inmates...who were residents and voters of the election district where the Home is situated, at the time they become such inmates, are still legal voters of that district."

Inmates from other parts of the state who are planning a temporary stay and do not plan on making the election district their permanent residence are ineligible to vote. Those who plan to become permanent residents, are 21 years of age, been a citizen 10 days, inhabitant of the state for one year preceding an election, a resident of the County four months and a resident for thirty days in the election district, can vote in said district. (This would set off heated debates in the years to follow as to the inmates' right to vote at the Soldiers' Home.)

By November 13, 1879, the Home was reported as full. In the barracks were 367 inmates; hospital-103; absent with leave-20; absent without leave-7; giving an aggregate total 497 members present and/or accounted for.

The slate roofing on the headquarters building had been completed and the hospital required only a finishing coat of plaster. The quartermaster and commissary storehouse was stocked with goods of that department. The icehouse attached to the commissary was sufficiently completed and ready for use while in front of the storehouse a foundation was laid for a huge Fairbanks scale.

M.F. Curtis, a musician who played in the 3rd Brigade Band during the war, had enlisted enough members for a Cornet Home Band. By Thanksgiving, they performed a concert for veterans at the Home much to their enjoyment. As their first gig, "the orchestra" gave a very "creditable" performance.

On December 12, 1879, the boys at the Soldiers' Home held a talent show. The audience consisted of a few trustees, the inmates and townsfolk who were entertained with recitals, music and dance. Superintendent Parkinson had allowed the veterans to erect a stage and G.C. Brydon, Director of Amusement and also the librarian, was in charge of the show. Mr. Brydon, who worked for Wallack's Theater in New York City, promised more shows in the future.

On December 31, 1879, it was recorded that there were 15 deaths at the Home to an average of 400 inmates. This figure was far lower than any other similar institution and also noted was that the deaths were due largely to already ill health prior to the veteran's arrival to the Soldiers' Home.

Although the Soldiers' Home grew rapidly the first year, the annual report gave full details of the inmates. Their disabilities, units they served with, if pensioned, married and so on. The Physician's Report (no signature was affixed to it but it was possibly made out by Dr. Wylie) listed 430 present and 30 absent on the roll. The total number admitted was 616. Of those admitted, 111 were disabled by gunshot wounds; eighteen suffered amputation of the arm, fourteen of the leg and sixteen wounded by shells. Of the disabled veterans who were now members of the Home, 138 came directly from pauper-houses of the State, representing fifteen counties. New York and Kings County provided the largest number being 61 and 51 respectively.

Superintendent Parkinson added that at least 90% of the inmates were "men of good habits, who by reason of their service...had become unable to support themselves."

Effective March 1, 1880, Superintendent Parkinson resigned his position and was replaced by General Thomas G. Pitcher. We see by his report that, while reporters praised their findings at the Home, improvements were needed.

In his report, we learn that 1,064 veterans had sought benefits at the Home since its opening. Of these, 127 men were "temporary at post," or sought temporary asylum but not permanently admitted. Also, he writes that more than one half of the current inmates came from alms-houses of the various counties in the state. Although it was a slightly higher expense providing for the inmates in the Soldiers' Home than other institutions of its kind, General Pitcher felt it was well justified considering it cared for men who had stepped forward to defend their country. He also felt it was much more honorable than to let them die in "pauper institutions."

General Pitcher also brings up the subject of pensions and pensioners. Here, he writes, there has been much debate over the disposition of the pension money; at times, very unfriendly. He attributes the negative remarks to those who had been discharged for non-compliance of the rules.

He explained that under the old regulations, a pensioner would forfeit a percentage of their pension towards the Home for their maintenance. At a meeting of the Board of Trustees on June 10, 1880 however, the regulations were changed to which seventy-five per cent of their pension money would be turned in to the commandant who in turn sent it to the pensioner's dependents. The other twenty-five per cent would be turned over to the Home and used under the discretion of the commandant. If there were no dependents, the entire amount would be reverted to the Home. Once this was explained to the prospective inmates and visitors, satisfaction with the process was usually expressed.

Of the 125 men who had received pensions throughout the year, eleven received two dollars a month, the minimum; while only seven received the maximum of twenty-four dollars a month. As of the date of this report there were only twenty-two pensioners on the roll; 103 having taken leave on their own application or have been summarily discharged.

General Pitcher next discusses discipline. He wrote that, considering the class of men, the want of regular employment and the lack of discipline, the overall behavior was good. He considered the discipline of these men as good as any other garrison of the same number of regular soldiers. Scenes of rowdiness and drunkenness had not been as prominent as it once was.

On March 1, 1880, when he assumed command, General Pitcher announced General Order No. 7 stating that inmates will no longer be required to have a written pass. They were free to come and go from reveille to retreat provided they were not on duty. They were also instructed to be dressed properly and act accordingly. Any inmates abusing the Order would have privileges promptly withdrawn.

Within three weeks, over 20 inmates had left the Home voluntarily or had been discharged. When interviewed about this, some of the older veterans verified the fact and stated that it ". . . served them right, they were drunken rowdies." The old men also mentioned how much quieter the Home had become since Superintendent Pitcher's arrival.

Of the new buildings, General Pitcher wrote that they were complete and occupied. Although the store-house was well adapted for its intended purpose, it was totally inadequate for the wants of the Home. The icehouse or "refrigerator room" as he refers to it as, was an "utter failure." He describes it as nothing more than an "air-tight room . . . surrounded on two sides with a wall of ice." During the hottest weather the temperature inside was the same as out. Measures were being taken to remedy the situation.

The hospital was all that could be desired for its capacity also. It needed to be enlarged immediately as it was now filled to its utmost capacity of sixty-five. Forty more sick and disabled inmates occupied the first floor of Company A for lack of space. Here, General Pitcher endorsed Dr. Wylie's recommendation for an addition to the hospital and requested an appropriation of $15,000 for that purpose. (This was approved the following February.)

The New York State Soldiers Home

Headquarters, Library and Chapel Circa 1885

The headquarters building was completed and occupied as planned, with offices on the first floor, library, reading and smoking room on the second and the chapel on the third. Although the commandant reported the library was in a good location, the reading and smoking rooms were inconvenient and inaccessible to the old and feeble. So much so, that the inmates themselves converted the front basement of each company into a "comfortable room."

The same was with the chapel. Because of its locality, it was a great inconvenience for those in poor physical condition. Here, General Pitcher makes the first recommendation for a chapel and request $7,000 in appropriation for such. It would not be until 1889 before a new chapel became a reality however.

General Pitcher next mentions the prior set-up of the gas-works and the dangers thereof. The general wrote about one narrow escape from a large-scale fire and, with the approval of the local committee, improvements and additions were made. He also mentions the boilers were in an unsafe condition by the end of the year and the problem corrected.

Additions to the laundry were made, making it a "very complete establishment of the kind" and the slaughter-house which was authorized earlier in the season was finished and ready for use.

When spring rolled around, General Pitcher found nearly all of the fencing in need of repair or replacing. This resulted in 3,399 lineal feet of five foot picket fence and 5,000 feet of four foot fence to be constructed.

Other work included 184 elms and maples, taken from the forest, 290 deciduous shrubs, 170 evergreens and 260 fruit trees planted. Over 2,000 square yards of sodding had also been put down around the barracks and superintendent's house. Three thousand, eight hundred feet of walks and paths had been blocked out and partially graded; nine hundred feet had been graveled. Work on the parade ground, sewers and roads were being performed as well.

The feeder of the reservoir was enclosed by a wooden building however; the exterior wall of the reservoir still needed coping and railing. A lack of funds, about $500, prevented the completion. General Pitcher first mentions here the dwindling water supply. He attributes this to the absence of the usual snowfall and the long drought of the summer. Since June, he reports, every possible step had been taken to conserve water. Unfortunately, more problems would arise in the near future.

As for the farm and garden, General Pitcher was pleased with the harvest. The garden had produced an abundant supply of vegetables throughout the season and the farm reaped 450 bushels of wheat and 800 bushels of oats.

A tract of land south of the superintendent's quarters had been stumped, cleared and broken up. This would allow an additional 75 acres of land for cultivation for the following spring.

General Pitcher made the first request for two small cottages for the adjutant and quartermaster to be constructed on the grounds. He felt that the good order and discipline of the inmates and also for proper care and preservation for State property require it. He requested $3,500 for this purpose. The first cottages would be completed in 1888.

Other requests made in his report called for removing and rebuilding barns, constructing a root-house, repairs and improvements to farm, grounds, stocks and farm implements.

In his report, Dr. Wylie reports that all 25 deaths for the year were caused by diseases far advanced when admitted to the Home. He also writes that there had been no acute or malarial character contracted to the Home since its establishment; showing the healthfulness of its location.

As stated earlier, Dr. Wylie laments the crowded condition of the hospital and vigorously urges an addition be constructed. He writes that the present hospital consists of a kitchen, a pantry and dining-room, wash-room, water-closet and bathroom (entirely insufficient for the number of patients), and four wards. With these limited accommodations, the number of patients, stewards and attendees far exceed the well-known sanitary rules. In his judgment, Dr. Wylie suggested hospital accommodation for 100 patients and the necessary attendants.

On January 30, 1880, Miss Ida M. Woodard, of Bath, an accomplished vocalist and organist, agreed to perform at services on Sundays at 3:00 p.m.

At the annual meeting of the Board of Trustees, a petition, signed by a majority of the inmates, was put before the board requesting the appointment of Reverend John Cowan as resident chaplain. Cowan reportedly served as chaplain with the 6th Regt., New York Heavy Artillery and was now a member of the Home. The request was approved and Cowan preached his first sermon to a large congregation of soldiers and civilians alike. (Cowan also served as the first librarian. He would later be dishonorably discharged in 1883 after making false accusations against the officers of the Home.)

During the summer, Senator Davenport proposed an "Excised Law for the Soldiers' Home at Bath." The bill was introduced into Senate on April 8, 1880 in hopes of passing an act, prohibiting sales or giving of spirituous liquors or wine to inmates. The charge would be a misdemeanor and the first offense was a $25 fine; the second offense was a fine not to exceed $50 and no more than ten days in jail. This law was to go into effect immediately.

The quarterly meeting was held in the new headquarters building in April. Among the order of business, John F. Little, after declining three times, accepted the position of treasurer and A.J. McCall filled the vacant position of secretary. Thanks were sent out to a Professor Stowits for the donation of books received from the Buffalo School Libraries. The library now contained over 900 books.

A piece appeared in the *Steuben Farmers Advocate* on June 23, 1880, relating the plight of the "soldier boys at the Home." The inmates were submitting letters reminding the paper that Governor Cornell had vetoed the $20,000 item for their hospital but yet spent $1,500,000 for that "gaudy capitol" in Albany.

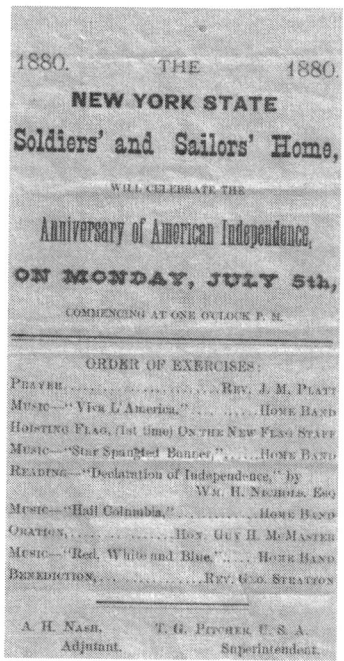

According to the *Steuben Farmers Advocate*, the Fourth of July in 1880 was celebrated on Monday. This would have been the fifth day of the month, probably due to the strict observance of the Sabbath. The crowd was light due to the slight shower at the appointed time, but it was reported that the inmates were "enthusiastic in remembrance of the day, and enjoyed the occasion and programme with visible delight." A new flagstaff had been erected and for the first time the stars and stripes floated in the breeze while the Home band played the Star Spangled Banner.

The New York State Soldiers Home

A letter to the editor dated October 20, 1880 relayed that a "poll" was taken and it was found that one-half to two-thirds were Democrats. The letter also stated that the members did not need no "Republican Whiskey" to stimulate them to do their duty. It was signed, a Veteran in Blue.

October 29, 1880 marked a special day for the citizens of Bath and the veterans at the Soldiers' Home. General Grant, campaigning for presidential candidates Garfield and Arthur, made a planned visit to Bath. At 2:00 p.m., the train traveling from Buffalo, which carried the ex-president, arrived in Bath, amid a large, cheering crowd. Grant made his way quickly from the train to the waiting carriage, drawn by "four magnificent greys." Because of the crowd, it took some time for the carriage to move but it finally got underway, escorted by one of the "finest organizations in the state", the Garfield Guards.

Also in accompaniment were the Bath and Cohocton Brass Bands as well as bands from Wayland, Pulteney, Savona, Bradford and several martial bands. The well-trained company of the Hammondsport Wide-Awakes, the Bath Boys in Blue and a long line of civilians also joined in the procession that led to Judge David Rumsey's residence where the famous general was to have lunch.

Around 3:00 p.m., General Grant was taken to Pulteney Square where he reviewed the Boys in Blue and the other organizations in front of the Courthouse. He then climbed a stand that had been erected in the park and addressed a crowd of 15,000. Dr. Dolson made the introduction and Grant delivered a short speech. The essence of his speech was that if the elections were based on the crowd assembled that the two candidates would undoubtedly be elected.

The former president then headed for the Soldiers' Home where he was given a quick tour of the buildings. He then took his lunch at Superintendent Pitcher's residence. After a short visit, Grant was taken to the depot and took the train to Elmira at 5:30 p.m.

The Home Band under the direction of Bandmaster M.F. Curtis began a series of free concerts in the Dining Hall on December 22, 1880. Although the band was lacking 4-5 members, the eight-piece band performed waltzes, polkas, and quicksteps.

In 1881, the census of New York State was at 5,083,173. President Garfield ad been assassinated and the population of the Home grew to over 600 members.

At the annual encampment held in Binghamton on January 26 and 27, 1881, an appeal was made on behalf of the comrades of the Home requesting reading material. In Circular No. 1 signed by Commander L. Young Coe on November 12, 1880, a plea for magazines, books etc. were called for. All contributions were to be sent to A. H. Nash, Adjutant of the Soldiers' Home.

By mid-February to the end of March 1881, appropriations had been made for the Soldiers' Home. The annual appropriation bill given by the Legislature for support was $70,000. Another $15,000 was appropriated to offset the cost of the hospital and the State Supply Bill gave another $5,000 for improvement of the grounds.

Reported in the *Steuben Farmer's Advocate* on May 18, 1881, the architect firm of Warner and Brockett, of Rochester, was awarded the contract for the second phase of the hospital, which they then sub-let to Thomas Fogarty and James Smith with a bid of $12,119.

A bandstand was also built in late May by Moses McChesney.

In the second week of April, Commander Young

introduced a bill into the Legislature directing the commissary-general and the chief of ordnance to issue 50 breech loading rifles, 50 sets of infantry accoutrements, eight NCO swords and belts and two six-pounders bronze field pieces with accoutrements. The bill was passed and in the second week of June arms and accouterments for the Home Police were provided, although it is not recorded how many. The Soldiers' Home had also received two brass cannons with carriage and caissons during this time. Governor Cornell also signed a law appropriating a supply bill of $5,000 for improvements of the Soldiers' Home.

6-pound Howitzer Circa 1887

On August 11, 1881, Superintendent Pitcher replaced Captain Nash with Captain Robert H. Gansevoort as Adjutant.

President Garfield, who had been shot on July 2, 1881, died on September 19. On Friday, September 30, the cannons at the Home were fired in tribute every half hour commencing at 6:00 a.m. until 6:00 p.m.

By November 9, 1881, a roof enclosed the hospital and walls and windows were being installed. The grading was an on-going process but every day the landscape was being transformed, giving the Soldiers' Home a certain domestic charm. Extending from the main bridge and around the guard shack, trees ran the length of Belfast Street heading toward Bath only to stop abruptly at the limits of the grounds. Posts for the gas lamps were now in place outside the buildings, ready to illuminate the dark recesses of the Home.

In his Soldiers' Home Notes", the author "c." reports that the population now numbered 464 inmates, of which 50 were in the hospital. The reporter also gives the figures for the rations used for one day as: 325 pounds of meat, 170 good-sized loaves of good bread, three bushels of potatoes per meal, 20 pounds of coffee per meal, 20 pounds of sugar per meal, and seven pounds of tea and twenty-two pounds of butter per meal. Vegetables were also listed as in abundance.

He also writes the men are supplied with clean clothes from the laundry once a week and Superintendent Pitcher insists the men bathe as often. But, he warns, ". . . do not approach us too carelessly; the flag floating from the splendid flagstaff, and the cannons fronting in front of the buildings show us to be a military community."

Women from the village were now holding religious-temperance meetings at the chapel of the Home. At these meetings, the veterans were urged to lead temperate and Christian lives.

By November 16, 1881, the population grew to 610. Harlo Hakes announced that the Home was now full and applications would be received and filed. In just one short month, there would be a total number of 680 inmates on the rolls.

At the semi-annual encampment held in Brooklyn on

July 28 and 29, 1880, a five-man committee, known as the "Starin Testimonial Committee" had been appointed with General Barnum as Chairman. The committee was charged with acknowledging the Honorable John H. Starin for his assistance and generous acts of courtesies afforded the delegates and members of the encampment; and to soldiers and sailors of the past war as well.

The committee proposed that $300 should be appropriated for such a purpose however; Starin requested that the money appropriated should be used for a library at the Soldiers' Home. It was decided to place in the Soldiers' Home a handsome bookcase filled with books relating to the "War of Rebellion." The name of the library would thus be changed to "The John H. Starin War Library."

It had been also resolved that a printed copy of this report and correspondence and acts of the encampment should be tastefully bound and inscribed and presented to the Honorable Starin. A similar copy would be placed in the library itself. A motion had been made to raise the contribution to $500 and was carried and amended unanimously.

By December 1881, after much preparations and correspondence, the total number of books purchased by the committee, with the exception of a very few expensive volumes, were over 300. At the sixteenth annual encampment held in Syracuse on January 25 and 26, 1882, past Department Commander Barnum reported that books purchased at the publishing house of D. Van Nostrand of New York, were bought at a 33 and a 1/3 per cent discount. The company also made a donation of 100 volumes. The house of Appleton and Co. had also donated 10 volumes to the library.

The total spent on books thus far was $392.86 and $100 was applied towards the bookcase and the memorial volume for Mr. Starin. The committee was receiving estimates on the bookcase and felt that $200 should cover the cost. They also felt that it should be built large enough to hold subsequent volumes obtained by the library.

On December 22, 1881, General Barry Post No. 248 was chartered. This G.A.R. post was made up entirely of the inmates of the Soldiers' Home.

On February 15, 1882, Dr. Joseph S. Dolson was appointed surgeon of the Soldiers' Home and on March 3, 1882, it was announced that all inmates would undergo an examination on the first day of April. (There were 556 men on the roll on March 1, 1882, 59 of which were in the hospital. This number was lower than the previous winter, probably due to the warmer weather.) This was to determine who may be well enough to be discharged in order that room could be made for more needing veterans. As it happened, very few inmates were deemed fit to be turned out.

On May 1, the cemetery reached the 100th mark. The local undertaker, Major John Stocum, was responsible for the burials.

Miss Kate DePuy, vocalist and accomplished organist, gave a concert, accompanied by her sister at the Home in September. The concert was held in the Grand Army room of the Barry Post No. 248. (This room may have been the main dining hall as no other building would be largest enough to accommodate a large crowd.)

On Thursday, December 14, 1882, the "Starin War Library" was presented. The Starin Testimonial Committee of the G.A.R. had charge of invites and the ceremony. The presentation took place on the third floor in the chapel. About 50 out-of-town guests were present and speeches were made.

After the presentation, Starin was invited to tour the Home. When he arrived at the hospital, he met 90 year old Peter Prime of Fulton. Prime mentioned that he had made a pair of boots for Starin in 1831. (Starin would have been 6 at that time.) If paid, he could return home to visit his family. Adjutant Gansevoort received a check from Mr. Starin for $20 a couple weeks later and Prime was able to visit his hometown.

The John H. Starin War Library

"Good nursing and care here are of more importance now than medical treatment, and if the old soldier must do without either I should say it would be better to dispense with the latter." J. S. Dolson

On April 30, 1883, representatives from the *Steuben Courier* accepted an invitation by Dr. Dolson, Surgeon of the Soldiers' Home, to accompany him on his daily rounds. The first stop in the hospital was the examining room. The patients came in, one by one, and described their ailments. The doctor examined them and dictated his prescription to the hospital steward, Mr. Eugene DePuy. There were thirteen men that day, fewer than usual. When the last man was seen, Dr. Dolson signed the requisition for the day's supply and then proceeded on his tour of the wards. During the month of March, 2,295 prescriptions were ordered and 19,554 prescriptions were filled during the year ending March 1, 1882.

The doctor went through the ward very methodically. Stopping at each occupied bed and interviewing the patient. In the reporter's opinion, Dr. Dolson was very professional in his duties, as he displayed utmost care and attention to those entrusted to his care. He also had nothing but praise for the body of nurses and his ward-master, Mr. Frank Kraus and the "skillful dresser," Mr. Frank Lloyd. The doctor was very thorough in his work. He was familiar with the medical, as well as the personal history of those in his care.

Hospital Ward

The reporters saw that the hospital that had begun of June of 1879 was now complete. The building was broken down into six wards designated B-G, with accommodation for sixteen patients each and six smaller rooms in which four beds could be placed. Closets and bathrooms were connected with every ward and numerous piazzas afforded the convalescents fresh air and a place to sun themselves.

The building was constructed so that every ward had windows on three sides allowing for light and ventilation as well as offering a magnificent view of the surroundings. The entire building was heated by steam and was equipped with numerous ventilation registers. One great asset to the hospital was as noted "the entire absence of disagreeable odors." Credit was due to absolute adherence to sanitary laws, and by the attention given on part of the surgeon and nurses.

Of the 598 inmates, 76 were patients in the hospital. A total of 20 personnel (all inmates themselves) were connected to the hospital staff, in the capacity of nurses, cooks and waiters. There had been 164 deaths since January of 1879, with 51 occurring in the past year. It must be noted that there were nearly twice as many inmates at this time and it had been eighteen years since the close of the war.

The tour took all of three hours and at the end, the visitors had nothing but praise for the doctor and his staff. They reported that all connected with the hospital and its management ". . . reflects the greatest credit upon General Pitcher and Surgeon Dolson." (This would undoubtedly come to the aid of the Superintendent and the surgeon in the months to follow.)

Near the end of May, General Rogers, Captain Palmer and Thomas Rogers examined plans for new roads to be laid at the Soldiers' Home. Improvements on the Home continued as shrubs and evergreens were placed in suitable locations. Approximately fifteen large iron vases, three of which released a spray of water were placed about the grounds. Two tasteful lampposts and water fountains combined, also adorned the grounds. Two additional fountains were also erected in front of General Pitcher's residence. One had also been placed in a pond below the residence, under the supervision of the engineer of the Home, Mr. Harold H. Havill.

The quarterly meeting held in the headquarters building on June 8, 1883, would be one not soon forgotten. The Board of Trustees performed the routine business such as voting on readmissions and authorizing General Slocum to arrange for the transport of disabled soldiers to and from Home at half-rate. General Slocum was also authorized to employ Harry Craske at a price not to exceed $200 per year, for the purpose of preparing all necessary paperwork for admission to Home for soldiers and sailors residing in New York City and Brooklyn.

Office in Headquarters Building

The board also wished to offer their thanks to Dr. J. L. Watson for his services as Examining Medical Officer of Applicants since the opening of the Home and that application of John Cross for transportation be refused.

It was also resolved to purchase 123.5 acres of the Charles M. Lang farm. Furthermore, the Quartermaster was ordered to prepare a book with full account of supplies purchased, from whom and price paid. This book would be made available for public use during normal business hours. Finally, the above resolutions should be published in all newspapers issued in Bath.

Quarterly reports of the Superintendent, Treasurer, and the Building and Grounds Committees were then read and accepted. At this point, Trustee Grattan H. Wheeler produced a letter from John F. Little in connection with charges reported by the newspapers that purchases of goods and supplies had been made for use of the Home by this Board or Trustees in complete violation of Section 3, Chapter 48 of the Laws of New York of 1878.

The letter also stated that certain trustees, now members of this board are interested in contracts for supplies used for consumption, which was also in violation of the Laws of New York of 1878. It was thereby resolved that the president of the board would appoint a three-man committee to investigate all contracts, vouchers and furnishings in relations to the home buildings. Wheeler would, later formally charge Jonathon Robie, Secretary and Treasurer of the Board, with this violation.

Wheeler also alleged that insufficient rations were provided to the inmates and the administration forced ill inmates to work. An ensuing investigation would threaten the very character and credibility of the men largely responsible for establishing the Soldiers' Home. A separate chapter is devoted to this and other investigations of the Soldiers' Home.

On June 27 and 28, 1883 the semi-annual encampment was held at the Soldiers' Home. On Tuesday evening, the guests began arriving. Department Commander John A. Reynolds, who had issued General Order No. 5, announcing reduced rates of transportation for comrades and families, arrived with his staff on Train 12 of the Erie Railroad. Members of Custer Post met them at the station and escorted them to the Nichols House, led by the Soldiers' Home's band.

Arriving from the west was Captain H. W. Linderman and a portion of his Linderman Battery, consisting of nineteen men and two field pieces. The guns had been placed in position on the rear car and reportedly fired a shot at every station along the route. Together at the Nichols House, the men enjoyed dinner and then speeches, stories and the singing of songs continued until midnight.

At 9:00 a.m. on Wednesday, Commander Reynolds arrived at the Soldiers' Home, welcomed by a thirteen-gun salute. General Wm. F. Rogers was acting superintendent for Superintendent Pitcher, who was in California at the bedside of an ill son.

Visitors arrived continually throughout the day, despite the weather. Although tents had been provided and set up about the grounds, the visitors found refuge on the third floor of the main building, where the beds had been removed. The men passed the time away, waiting for new arrivals, with speeches. For the latecomers, dinner could be had downstairs in the dining hall. About 400 meals had been served. After an hour of inspecting the buildings and grounds, not a derogatory remark was made. The encampment then went into session.

Barry Post No. 248 had the honor of providing the Officer of the Day, an Officer of the Guard and a twelve-man detail to provide guard duty for the duration of the Session. By 5:00 p.m., the meeting had adjourned. Many of the visitors headed immediately for town to catch the evening trains for home.

On Thursday morning, the weather began to clear. About one hundred and fifty visitors who remained overnight took the Bath & Hammondsport line to Hammondsport. There they toured by boat over Keuka Lake to points along the lake. At last, the encampment came to an end. It was reported that between 500-800 visitors were present over the past two days and that a good time was had by all.

Another bandstand is mentioned being built around the flagstaff in August of 1883. This may be that the first was not large enough for the concerts given or it was not placed in an optimal area for which to give concerts. In September, six torchlights were erected around it, providing light for light for the dark hours when concerts were given.

Except for the recent unpleasantness in July, the inmates appeared to be well satisfied with their home. One man had built a "summerhouse" near the Home, made up of limbs from the numerous trees, his yard adorned with flowerbeds. Other inmates found employment during the hop-picking season at Mr. Holmes.

There were 162 interments in the cemetery and getting drunk and landing in the Bath jail qualifies a summary dismissal from the Home.

'Notes from the Soldiers' Home' as printed in *Steuben*

Farmers Advocate on August 29, 1883, mentioned one black inmate at the home. The second black inmate arrived on October 24, 1883.

In the third week of September, the Soldiers' Home Band made their first appearance at the Steuben County Fair to the crowds delight. Several inmates had won $10 prizes for their agricultural entries, while cattle from the Home also took premiums.

Superintendent Pitcher still maintained discipline at the Home however. General Order No. 221 had been issued, confining any man to 30 days "on the limits" for appearing in town in an unkempt conditioned. It was also said that the superintendent owned a bobbed-tail dog that would sound a "give-away" bark, when a soldier in an inebriated condition crossed the bridge.

Superintendent's Residence

On October 15, 1883 a bronze statue with fountain, spraying a fine mist finally graced the Home. With the coping stones set in place around the base a month prior, the larger-than-life civil war soldier stood vigilant amidst a host of cherubs in front of the Main Building.

Statue with Fountain

In November, a large conservatory (greenhouse) was being erected along the southern side of the headquarters building. The Home Band moved their concerts inside, playing in the Main Building. Double-breasted vest of good quality, made of a dark blue cloth was issued to the soldiers of the Home. Many of the inmates were very satisfied with their new garment.

In the third week of November Fred Arnd, who owned a saloon on Home Ave. (this was probably Belfast Street), received a license to sell ale and lager. Almost immediately, the saloonkeepers in town would realize a loss in business. This would become the subject of a much-heated debate over the course of the ensuing years.

On November 24, 1883, Superintendent Pitcher sent letters to be published throughout the state that the Soldiers' Home was again full. He asked that applicants not arrive in person expecting to be taken in.

In December of 1883, a one-horse powered, two wheeled mail wagon was constructed and christened "S. & S. Home Mail." The vehicle was used for transporting mail to and from town. Also announced was that two former inmates of the Home, Mr.

S. S. Home Mail

Sullivan and Kelly, were about to open a grocery establishment on Home Ave. near the D. & L. R. R.

The Christmas dinner of 1883 consisted of 450 lbs. of turkey with oyster dressing. In the hospital, baked goose with stewed oysters was served with all the trimmings. Approximately 510 inmates partook in the meal.

In his Surgeon's Report, Dr Dolson describes a case of smallpox, which occurred at the Home. John Kay was admitted

The New York State Soldiers Home

to the Home from Peekskill on October 16, 1882 and was immediately admitted to the hospital. Within ten days, Dr. Dolson had recognized the signs of smallpox and had the patient removed to the "pest house", along with his clothing and bedding he had used since his arrival. A nurse who had at one time suffered from the disease accompanied him. After 23 days, he was returned to the hospital but complications developed and the patient died. All the patients, nurses and employees were ultimately vaccinated and no other cases were reported.

Rumors were circulating in nearby communities surrounding Bath that smallpox existed in the village. This had prompted Dr. Wylie to give notice in the Farmers' Advocate that there had been but one case and it had been contained. He also assured the public that there was no danger in the disease spreading.

Although he praised his skills, Superintendent Pitcher felt that Mr. DePuy, the steward and pharmacist, lacked the administrative and executive abilities needed as steward. Dr. F. A. Wygant, a graduate from the University of Michigan, ultimately replaced DePuy.

A small item of interest occurred on June 11, 1883 when Dr. Dolson removed a Minie ball from the back of George Hedrick, an inmate who had carried it since May of 1864.

Another item of note was that the board had praised Pitcher for his abilities in managing the Home. The Annual Report gives slight reference to the investigation in July but holds refrains from details.

By January 11, 1884, there were now 624 inmates at the Soldiers' Home. Of these, 120 were in the hospital. The crowded condition at the Home was not surprising as the weather had grown colder and more aged veterans turned to the Home for refuge. The G.A.R. decided, at their Annual Encampment in January, to ask the State for $25,000 for a new barracks. The Annual Appropriation Bill went before the

The New York State Soldiers Home

Legislature in February however, asking for $80,000 plus an additional $50,000 for a new barracks and enlargement of the hospital. On May 23, 1884, Governor Cleveland signed the bill.

A bill had been passed in the second week of April, authorizing the loan of four 12-pound or four 6-pound Bronze cannons to the Home. (It is thought that these cannons, six in all, along with the statue was scrapped during the war effort of WWII)

On May 7, 1884, a local paper had reported that Mr. and Mrs. Rodell accepted positions of cook and matron respectively. This is a mystery, as female nurses were not added to the staff until 1891.

On May 30, 1884, Captain Palmer met with Mr. Walter Dixon, an architect from Albany and A. J. Warner, to decide on the new barracks and addition to the hospital. The Executive Committee wanted a barracks large enough to accommodate 300 new inmates and have the hospital enlarged to allow an additional 50 patients. It was believed that the additional buildings would provide the capacity for 1,000 members.

Plans were drawn up and sealed bids were accepted and on August 6, 1884, the bids were opened. Of the eleven bids submitted, the firm of Allington, French & Gerity won the contract with the low bid of $38,000. Ground for the barracks was broken on August 12, 1884 and by October 9, 1884; the cornerstone was ready to be laid into place. The event did not draw as large a crowd as in the past however; it was still a time to celebrate. Of the items deposited into the cornerstone was a bottle, which contained a sample of the whiskey used in the hospital. It was rumored that it was also sampled by several of the dignitaries who were on hand that day.

By Thanksgiving Day, there were 682 members at the Home. Of these, 139 of which were in the hospital. The following is what the fare of the day consisted of: 689 lbs. of bread, 73 lbs. of butter, 60 lbs of cheese, 32 lbs. of coffee, 100 lbs. of mutton, 633 lbs. of turkey, 10.5 lbs. of tea, 100 quarts of cranberries, 10 gallons of oysters, 10 bushels of potatoes, 4 bushels of onions and 100 gallons of cider.

Dr. Dolson relates in his Surgeon's Report that not one case of typhoid fever has been exhibited at the Soldiers' Home since his arrival. He mentions this because the Village of Bath, he writes, has not been free of the disease since the Home opened. Dr. Dolson credits this with the sanitary conditions of the Home such as the drinking water, proper sewage removal and good ventilation of the hospital and barracks.

Dr. Dolson continues to state that the food is very good and he is granted most all that he requests for medicinal purposes.

The Annual Report for 1884 also gives a Librarian's Report, submitted by the librarian John Kay. The reading room contained eleven daily papers and two Sunday papers and fourteen weekly papers as well. These papers came from New York City, Brooklyn, Albany, Buffalo as well as local towns. German books and newspapers were subscribed to or donated as well.

The Starin War Library contained 275 volumes of history and 86 fictions. The aggregate total of books, magazines and newspaper was 3,997.

One donation made in April by Captain M. A. Reed of New York City, consisted of one bookcase and 182 volumes.

Canteen (Home Store) Circa 1887

This was another big year for the Soldiers' Home. In the last week of January, 1885, the first canteen, known as the "Home Store" was opened. It was located between the hospital and Company A, where the road that ran behind the hospital intersected with the lane which ran alongside the barracks.

Superintendent Pitcher's issued General Order No. 17 stating the guide lines concerning the sale of ale, beer or cider. No more than three glasses of such beverages could be sold to any individual in one day's time; two in the forenoon and one in the afternoon. The rations were increased to four glasses by General Order No. 236 on November 20, 1885. Ironically, a bill was passed in 1896 by Governor Levi Morton, approving the sale of beer and ale at the home.

On September 17, 1885, a bowling alley was opened somewhere on the grounds. (This was probably out behind the barracks.) The men greatly enjoyed this new entertainment, which was opened the same hours as that of the canteen.

On Friday, October 23, 1885, the new barracks was nearly ready for occupancy. Due to inclimate weather, the Building Committee had extended the completion date. Lots were to be drawn to see who would be transferred. Company A would transfer 41 men, Company B, 36; and Company C, 48. The crippled and feeble men would not be transferred unless they so desired. The veterans chosen to move were also allowed to trade if they found a partner willing to switch places. It appears that the official transfer did not take place until January 6, 1886.

John Stocum and Son, local merchant and undertaker had received the contract for 350 mattresses and pillows for the new barracks. The completion of this building came none too soon as there were now at this time 712 veterans at the Home.

In his report, General Pitcher states that discipline and conduct of the inmates have been good. They appear content with little complaints towards the few restrictions made upon them.

General Pitcher also reported that the water supply for the year had been abundant. However, at least fifty percent came from sources other than the original spring. The more-than-average rain and snowfall throughout the year did not revive the "big spring" and it was now perfectly dry. To overcome this, the board decided to tap into sources on the Home property. One obstacle needed to be resolved first. The water source was being polluted by the run-off from the barnyard. To remedy this, the board authorized the removal of barns to the south of the farm residence.

Also mentioned is the propagating house and brick dead-house being completed. The dead-house was located near the hospital and replaced the unsightly, old wooden building.

Dr. Dolson report's that there are 96 patients in the hospital at the time of his writing. He praised the nurses in their duties but allowed that they are beginning to grow older and weaker. Dr. Dolson makes the first call for two civilian nurses to care for the more serious cases. He also tells of how discouraging it is to treat men of great age and broken-down condition.

On the positive side, he writes that there had yet to be a case of typhoid fever at the Home.

Even with the completion of Barracks D, E and F the previous year, the Home was again nearing its capacity. The average population had grown to by nearly 130 veterans and by February 18, 1886, the actual number of inmates seeking benefits of the Home since it originated was 2,576. Of these, 570 had been discharged and readmitted. Only 58 had thus far been admitted from Bath. Of those, fifteen were discharged by their own request, twelve were summarily discharged, seven had died and fourteen deserted, leaving ten Bathites present. In addition, forty-nine transient men would receive some form of care at the Home in 1886.

Companies D, E and F

In his report, General Pitcher relays that the cost of maintenance afforded each man compares favorably with that of similar national institutions. The general also added that the plaster ceilings of the old barracks had been replaced with yellow pine and were at the same time thoroughly cleaned, kalsomined and painted throughout.

The gas, water-works and steam-heating apparatus were all in good condition and the cost of gas per thousand was $1.65. (The capacity for gas production was doubled the previous year to in order to keep up with the demand.) Little work was needed in maintaining the roads and grounds which were reported to be in good order.

Dr. Dolson goes into greater detail in his Surgeon's Report for 1886. Not only does he give the number of men admitted to the hospital and those discharged, he also gives the number of exams given for first-time admissions, 585. He also breaks down the deaths for the year, 76, by months as well as prescriptions; 29,945 total.

Dr. Dolson also writes that of the 585 new admits, 273 were born in the United States, 163 were from Ireland, 91 were from Germany, 32 were from England 19 came from Canada, six came from France and one was from Greece.

We also learned that 352 were Protestants and 233 were Catholics; 284 had never been married, 170 were widowers and 131 were married.

Of the 585 new members, 517 were considered unable to perform manual labor.

Dr. Dolson calls attention again for the need of trained nurses. Two of his best nurses had died during the year and the remaining members serving as nurses, as well as the inmates themselves are becoming older and more feeble and require better care. While the nurses have gained the critical experience serving in the capacity of care-giving, they are no longer able, he explained, to keep up with the demands of their duties.

Also recommended was "the best and the most skilled cook" for the old men now in their second childhood. The doctor felt that young, healthy workingmen would be better suited preparing the special diets for the "broken down soldiers, who do little but eat, drink and sleep, and drink, eat and sleep again." Proper cooking and food preparation is as important as the preparation of medicine administered the inmates, Dolson felt.

The 1887 Annual Report gives a list of foods consumed that year which includes: fresh beef, 66,540 lbs; ham, 4,750 lbs.; mutton, 36,074 lbs.; turkey, 24,134 lbs.; ice cream, 28 gals.; lobster, 7 lbs.; whiskey, 218 gals.; wine, 156 gallons, and nearly four pounds of canary seed.

The doctor suggests that the nurses be compensated in some way for their dedication and devotion to duty. He points out that a nurse who has had charge of a ward for a year is receives no more pay than that of one who has had charge of a ward for a week. As an alternative to a monetary compensation, Dolson recommended that the nurse who does his duty well for a year or two, receive a month paid vacation or furnished transportation to and fro his former home.

He feels that all men would like to feel that "work well and faithfully done" is appreciated and will be rewarded. "'Well done good and faithful servant!'" he continued, "is as sweet and cheering to faithful workers here as it can be in the great hereafter to those who may be so fortunate as to hear it uttered, and it need not be said in a set speech, but in a way I have suggested or in some other way that your judgment may deem proper."

On March 10, 1886, a bill was passed extending the Corporation of the Village Limits of Bath to the grounds of the Soldiers' Home. The population was increasing, approximately 950 by this time, at the Soldiers' Home, as was the visitors. It was only a matter of time that improvements to road leading to the Home, would be made.

In less than two weeks of the extension of the Village Limits, a petition was circulated, requesting a walkway from Cook's Point to the Main Entrance be laid for foot traffic. Without it, it was argued, access to the Home on foot was possible only four months out of the year. Of course, this may have been a bit of an exaggeration but to the aging veterans the distance to town was becoming harder to negotiate.

On May 7, 1886, the Home paid $40 to the Board of Excise for an Ale and Beer License. By Memorial Day there were 311 veterans buried in the cemetery.

During the year of 1887, over $800,000,000 paid out of the U. S. Treasury for pensions since the close of the Civil War. General Isaac F. Quimby would resign as trustee in January, to be replaced by Frank Campbell of Bath and the population at the Soldiers' Home would reach the 1,000-man mark. Also, the East and West Barracks would finally be completed.

On January 27, 1887, an explosion rocked the yard behind the main barracks. Around 9 a.m., the roof of the gashouse was blown into the air and the walls shattered. There were no reported injuries and the gas was restored by the evening meal.

Accepting the invitation of Dr. Dolson, correspondents from the Steuben Courier once again visited the Soldiers' Home on May 2, 1887. After traveling with the surgeon to the Home, their first stop as usual was the hospital. The assistant-surgeon Dr. F. A. Wygant met them in the ward and accompanied them throughout the hospital. In the news account in was noted that of the 163 patients, many would remain there until they are removed to the cemetery on the hill.

One patient, George Beniski, a Poland native, was said to be Grover Cleveland's conscript during the Civil War. A member of the Home since January 16, 1886, he reportedly produced a newspaper containing an interview with him, in which he gave his account of the circumstances of being made a conscript. (Beniski died at the age of 53 or 54, of fibrous phthisis in the hospital on August 18, 1887, a year after he had applied to the government for a pension in 1886. He is buried in the Home Cemetery.)

General Pitcher then took over the tour. While driving around the grounds, he pointed out the numerous improvements being made and the others in progress. Among the improvements were two rustic summerhouses built under the direction of the florist, Mr. Henry L. Drummer. Also were fifty chairs, which he built during the past winter. The 25' x 125' greenhouse, which consisted of 3,000 square feet of glass, contained 40,000 plants, which were ready to be put out in the numerous flowerbeds within a few days. The coming summer, the greenhouse was expected to be expanded. A $1,000 had been proposed from the Post Fund, which realized its profits from the sutler's shop. Seventeen vases, eight of which will be fountains, were also to be placed upon the grounds this summer, adding to the dozen already there.

The next stop was the commissary building, which, the visitors noted, resembled a wholesale grocery and meat market. The quartermaster, Mr. Leavens, was engaged in tending to the ". . . day's rations for his little family of 745 people . . ." that being the total number of inmates for that day. In the Home cemetery, there were 364 graves. A portion of the headstones was furnished by the state and the remainder would be supplied and placed by the federal government. By May 25, 1887, there were 410 graves in the cemetery but only 320 had headstones.

The guests had reported that the General Pitcher knew every inch of the grounds and buildings. He was complimented as a model Superintendent and ". . . a piece of rare good fortune for the Home, the State and the town, that he holds that position."

On August 10, 1887, Jonathon Robie resigned after being found out that he had borrowed Post Funds. An audit showed a $9,000 deficit upon which Robie admitted to using to pay off his own business and personal obligations.

On September 29, 1887, the Soldiers' Home got a rare treat when Governor Hill visited the Bath Fair. He met with several dignitaries and later toured the Home and upon being impressed with the state of the facility, addressed a crowd of 500 cheering veterans.

On October 15, 1887, General William F. Rogers became the new Superintendent when General Pitcher tendered his resignation on October 6, 1887. General Rogers lauded Pitcher's efforts and wrote "His administration of the affairs of the Home had been entirely satisfactory, and he left this field of his labors with the respect and esteem of all connected with the Home." It had been reported that General Pitcher turned the Home from a nuisance into a positive blessing.

In Dr. Dolson's final report as Surgeon of the Soldiers' Home for the 1887, he reported that 104 "transient men" had received aid throughout the year. On the date of his report, August 31, 1887, Dr. Dolson reported that most or all of the 126 patients in the hospital were suffering from incurable diseases. Nearly all the diseases contracted while in service of the country or from drinking habits while very few were contracted since entering the Home.

Dr. Dolson again urged the importance of employing trained nurses to take the place of the soldiers whose health diminishing. He also felt that, while the food in the hospital was as good as could be expected, improvements could be made here also.

One last recommendation was the necessity of a dayroom or rooms, which could be flooded with fresh air and light every twenty-four hours.

Dr. Dolson was replaced by Dr. G. C. McNett as surgeon of the Home on August 31, 1887. Dr. F. A. Wygant resigned his position as assistant-surgeon on September 2, 1887, and was replaced by Dr. Lewis W. Rose, of Hammondsport.

In an article in the Steuben Courier dated March 2, 1888, General Rogers reported that the Home had reached its maximum capacity. During the past winter, General Rogers stated that every available space was being used for the welfare of the inmates. He also added that in December he was forced to give notice that all application for admission could not be entertained.

Throughout 1888, 129 veterans passed through the Home, receiving aid of some sort. He went on to say that the population in the National and State Homes across the country was steadily rising. The National Home in Dayton, Ohio reported over 4,000 inmates present and of this number, some 50 of these were sleeping in beds on the floor.

One item of interest was that Rogers advised the Home's agents to forward only those with absolutely no means of support. [Note: while researching the practices of admission to the Home, it would appear that agents were stationed in cities about the state; assisting veterans with the application process.]

As of February 25, 1888, the Soldiers' Home had 1,010 on the rolls. General Rogers had concurred with Dr. Dolson's last report and suggested that an addition to the hospital was an absolute necessity. The hospital contained 170 patients with three empty beds on the day of the interview. The dayroom, which was occupied by convalescents, was clouded by tobacco smoke. It also contained several beds, some of which were occupied. It was apparent that all the wards were overcrowded. The State Board of Charities had condemned the condition of things, citing the beds to near together, not more than three feet apart and made recommendations to the Board of Trustees that a more suitable dayroom be provided.

Other improvements suggested by Rogers were the need of a new headquarters building, merely to contain the office space needed for the Superintendent, Adjutant, and the clerks. An addition built onto the existing headquarters building and converting it into barracks, it was thought, would be adequate to house an additional 200 inmates. This would bring the housing capacity up to 1,200 men.

A new chapel was considered an absolute necessity. Currently the aging, disabled veterans had to climb the winding stairs to the third floor of the present headquarters building to attend religious services.

For diversion and entertainment, Rogers suggested an Amusement Hall be built. Inmates either climbed a steep pair of stairs to the second floor reading room in the headquarters building, strolled over to the little cottage over which a Mr. Murphy (p)resides, to play "ten-pins" or enjoy a glass of beer or he could go to the basement of one of the barracks to play cards and smoke. Here in the depths, the light filtered thru narrow windows giving off a gloomy atmosphere. Because the basement was shut airtight to prevent fumes from entering the living quarters upstairs, ventilation was non-existent. The smoke would be so thick that it was said it could be ". . . cut and rolled into a cigar."

In the Basement

Due to the fact that for the greater part of the year the aging veterans spent their time indoors, it was highly recommended that a place of assembly could be provided above ground; a place where they could read and smoke or enjoy a band concert without climbing stairs or ladders.
General Rogers also suggested that the blacksmith's shop, carpenter's, tailors and barber's shop which were all little wooden structures be replaced by a brick structure sufficient to

accommodate them all and the construction of a new bakery. General Rogers felt that $40,000 in addition to the annual appropriation would be sufficient.

After consideration of these suggestions, several trustees headed to Albany on March 14, 1888 seeking an additional $50,000 for the proposed improvements. For their efforts, $55,000 had been appropriated on June 15, 1888 for a new Headquarters building, a Chapel, an Amusement Hall and two cottages.

On that same day, the Building and Grounds Committee began examining plans submitted by Architects Fuller and Wheeler of Albany for the new buildings. After examining the plans, a group of trustees headed to the National Homes in Dayton, Ohio and Milwaukee, Wisconsin for new ideas. Upon returning, they began comparing the Homes. It was reported that the Dayton Home now had 5,000 veterans and the Milwaukee Home had 1,700. They had elevators and we did not; however, we had our own garden thus producing better food. Also, the western homes were governed by military rules whereas; we were comprised of a more relaxed state. Bath was thus reported as "by far superior."

By July 4, 1888, successful bids for the proposed buildings were in. All work was to be completed by November 1, 1888 with Mr. R. J. Davison to superintend all the work. On July 17, a contract was awarded for a steam heating apparatus for the new buildings to Gould & Hardenbrook and LeValley & Crow (Knowl) of Elmira in a joint bid of $7,500.

Company G, Library, Union Chapel, 1889

General Rogers brought other matters of importance to

the attention of the Legislature. The first was the present laundry facility which was now unable to keep up with the demands of its services. It had been in service for eight years and was in need of constant and extensive repairs. Rogers suggested a new building to include a more commodious bathing facility be erected. The present building could then be converted into a machine shop which it was well suited for and greatly needed.

The reservoir from which the Home's water supply was obtained was in need of cleaning due to the vegetable matter growing on the bottom. It was suggested that a pond be constructed above the reservoir and diverting the numerous springs in the immediate neighborhood to it. Water could then be obtained from the pond while the cleaning and repairs to the reservoir were made.

The storage-room of the quartermaster's department was deemed "entirely inadequate" and should be enlarged.

The first mention of a new dining facility is mentioned in the Annual Report of 1888. Rogers suggested "adding an L one story in height, to connect it with the rear ends of barracks A and C." This would allow all veterans to be served at one time thus, serving the meals hot and saving work. The old method used included the tables had to be set up and food placed on the tables and then cleared off and repeated for the next group. This resulted in the meal not being served at the optimal temperature the veterans deserved.

Should these proposals be approved, Rogers stated that the gas works would then be overburdened. He recommended that a new, larger plant, needed to accommodate the growing establishment, be built in a more remote location from the buildings.

On August 27, 1888, the sum of $100 per annum was to be paid to each State Soldiers' Home and other like State institutions for every inmate it fully maintained. This was payable by the United States Treasury, apportioned and distributed under the direction of the Board of Managers of the National Soldiers' Home. Based upon the average amount of inmates for the past year, 873, the Home would be appropriated over $87,300 relieving the State to this extent in the yearly appropriations for its current expenses. (Out of the twelve northern states to have a State Soldiers' Home, Bath was the largest.)

Since the State had already provided for maintenance of the Home for the current fiscal year, General Rogers suggested diverting approximately $30,000 from monies now appropriated by Congress towards these recommendations.

General William W. Averill, Assistant Inspector-General of the State Home for Disabled Volunteer Soldiers, began a tour of all National and State Homes.

As the population of the Home grew so did concerns by the people of Bath over the disposal of the sewage from the Home into the Cohocton River above the village. The Bathites had legitimate concerns over contamination of their water supply in the village, which could result in serious health issues.

The Board of Trustees contacted the State Board of Health in regards to the sanitary conditions of the Home. Mr. Emil Kuichling, an experienced engineer, was sent out by the State Board with a view of inspecting the grounds and surrounding areas and to report back with his findings and suggestions. Kuichling rejected the idea of the citizens of Bath of building a sewer through the village and emptying into the river below the town. Not only was there too slight a grade for this to be practicable but towns further down would also have good cause for complaint.

Backed by one Dr. Balch, the executive officer of the State Board, on his opinion, Kuichling suggested that a system of tanks be set in place and the refuse could here be collected. The sewage could then be chemically treated; the breakdown resulting in the effluent passing harmlessly into the river and the residuum used as a fertilizer, free of offensive odor. (This process was noted as being used successfully in Long Island and other places at the time.)

Mr. James J. Powers, a sanitary engineer of Brooklyn, drew up the plans and specifications for the system. After Powers explained the process in great detail to the Board, the plans were adopted and the State Board of Health gave their approval. A contract had been entered into for the construction of the treatment plant and the Legislation approved $15,000 for the project.

The Memorial Day ceremony held at the Home was under the auspices of Barry Post No. 248 with a fine oration given by Superintendent Rogers. There were now 450 graves, all of which were decorated

In a bid to obtain a new organ for the chapel, General Rogers requested $1 from each G.A.R. post. One veteran however, replied to the request by writing a complaining editorial to *The Plain Dealer*. The writer suggested that the funds should come from the "Home Gin Mill" which is said to be the "best paying bar in the county." General Rogers was also hoping to expand Company D, E and F.

With Dr. McNett's first report, we find the first standard bill of fare "issued to the convalescents and employees." He describes the food as wholesome and well-cooked under the supervision of a professional chef. The special dietary list is prescribed by the surgeon and felt to meet the requirements of all diets with little complaints.

He cites that the sanitary condition of the Home and the health of the inmates is all it could expect to be. Considering the work is done by "broken-down men," the buildings are all in a state of cleanliness. He also writes that there have not been any contagious or infectious diseases and all the men have been vaccinated.

During the year there had been a number of emergency cases requiring "'capital operation' to save life." With the growing number of patients and increasing amount of surgical skills needed, Dr. McNett reiterates Dr. Dolson's call for a physician or skilled nurses. This, he feels, would give the patients the best of care they require.

Dr. McNett also called attention to Ward D, which was occupied by the demented and partially insane patients. He felt that ventilation was insufficient here and that the foul odor would permeate into the main hall and throughout the entire building. His recommendation was to have a separate building house "such unfortunates," this would also help eliminate the tranquility of the hospital itself.

He mentioned that for the month of January, 1888, 4,600 prescriptions were put up and over 150 were put up daily. Money spent on drugs, surgical equipment and appliances during the year amounted to $1,872.16.

One of the first serious crimes reported at the Soldiers' Home was committed on Monday, May 14, 1888, when Sergeant Patrick Dowling, of the Home Police Guard, was shot and mortally wounded by fellow inmate Thomas Redding. It was reported that Dowling intercepted Redding, who had been drinking throughout the day, around 7:00 p.m., about an hour after "retreat." Redding was who was walking along the tracks towards Kanona when Dowling noticed him and called him back. Redding continued on, but then turned around. As Dowling approached, Redding pulled a pistol out and fired five times, the first shot proving the fatal shot, hitting just below and to the left of the navel.

Dowling headed back to the Home but made it as far as the quartermaster's building before lying down on the bench. He was soon discovered and brought to the hospital where he was treated by the surgeon, Dr. McNett and his assistant, Dr. Rose.

Dr. McNett then drove to Kanona and swore out a warrant for Redding's arrest. Redding was apprehended shortly after in a dive in Kanona that was known for selling liquor without a license.

Sergeant Dowling died Wednesday evening of peritonitis. He served with Company H, 70th N.Y. Infantry and had been a member of the Home for the past four years. Dowling's son came and retrieved the body and returned with it to Troy, from which Dowling had hailed from. Redding, an Irish native, served with the 60th N.Y. Volunteers and had been a member of the Home since 1879 where he acquired a bad record. He was found guilty in November of 1888 and sentenced to life in prison.

The year of 1889 saw four territories, Washington, North and South Dakota and Montana admitted as States and Benjamin Harrison sworn in as President. The Soldiers' Home now had 1,200 inmates on the books.

On February 1, 1889, Trustees Little and Campbell left for Albany in hopes of securing an additional $89,000 for much needed improvements. This was broken down as follows: converting second floor of Main Building into dining hall, $1000; improvement of grounds, $15,000; electric lighting, $10,000; additional barracks, $30,000; laundry and bathroom plus machinery for new barracks, $23,000; furniture and fixtures, $5,000; bathrooms, washrooms, and additional improvements for hospital, $14,000 and for cleaning of reservoir, $1,000.

The State Board of Charities had also inspected the Home and concurred with the proposal except for minor changes in the plan. In their annual report, they suggested that a new laundry facility, with a separate department for the hospital, be constructed and outfitted with all new and modern machinery. The present laundry house is entirely too small for the current population and continual growth.

Also, a detached bathhouse with an enclosed approach should be erected for the hospital and the old bathtubs done away with. The old wooden floors should also be removed from there and replaced with tiles. At present the water closets and lavatories are in rooms that open into the wards. They were small and poorly ventilated which caused odors to permeate throughout the hospital. By making these changes, the welfare and atmosphere of the hospital department would be improved greatly.

The call for a competently trained matron was again made and the need to place the sick and disabled veterans under the care of female nursing attendants. This idea was heartily endorsed by the *Steuben Courier* who expressed that "These dying men are certainly entitled to that care and attention which they can only receive at the hands of women." The average number of patients in the hospital department is about 125, many of whom are suffering from consumption, chronic rheumatism, paralysis, dementia, and other debilitating diseases. At present, the nursing staff consists solely of inmates, many of whom received their training as army and navy hospital nurses.

Although supervised by the resident and assistant physician, these moderately paid inmates are inadequately trained to perform the duties of capable, trained nurses. Also, the attending inmates themselves will soon fall victim to advanced years and with the ever increasing population, there will be no one left to tend to these men.

To help ease the crowded condition, another suggestion was made to furlough eligible inmates, approximately fifty, who had relatives that were able to care for the veteran. The veteran would receive pay equal to the cost of housing him at the Home, about twelve dollars a month. It is unknown if this ever came to be.

On Sunday February 17, 1889 nearly 300 inmates, of whom many were standing, attended the long awaited first service at the Union Chapel. The opening services were the charge of the Reverend P. S. Vreeland. He was accompanied by four of the ministers who conducted services in the rotation of Sunday worship at the Home- the Rev. M. N. Preston, of the

Presbyterian Church; the Rev. A. P. Brush, rector of the Episcopal Church; the Rev. T. E. Bell, pastor of the Methodist Church and also by Rev. S. Nichols. The Baptist Choir furnished the singing and the Home Band provided the music. Among the Board who attended were General Rogers, Trustees Little and Campbell, Adjutant Leavitt, Quartermaster Leavens, Drs. McNett and Rose.

Heated by steam, the sanctuary was described as light and airy and possessed excellent acoustics. The seats from the old chapel were used until appropriations for new ones were made by the State.

On Friday, March 1, 1889, Major Leavitt, Adjutant, and his wife took occupancy of one of the new cottages built outside the main gate.

Amusement Hall or Annex C

The amusement hall, or Annex "C", was opened on March 22, 1889, with a show called "A Cold Day Company." The show featured live music, singing and "lots of fun."

Ever mindful of the comforts and care given the residents at the Home, the Board of Trustees began entertaining the notion of electric lighting since December of 1887. After interviewing representatives from various electric companies, the Building and Grounds Committee approved and awarded a lighting contract in at their quarterly meeting in July of 1889 to the Western Electric Light Company of Chicago. The said contract was to provide 700 incandescent lights, 12 arc lights, four dynamos, and Woodbury engines to furnish the power.

The electric company was to give three months trial after completion to test the efficiency of the works and an electrical expert was to examine the works at the company's expense. The total cost was $12,600. The light-plant was completed that summer and all the buildings had been wired. Poles had been placed upon the grounds and were wired and waiting to be connected to the dynamos, which had not been received.

Also voted on and passed was the authorization to employ a Dr. Wheelock Rider of Rochester, as a consulting oculist (Ophthalmic Surgeon). This was to be on a six-month probationary period and his salary was not to exceed $150.

Dr. George C. McNett turned in his resignation on August 9 and temporarily replaced by Dr. William B. Brown, Secretary of Board of Pension Examiners. Unfortunately, Dr. Brown passed away suddenly of heart failure on November 30, 1889 at the age of thirty-one. General Rogers recommended Dr. C. T. Stewart as acting surgeon until his resignation in December of 1889. Dr. E. H. Tweedy as a temporary replacement succeeded him. Dr. Tweedy, a graduate of Buffalo Medical Collage, appointed Dr. G. W. Wende, of Buffalo, as assistant-surgeon.

In his annual report, General Rogers reported that the Soldiers' Home was now required by law to purchase clothing from the prison department, which added a twenty-five per cent increase to the cost of goods than what could be obtained in the open market.

During the Steuben County Fair, the florist Mr. Drummer displayed a magnificent floral arrangement. Set up in the main building, the display consisted of two moss mounds, built up and covered with flowers. Situated between the two was a small pond adorned with aquatic birds. Several doves had been pinioned to the lowers. In the produce section, four cabbages from the Home were entered, the largest weighing in at 50 pounds. Mr. Drummer would also publish the first in a series, an album of photos of the Soldiers' Home. It was tastefully done and made a very nice souvenir booklet.

Over the course of the summer a roadway, today known as River Road, was constructed along the river from the main entrance and intersecting with Longwell Lane behind the buildings. This build-up of earth contained the river during the spring months when the river would flow over its bank and damage the gardens. A large quantity of rich loam had been excavated from the site of the new road and replaced with stone from the gravel. This was then topped with gravel, making a very sound roadway. The excavated loam was deposited into depressions in the garden made by the flooding thus enhancing its yield.

Mr. Leavens, who had been quartermaster of the Home since it opened, turned in his resignation effective October 1, 1889. He had been praised for his honesty, intelligence, and integrity in performing his duties. Frank P. Frost, of Horseheads, succeeded him.

In December, every inmate of the Home received Christmas cards from Miss Florence Way of Brooklyn. Miss Way was a frequent visitor of the Soldiers' Home.

SUCH A LOVELY PLACE
1890 - 1899

The year started out brightly at the Soldiers' Home as the buildings and grounds were fully lit up by use of the new electric light plant. There were now 644 Grand Army posts in New York State, and the population at the Soldiers' Home had grown to over 1,000 veterans.

In January of 1890, questions and rumors began circulating in the Legislature concerning invalid vouchers and expenditures of the Home. On January 27, 1890, a 10-man committee was formed to investigate the Home and the books and was ordered to file a report of their findings.

On February 21, 1890, five of the committee members visited the Home, inspecting the grounds and buildings. They continued on to the books, accounts and vouchers until they were satisfied they had made a thorough inspection. Upon completion, a report was then drawn up and presented to the Assembly.

At the time of the report, there were approximately 1,172 inmates present at the Home. All space available was being used and the board members informed the investigating committee that during the past year, 200 members had to be denied entry, due to lack of accommodations. The report then mentioned the neat and sanitary condition of the Home, the sewage system and disposal works being the most modern and efficient available.

The inmates were provided with clean and comfortable clothing and beds. The food was first- rate and abundant. However, the Investigation Committee reiterated the need for a new mess hall. With the number of men now on the rolls, the meals had to be served in three shifts. Appropriations for a new dining facility were not asked for due to the deficit of the last fiscal year.

Due to the growing membership and the maintenance of the numerous buildings, requests for adequate appropriations proved futile. Weather was a factor, as crops were damaged, thus affecting the cost of rations, and buildings were damaged, as well, which resulted in a deficit.

After the investigation, the committee reported that all uncertain vouchers and questionable charges were addressed and deemed justifiable. The committee expressed approval of the management of the Home, and the administrators of the Home were commended for their efforts. The report not only found no basis to the rumors but praised the members of the administration of the Home, especially Treasurer Frank Campbell.

In August of 1890, Trustees Slocum, Greenleaf, and Little were appointed a committee to hire a matron and two female nurses. General Rogers stated that apartments would be provided on the second floor in the front portion of the hospital. A new special diet by the surgeon would also be provided as a relief to the patients.

Decoration Day was rainy but the ceremony was still attended by a large crowd. There were now 568 graves in the Home cemetery.

In October of 1890, General Averill embarked on another tour of the State and National Homes. Of the 19 State Homes now operating, General Averill reported that Santa

Monica, Minneapolis and Bath were the three most beautiful. Twenty-three thousand soldiers now occupied these Homes. In March of 1889, 14 State Homes housed 4,225 men. Bath was credited with housing 1,174 of them.

Since the Disability Act of 1890, signed into law on June 27, 1890, many veterans were applying for admission to the Soldiers' Home. Upon acceptance, as the law read, the veteran indeed deserved this "prima facie evidence" of a pension. Under this act, the amount for said pension was no more than $12 and no less than $6. Once the veteran received his pension, he could then apply for and receive a discharge.

In his annual report, General Rogers mentioned that, because of the Disability Act, all members of the Home would eventually be receiving pensions. He recommended that if a pensioner did not receive a sufficient pension to support himself outside the Home, then, if he had no dependents, he should contribute a portion to the Home in return for comforts the Home provided. The State would benefit in either case. If the pensioner decided to take his discharge, this would make room for veterans willing to pay a small share to take advantage of the benefits the Home had to offer and at the same time alleviate the cost of maintenance of the Home.

General Rogers again stressed the importance of building and furnishing a new mess hall. He made a request for special appropriations of $50,000 for fiscal year 1892. This, he believed, would relieve the strain of the current dining problems and give room to house another 100 veterans.

The general's report also mentioned a severe flood in September which caused damage to the grounds and buildings. He estimated a cost of $5,000 for repairs and preventative measures to avoid a similar occurrence.

The total value of the Home buildings at this time was estimated at $267,720.15.

In his Surgeon's Report for the year 1890, Dr. Burleson mentioned that a disease known as *la grippe* plagued the Home for three months during the winter and spring with fatal effect in many cases. The report mentioned no real remedy for the disease and many of the deaths that year were due to complications from said disease.

Dr. Burleson also brought attention to the water closets in the barracks. He felt that these facilities were inadequate for the number of men now being housed. He also stated that the wooden floor and other features, which had begun to decay, should be replaced with a material that would not absorb water or decay, thus eliminating offensive odors.

Changes in the medical staff took place. Dr. Tweedy, who was appointed as surgeon on May 9, 1890, was replaced by Dr. Ten Eyck O. Burleson, of Pulteney. Dr. Tweedy resigned in August and Dr. Burleson assumed his duties on August 25, 1890. Dr. G. W. Wende was appointed assistant-surgeon on December 19, 1889.

The Excise fee for the Home was raised from $50 in 1889 to $100 in 1890.

The headlines for 1891 were the deaths of General William Tecumseh Sherman and past-Governor of New York Lucius Robinson. Rochester was the site of the twenty-fifth department encampment for the G.A.R., and Bath was announced as the lowest in average expense per inmate in the State Homes and the second lowest in the National Homes, which was a testimony to its administration.

By January of 1891, a Veteran Bus Line began making trips to the village from the Soldiers' Home. Under the supervision of John Meddick, the bus would depart the Home five times a day, making stops at all the hotels on

An early mode of conveyance

the way to the Cornwell House. Here, it would begin its return.

A decrease in members was realized with the introduction of the Disability Act of 1890. The average population began to decline when veterans, after entering the Home and becoming eligible for their pensions, then asked for a discharge. This was short-lived, however, when it was seen that their pension would not sustain them at the level of care that many of the aging veterans were now requiring.

On Saturday, March 7, 1891, the usual peaceful atmosphere of the Home was broken when the Sergeant Major read a resolution to Rule 10 of the Rules and Regulations of the Soldiers' Home. Rule 10 stated that any member of the Home who was a pensioner must sign over his quarterly pension check to the superintendent, who would then dispose of it as he saw fit. The resolution stated that the superintendent was to pay the pensioner a sum not to exceed $6 a month.

Of course, the misunderstanding led to a bit of a disturbance and General Rogers hastily drew up a clearer explanation of the rule. It was then posted on March 9, explaining that the men were entitled to $6 a month and the remainder would be held for them, should they take their discharge or ninety-day furlough. Also, any member who had a dependent family could have the Board forward some or his entire pension to them.

This cleared the air. However, at the time of the reading, 402 of the 435 pensioners at the Home were present and by Monday, 149 took their discharge.

Twenty thousand dollars had been appropriated for repairs and improvements of existing buildings. At the quarterly meeting in May, the board recommended constructing a vault in the rear of the headquarters building for the safekeeping of books and papers. They also recommended the extension of the barn on the hillside and repairing or rebuilding of the slaughterhouse, building a pest house and removing the sheds near headquarters. It was also recommended to raise the quartermaster's cottage up three feet and then raise the cellar floor above the water line. Also, the painting and repair of all buildings and outhouses was deemed necessary.

Other recommendations were to supply water to the cottages if the expense did not exceed $600 and to build additions to cottages, not to exceed a cost of $125.

Over $12,000 had so far been expended throughout the year for such repairs. Some existing structures, however, required more repairs than previously thought. The verandahs were rapidly decaying, presenting a dangerous situation. Attention was also called to the water closets in the barracks. The wooden features had been deteriorating now for some time and it was recommended to have them repaired. As for the hospital, the water closets were situated adjacent to the main corridor, where foul odor would permeate. Dr. Burleson called to have them removed and relocated behind each ward.

In July, a new barn had been built on the hill near the house of the Home farmer, Baskin Freeman. A new cottage located east of the river was being erected for Captain Frost. The quartermaster and 30 men were busy, under the supervision of Mr. Drummer, excavating a new pond in the cemetery. The pond was to collect the excess water from run-off due to heavy rain. A circular drive was also being constructed from the bridge to the main drive.

In August, the Home Band had the honor of traveling to Detroit, Michigan, where the twenty-fifth national encampment of the G.A.R. was being held. The band was positioned at the head of the New York Division and led the four- and-a-half mile march. Over 42,000 members were present.

A drought had drastic effects on the hay and oat crops, but later, frequent rain produced a bountiful crop of other farm products. Due to the flood the previous September, potatoes had to be purchased at a cost ranging from $.85 to $1.20 a bushel from February until July, when the new crop came in.

Female nurses had finally been added to the staff, with positive results. One matron and four nurses, one being Miss St. John of Pulteney, were under the supervision of the surgeon. They took care of all housekeeping, bedding and linen. Other duties included the distribution of medicines and the dietary list. They also enforced the rules of the hospital. The addition of these trained nurses greatly aided in producing more efficient service of the other attendants.

Nurses, Doctor and Asst. Surgeon

The overall condition of the Home was thought to be satisfactory but continual improvements were being made in the medical department. Requests for funding to upgrade ventilation, sewage treatment and the bathing facility however, were made annually.

As foreseen by General Rogers two years prior, many of the inmates were now pensioners. Of the 829 present as of October 1, 1892, 625 were receiving pensions. However, the population was beginning to diminish during these years, especially throughout the summer months of the fiscal year. He stated that most able-bodied pensioners applied for a ninety-day furlough during the warmer season, between March and October, searching for work, and, for whatever reason, failed to apply for an extension or request a discharge. They were then "dropped from the roll" and collected their pensions wherever they happened to be. Ultimately, the weather forced the veterans to seek sanctuary and they were once again accepted at the Home.

Since the Disability Act of 1890, many applications were from New York veterans living in National Homes and from first-time applicants. General Rogers noted that a trend was not being set here as the veterans were aging and the pride that had once kept them from the doors of the Home had now begun to wane. The aging soldier now wished to become less of a burden on his family and to take advantage of the care and support he deserved and the Home could provide.

At the quarterly meeting in August, it was decided that the superintendent was the only person to contract out and receive payment for the Home Band and disburse the money from it as he saw fit. By now, the band was sporting new uniforms consisting of military blue blouses and pants, caps and an extra pair of white duck pants. These were to be worn only when performing.

General Rogers again mentioned work on the boiler house and a larger water supply. He also made a request for a larger icehouse and cold storage room.

Dr. Burleson reported that the year 1892 saw the lowest average population in four years, 864. The largest number of deaths for the same year was 109. One reason was that *la grippe* once again appeared at the Home. Although less severe than when it first appeared two years prior, it still took its toll on the aging veterans. About thirty cases had been treated from December 20, 1891 to March 1, 1892, with more positive results. Another reason listed for the high death rate was the age of the patients being admitted. Many inmates did not enter the Home until forced to do so, and by then, their health had already deteriorated to a weakened state.

It was decided at the quarterly meeting in August that the rate of pay for the female nurses, except the head nurse, would be $15 a month for the first six months and $18 a month thereafter.

The overall conditions were satisfactory. However, he called once again for improvements of the water closets.

In 1893, past President Rutherford B. Hayes and Confederate President Jefferson Davis both passed away. At Ellis Island, 364,674 emigrants would have arrived to fulfill their dreams in America and over 8,000 veterans would have made their way to the New York State Soldiers' and Sailors' Home.

By June 30, 1893, three branches of services were represented at the Soldiers' Home. These were broken down as follows: regular army, 128; volunteers, 4,799; navy, 3,480. The average number of men present was 897 with an average age of 62.79.

On May 1, 1893, the board allowed a branch of the Leslie E. Keeley Institute, known as the Keeley League, to be established at the Home. Based in Dwight, Illinois, the Keeley League was an anti-addiction program. The first class of Keeley League No. 16 consisted of thirty members, of which twenty-eight were announced as cured. Of the two backsliders, one veteran was in the last stages of morphine poisoning and the other had used whiskey for many years to escape the pain of having his eye shot out.

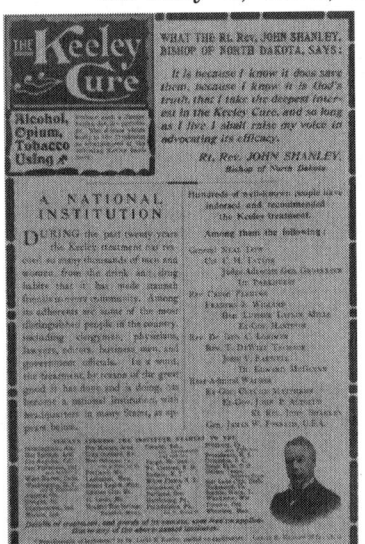

The cost of the cure was normally $25. However, pensioners at the Home could receive the cure for $10 and non-pensioners could receive it free. Veterans of the state who were not members of the Home could receive free board at the Home while enrolled.

By September 30, 1893, 171 members had been treated. For alcoholism, 167 were treated; for morphine addiction, 3; and for opium, 1. The record to date was 15 currently under treatment, eight failing to graduate, and 22 going back to their old habits.

The league had been provided with its own clubhouse opposite the Amusement Hall. It was set up and well provided for in its accommodations. Only graduates were allowed membership and privileges of the clubhouse, which was frequented often by those off duty. It was reported that the Keeley League, as a whole, had a positive effect on the Home. The Keeley Institute would last at the Soldiers' Home until November 1, 1894; however, Keeley League No. 16 would remain in existence for several more years.

Keeley League

The recommendation made in 1891 to overhaul the steam plant was finally heeded. Four new boilers replaced those which had been in service since 1878. The total of nine boilers were then probably placed "in battery," or aligned to improve economy of service, as had also been recommended.

The reservoir was completely cleaned of a large amount of sediment. To avoid interrupted service, a by-pass was installed around the reservoir, and the water continued to flow in great abundance.

A severe hailstorm occurred on September 7, 1893, causing considerable damage. Hailstones one inch in diameter broke a majority of the glass on the greenhouse. Nearly all the sashes on the windows suffered damage, as well as the crops and fruits. Oddly, General Rogers submitted in his annual report that the farm and garden, under direction of Mr. Drummer, had produced a product better in quality and quantity than in previous years.

General Rogers also mentioned several reunions taking place on the Home grounds during the summer. The 30th Separate Company of Elmira and the 47th of Hornellsville

The New York State Soldiers Home

went into camp for three days in September. The Home Band took part in the encampment and the visitors entertained the old soldiers with drill and maneuvers.

A mild epidemic of dysentery had prevailed at the Soldiers' Home during August and September of 1893. Thirty-five cases were treated but eight had proven fatal.

Appropriations of $25,000 finally came through for the changes recommended in 1889 to the hospital and barracks' water closets and lavatories. The progress of the work had advanced to a point in September that by the end of the year the job would be complete. The new tiles were laid and the modern flushing apparatus left the department nearly odorless. The alterations thus far were reported as a great improvement.

On March 28, 1894, a contract was awarded to a Mr. Page of Avoca, to raise the main bridge eighteen inches, for the sum of $125.00.

On April 14, 1894, a terrible sadness fell over the Soldiers' Home when news of the death of Major-General Henry W. Slocum, U. S. V., President of the Board of Trustees, was announced to the officers and men of the Home via general orders. The flag at the Home was ordered hung at half-staff until the funeral. Mr. Drummer sent a four-and-a-half foot column of roses, carnations and lilies as a tribute on behalf of the Soldiers' Home.

Barry Post No. 248 resolved that a portrait of General Slocum be draped in mourning for thirty days and that the members in the post would unite in expressing their sympathies to the family. A copy of these resolutions would be forwarded to the family as well. Keeley League No. 16 took the same action as that of Barry Post No. 248.

During the summer of 1892, the Soldiers' Home had been the recipient of a $5,000 bequest from the late Samuel Dietz, of New York City. There were no stipulations in regard to how the funds should be used, so the Board of Trustees decided a monument erected in the cemetery in memory of the soldiers and sailors would make a fitting tribute. Trustees Campbell and Little made a trip to Gettysburg in January of 1893 to get ideas for the design of the monument. After deliberations, a decision was made and work commenced.

On July 18, 1894, after a year of construction, the monument was dedicated. Two companies of the National Guard, the 30th Separate Company, Infantry, and the 5th Battery, under the command of Captain E.M. Hoffman of Elmira and Captain L. M. Olmstead of Binghamton, respectively, were named by the Adjutant-General for escort duty. The G.A.R., members of the Home, the fire companies and other civic societies accompanied the guard units in procession to the cemetery.

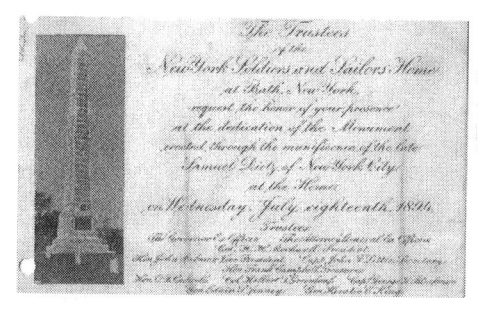

Invitation to Dedication Ceremony

A large crowd had gathered at the cemetery which now contained nearly 900 graves, to witness and participate in the ceremony. Major Rockwell, President of the Board, made a brief address, speaking of the bequest of Samuel Dietz and the decision to erect the monument.

He also spoke on the passing of General Slocum. In closing, he said: "In another year, the number of these graves will exceed that of the living members of the Home. And so they will increase, year after year, until the institution will no longer be required. But these graves will still [sic] remain. The names inscribed here will forever constitute an honor roll of citizens of the Republic who periled their lives and lost health, strength and opportunity in defense of the integrity of the Nation."

The guest speaker, General Stewart L. Woodward, gave an elegant speech, which held the crowd in "rapt attention."

The ceremony was ended by a national salute of the battery and noted as a "red-letter day in the history of the Home."

In August, the care of the garden and farm was transferred to the Quartermaster's Department.

On October 24, 1894, Governor Flower made an official visit to the Soldiers' Home. After visiting the hospital, barracks, buildings and grounds, he gave his overall approval of the state of cleanliness and the conditions he had observed.

On November 1, 1894, the Keeley Treatment was discontinued but the Keeley League would exist at the Home on for some time. Also, Professor Sutton, of the Home Band, was relieved of his duties after five years and replaced by E. G. Hollenbeck. No reasons were given for this.

During the past year, first-time applicants for admission the Soldiers' Home had grown. The average population was 1,015 with the average age 53. As time passed since the close of the war, aging veterans grew more dependent and less capable of earning a living. Those who wished to be less of a burden to their families turned to the Home. Again, it was necessary to give notice that, applications would not be considered at this time but while less frequent, they still came in. While some had been denied admission, there were those whose condition made it necessary that they be accepted.

The Home now had a capacity of 1,200 but 1,400 names was carried on the rolls. General Rogers pointed out that a deficiency in the financial report was due to the increase of membership. Due to the increase (97 more members than the previous year) the appropriation, he stated, should adjusted so the deficiency would be covered and avoided in the years to follow.

In his annual report, General Rogers made another plea for a new mess hall and appliances that were more modern. He also pointed out the need for a cold storage room and a larger icehouse. He mentioned the present cold storage as very deficient and the icehouse as being entirely too small.

He also took this opportunity to make note of the crowded conditions in the hospital. Here, he pointed out that in the near future the hospital should be properly suited to handle the caseload of patients. He made a recommendation to begin thinking of building an annex adjacent to the present hospital building.

It was also noted that a female nurse had been added to the roll for service during the night, replacing a member of the Home who formerly held the position. The female nurses, under the direction of the physicians, were now in charge of all diet and the administering of remedies prescribed. This greatly improved the care given the men.

All buildings connected with the Home were clean and the sanitation was good.

For Easter breakfast in 1894, 300 dozen eggs were served, each man receiving three each. Also, it was resolved that no soliciting should take place on the grounds except for that of newspapers.

In late May, according to the Steuben Courier, a bill authorizing the Board of Trustees to sell beer and ale at the Post Exchange was in the hands of the governor, which was expected to be signed. A special committee had visited the Home earlier in the month to investigate criticism by some state organizations. The committee reported favorably on behalf of the Home explaining that the several thousand dollars which derives from the Post Exchange goes towards support of the band, library and greenhouse and the occasional entertainment given at the Home.

It was also reported that about 300, mostly of German nationality, out of the nearly 1,000 members are regular patrons of the Post Exchange and rarely leave the grounds.

Even the Association of Military Surgeons of the United States which met in session a week before in Buffalo approved of the system at regular army posts. It was their belief that such arrangement was the cause of "decided improvement in morals, health and discipline of the soldiers- a sort of safety-valve arrangement which prevented excesses elsewhere."

It had been rumored that liquor dealers of the village had sent a representative to Albany to lobby against the bill. If that were, in fact true, wrote the reporter, that should be reason enough for the governor to sign the bill.

The call for a new dining facility, kitchen and cooking facility had finally been heeded and an additional $25,000 had been appropriated for that purpose. On August 15, 1895, the excavation began and by the third week of September, the foundation was completed and the brickwork had begun.

Even with a deficit of $4,132.09 from the previous year, General Rogers put out a call for a new assembly hall. The amusement hall, completed back in March of 1889, was not able to accommodate all the members during the winter months. Also, the Keeley League now occupied the building, allowing more space for members. Applications were being received for membership into the league although it is uncertain if they were required to take the cure.

Citing that the other Homes were fortunate enough to possess such a facility, he felt that the members here could benefit from such a building. There was enough talent here at the Home, he stated, that this would be incentive enough to awaken the aging veterans and to get them out to enjoy amusement with their fellow comrades.

Fire had broken out at the Post Exchange about 9:15 p.m. on Friday October 4, 1895 destroying the rear quarters occupied by the band. The main building was badly gutted but by the next day, business was carried on as usual. Repairs began on Monday; the loss amounting to $300.

Again, the crops were in abundance. It was said that the yield thus far was the largest yet. Every vegetable known to grow in this area had flourished and had contributed greatly to the generally good health of the residents.

Dr. Burleson conveyed again that the sanitary condition

at the Home was good. He noted that the free use of disinfectant in the closets and lavatories rendered the hospital almost odorless. General Rogers also wrote that the corps of female nurses was very assiduous in their duties and popular with the patients.

The Home received a bequest of $2,000 by Lizzie Perkins of New York City.

General Rogers reported that because of the rising population, more funds were needed for maintenance. He gave one example in his report that showed the magnitude of the responsibility of providing for the men: 295,550 pounds of flour were used in producing 156,070 loaves of bread. Because the population increased and decreased with the seasons and new veterans were applying for admittance, it was a difficult task when asking for appropriations. Prices on the open market also played a vital role in the care and welfare of the inmates.

On March 27, 1896, the Legislative Committee of the Assembly, known as the New York State Soldiers' and Sailors' Committee, made a visit to the Home in an official capacity. After a thorough investigation of the buildings and grounds, they expressed their approval of the conditions and the management.

On May 26, 1896, with the approval of Governor Levi Morton, a law was passed authorizing the sale of ale and beer upon the grounds. The net proceeds were to go toward support of the reading room and library and other such comforts or amusements deemed best for the residents.

In mid-September, General Averell conducted his annual review and inspections of the inmates at the Soldiers' Home. Accompanied by most of the officers of the Home, Averell watched as nearly 900 veterans passed in review. He was so impressed that he remarked the review was the best of any institution in the country and it showed "the officers took pride and maintained excellent discipline."

By the end of September, the new Victorian-style dining

hall was near completion. All that was needed was to have the kitchen apparatus installed. Trustees Smith, Blackman, Palmer and Shoemaker had visited the National Home in Hampton, Virginia on June 26, 1896 to inspect their dining facility in this regards.

Due to the high ceiling, installed for an airy, ventilated atmosphere, the dining hall gave the appearance of a three-story structure. The new facility would have the capability of serving 750 meals in overlapping shifts.

On November 26, 1896, Thanksgiving Day, the dining hall was officially opened. The meal, served to over 1,000 inmates, consisted in part of 65 gallons of scalloped oysters. The Home Orchestra played music throughout the day.

Dining Hall

The construction of the new mess hall brought up new concerns. Dr. Burleson worried that with the old dining facility in the main building being converted into more barracks, this would bring in more residents of an advanced age. Dr. Burleson suggested that two additional wards be added to the hospital. This would allow convalescing patients to remain nearby rather than be returned to their barracks. He also assured that there would be no need for an increase in staff for the improvement.

Dr. Burleson also related that the percentage of deaths showed a marked decrease during the year. He credited the fact to two reasons, the first being that no epidemic disease prevailed throughout the year and the second being the nurses. He gave great credit to the hospital staff and attendants for the faithful and patient attention given their duties.

On December 5, 1896, the Board of Trustees appointed a special committee in regards to dispensing employees not needed over the winter. No reasons are given for this but we do know that Superintendent Rogers was given a three-month furlough, until February 27, 1897, when his term would expire. Trustee Blackman filled in as acting commandant until that time when Colonel Charles O. Shepard was elected as superintendent. In addition, master mechanic and architect Thomas Fogarty's salary was reduced from $100 a month to $75, Engineer George C. Densmore's was reduced from $125 to $100 a month and eleven employees were laid off.

In 1897, a Buffalo newspaper reporter had declared "the New York State Soldiers' and Sailors' Home . . . a delightful place for the men who fought for the Union to spend their last days." The article also went on to say "the home was splendidly and economically managed and men were contented and well cared for."

The reporter had visited the Home to see for himself how the men were faring under the new management of Colonel Shepard, who became superintendent on February 27, 1897. During an interview, Colonel Shepard told the reporter that at first he was not well received. He said that when he took control he turned the Home upside down. This was evident by an article in the *Farmers' Advocate* published March 24, 1897, stating rumors were circulating about the Home. The most prominent was that Shepard had resigned his position.

The upkeep of the Home was accomplished by the inmates, who were paid a nominal wage. Paid civilian employees performed other jobs which called for skilled laborers. Colonel Shepard held court nearly every morning and as part of the sentencing, some of the men guilty of minor infractions were made to work, which they resented.

Another cause for ill feelings towards him was that he ordered 20 cats that were killing birds and squirrels to be drowned. The men thought of these cats as pets, and they gave the Colonel dirty looks or muttered curses when he passed by. The men generally avoided him whenever possible.

This did not last long, however. First, the men also noted that the quality of the meats and provisions were improving. The men were also surprised when the colonel had ordered mince pie to be served for supper and witnessed him in the dining hall eating a piece himself.

Another step towards being in the men's good graces was taken when he had the doors of the Keeley League clubhouse thrown open. About a dozen men who had backslid now occupied the building, which had been off limits to those who had not taken the "cure." These men were turned out and the building was then used as a card and smoking room. Also, a quiet, shaded lane, which for years had been closed because of a "troublesome grog shop" located there at one time, was reopened. He also extended the time the men were allowed off the grounds three hours on Sundays.

On the anniversary of Lee's surrender at Appomattox Courthouse, Colonel Shepard arranged for a small service in which his gave a short but elegant speech. Songs were sung and an informal poll taken revealed that about 400 of the approximate 1,200 veterans were present at the surrender.

Evening Formation Circa 1897

Another welcome change was that Colonel Shepard had

a detail of volunteers make a clearing on the hill overlooking the valley. Supplied with tables and seats, the men were treated to a picnic on Saturday, July 3, in honor of Independence Day. Games and other contests were held and each man received three coupons, each good for one glass of beer. Eight barrels of beer were consumed and 250 pounds of candy was dispensed.

Because of these and other improvements and additional privileges, the Colonel was now affectionately known as "the Little Man."

The reporter next turned his attention to the new mess hall. Measuring 100 X 150 feet, the dining hall was capable of seating nearly 1,000 men. When the bugler sounded, the men would come from all parts of the grounds and congregate outside the mess hall. At the sound of a gong, the men then entered the building; a second gong signaled the men to take their seats. Utensils and condiment servers had been set upon the tables.

A mess captain who was assigned six to eight men would serve the meal out of a big pail with a tin dipper. Except for the meat, the men were allowed extra helpings, providing they ate everything on their plates.

The Home cemetery we discover was actually two cemeteries divided by a roadway. One was for the Protestants and the other for Roman Catholics.

Colonel Shepard said that the greatest problem with the Home was the half-mile of road leading up to the grounds. The road, he contended, was lined with neatly painted "Soldiers' Rests" or saloons built with soldiers' money. Colonel Shepard said he was taking steps in passing a law, keeping "drinkeries" a long distance from the Home.

The Home Band was boasted as the "finest in WNY." On Sundays, 5,000-10,000 patrons would gather at the Home to hear concerts performed in the bandstand. One advertisement for the steamer "Urbana" offered passengers a Special Excursion from Penn Yan to the Soldiers' Home and return for only 50 cents. They would leave Penn Yan at 10:00 a.m. and arrive in Hammondsport at 12:30 p.m.

From there the passenger could dine and shop for an hour and a half and then catch the 2:00 p.m. train to the Soldiers' Home. After a two-hour "Grand Stand Concert," beginning at 4 p.m.., the passengers would arrive back at Penn Yan at 9:00 p.m.

Baseball games between the nurses and members of the different wards were also played.

Collectively, the positive results of Shepard's action may have been the deciding factor of having a branch of the Union Veteran Legion established at the Home at the end of June 1897. Organized by General J.P. Donahue, National Commander, twenty-three men were mustered into what would be known as Encampment No. 150.

An announcement dated July 12, 1897, was published stating sealed proposals were being accepted for a farm residence to be built on the grounds.

Dr. Burleson pointed out in his report that three more female nurses had been added to the roll throughout the year. Although the number of patients confined to the ward was about the same as the two previous years, the number admitted and treated increased by nearly one hundred patients. This condition again caused Dr. Burleson to ask for additions to the hospital.

Over the summer a number of wards had been repaired, new floors had been laid and steel ceilings had been put in. The improvements were not only pleasing to the eye but the sanitary condition was greatly improved. Remaining wards were yet to be up-graded.

Each of the completed wards was painted a different color and the furniture and fittings for each were repaired and painted to match each ward respectively. Rocking chairs had been supplied but the cane-seated chairs that were purchased had not yet been received. Twenty-four rocking chairs at a cost of $1 each were listed in the 1897 Annual Inventory.

Staged Operation

The operating room had been entirely lined with steel, and tile flooring had been laid. This had been done to eliminate the dangers of germs of a putrefactive nature. Also added to the room was a glass and iron operating table, an instrument case and stand, a large galvanic and faradic battery, microscope and galvano cautery, together with incidental instruments and appliances. The hospital was thus rendered well equipped for the most difficult operations.

In closing, Dr. Burleson writes, with a great degree of satisfaction, that ". . . the New York State Soldiers' and Sailors' Home ranks as one of the best of its kind."

Under the Laws of 1897, Chapter 413, an Annual Inventory and Report of each State charitable institution, State hospital, reformatory, house of refuge and industrial school was required to be filed with the State comptroller no later than October 20 for the preceding fiscal year. According to the first Annual Inventory of 1897, five barracks housing Companies A-G had been established at an estimated value of $153,000.

By 1897 the New York State Soldiers' and Sailors' Home had become the largest State Home in the nation.

In 1898, the average number of men present was 1,271. This was more than ever before and the hallways and basements, filled to utmost capacity, were being used as sleeping quarters. Even the basement of the hospital was being utilized by the sick. Yet, still they came.

On January 19, 1898, Governor Black received a visit by a delegation of the trustees, imploring him for immediate appropriations. General Horatio C. King, spokesman of the group, informed the governor that the Home now exceeded its capacity of 1,200 members by 242. Beds were now being placed within eighteen inches apart and the Home could not wait until June for its appropriations.

The general declared that the situation demanded immediate attention. The group was seeking $108,000 for the following: $34,000 for a new barracks to house 250 veterans, $20,000 for providing and equipping additional hospital accommodations, and $9,000 for constructing a cold storage area.

An additional $30,000 was also asked for a library and reading room. Another bill introduced called for $108,000 and while yet another bill would re-appropriate $3,490 of the unexpended balance of the previous year. This was intended for lighting the house of the adjutant, quartermaster and surgeon with electricity; for radiators and heating apparatus; for steel flooring and painting the different rooms in the hospitals and for a steam heater in the commandant's house.

On February 25, 1898, an appropriation of $78,000 had been received for construction of a new barracks which would house Companies H and I, the hospital addition and the cold storage area. Funds for the library and reading room were cut.

Plans and specifications had been drawn up by the superintendent of construction and approved by Mr. Perry. The contracts were then let on June 15, 1898.

Work had progressed rapidly on the new barracks until it was discovered that plans for the heating, lighting and plumbing were not yet drawn up. Under the advice of the Capitol Commissioner, it was thought that lower prices could be obtained if the contracts were let out separately. Unfortunately, the plans were not completed and forwarded until October 10, 1898.

The plans, being very elaborate and detailed, were immediately advertised and when the bids were opened, they were discovered to be in great excess of the appropriations. New plans and specifications were then made by the Commissioner and forwarded. By November 26, 1898, the bids were opened and awarded to the lowest bidders.

This delay would not only stall the occupation of the new barracks until early spring of 1899, but the plans of tying into existing heating ducts would have costly repercussions in years to come. The immediate consequence of the delay was that the expense of employing an architect, inspector, sanitary engineer, heating engineer and electrical engineer set back the appropriated funds to a point that the cold storage system could not be purchased. A new farmhouse had also been constructed at a cost of $5,617.78.

Two wards had been added on to the hospital. This was hoped to temporarily relieve the over-crowding of patients. This addition increased the hospital capacity to nearly two hundred patients, but it was feared that this would still not be enough. The number of

Hospital Ward

patients in the hospital on October 1, 1898, was 126, while 431 were admitted throughout the previous year. Dr. Burleson deemed it necessary that the hospital staff be enlarged. He requested not only more medical and surgical attendants, but also more female nurses.

Dr. Burleson recommended electric fans for use in the various wards. These would serve a dual purpose in that they would move the air about, improving circulation in the winter, and they would provide cool, refreshing relief to the patients confined to their beds during the hot summer months. The surgeon also made a request for a shower and Russian bathroom. This was to alleviate the difficulty of handling, bathing and sponging the patients suffering from renal, rheumatic and neuralgia afflictions.

Dr. Burleson rated the overall sanitary condition of the Home as good except for the water-closets in Companies D, E and F, which he felt should be repaired at once. He recommended that new flushing apparatuses and cement floors be put into place.

The large two-story building being erected behind the hospital was a much-needed improvement, he felt. This structure would provide relief for the hospital staff by allowing them a kitchen, dining rooms, a cold storage and dormitories.

Dr. Pixley, assistant-surgeon for more than eight years at the Home, resigned on October 15, 1899, and was replaced by Dr. Arthur P. Shellman.

On February 25, a new bill was introduced regarding excise law. Barry Post No. 248 also held its first campfire which was another name for encampment.

Not all was as harmonious as Colonel Shepard had related a year earlier. Friction and dissension between some of the trustees and the commandant had been evident ever since Colonel Shepard had been appointed.

Two local trustees, Messrs. Smith and Campbell, appeared to be the main adversaries of Colonel Shepard, and when he created an office for a Home Chaplain in November of 1898, Colonel Shepard received a warning from Campbell stating that "that would finish him." Supposedly, this final act split the board and the commandant.

It had been the practice of the Home since it first opened to have pastors of Episcopalian, Presbyterian, Baptist, Methodist and Roman Catholic churches from Bath provide the services at the Home. The pastors rotated weekly services and each received $300 a year for his efforts. However, arrangements for scheduling could not always be made among the various chaplains, and it was impossible for the visiting chaplains to gain any knowledge of the men. Thus, Colonel Shepard thought it best for the men to have a resident chaplain. The Roman Catholic chaplain was retained, as most of the men were of this denomination and would not attend any other services. The Reverend John J. Arnaud of Brooklyn was elected to fill that position.

Stained glass given by members of the Home to St. Mary's Church,

Providing a resident chaplain meant a slight increase in expenses, but only Trustees Smith and Campbell raised any objections. They made the case that the residents of Bath had been against the change because the parishioners of the churches "like[d] to see their pastors prosper."

Charges would be brought against Colonel Shepard a year later. The chapter Investigations covers this incident.

In 1899, an appropriation of $20,000 was received for a new assembly hall. (This would cover about half the actual cost.) However, the Board of Trustees was unable to obtain bids low enough to meet the amount appropriated. This large multiuse facility would not be completely finished for several years due to upgrades and other necessities.

Money appropriated for houses and stables for the inspector and chaplain, and for a vegetable cellar, $5,800 total, would not be enough to cover the estimated cost specified by the State Architect. Additional funds would again be asked for to meet the cost.

With the additional wards to the hospital, Dr. Burleson repeated his call for electric fans and a Russian shower. He felt that the expense would be relatively small and the benefits these minor improvements would give were a fair exchange.

While some annual reports can be rather vague in describing happenings and everyday life at the Soldiers' Home, we are fortunate that inmates sometimes find a want or need to put to paper how they viewed their surroundings. Such is the case of one veteran who, judging by his style of writing and use of the English language appears most proficient in the art of literature. This is a good example that all classes were affected by the war and its aftermath.

The author, known only as F.N.A., wrote several letters to the editor of the *Brooklyn Eagle*. The first I discovered, and there may have been previous letters, was published on June 3, 1899. It was signed F.N.A. Corning, N.Y. and dated May 31, 1899. In this letter, our writer states that he is merely a tourist and, finding himself in Corning, decided to visit the "much criticized and maligned Soldiers' and Sailors' Home." The following letter published on July 30, 1899 states F.N.A. has been a member for over a year.

This letter was written in the language in which you might hear on the Brooklyn streets and is not as articulate as his following writings. He describes upon his visit to the Home of being met at the bridge by a "squirrel cop" and is courteously referred to the adjutant's office where he is courteously received. He is then given every facility to see the Home and its belongings. When asking for the Brooklyn boys, he is furnished with names of the men who hailed from the City of Churches.

He now describes meeting an old acquaintance and is given the "grand rounds." The first company he mentions is designated as Hogan's Alley because it was compose mostly of irreclaimables [sic]. Another company he mentions was known as Kelsey's Alley, because as one member informs him, "We're from South Brooklyn and play nothin' but forty-fives and can put the culkush on the cards like old times." He is next introduced to the corporal in charge of Paradise Park, so-named because there are no incorrigibles in his company.

Passing down a foot path, our writer describes encountering a "genuine specimen of the Bowery b'hoy with the Saxey roll and a Mulligan mouth." Our writer's guide hailed the man with "Hello there, Patsey Tough, from the Hook" to which came the response "Every time, by the mortal."

On Gettysburg Ave. circa 1900

Our writer now gives a glimpse of the variety of hats and caps which could be seen. An array of "white hats with red, blue, white, orange, green and black ribbons, rough riders, golf caps and, occasionally, a genuine 'caubeen.'"

On Saturday, our correspondent attends a "genuine soldier's funeral" and gives a full description of the affair. On Sunday, he visits the dining hall where he observes an "orderly lot of men eating a good and substantial dinner." He notes that he never saw in such a large crowd so many "genteel eaters."

The evening memorial service in the chapel is largely attended. The Reverend J.J. Arnaud of Brooklyn conducted the services, which he did "impressively and feelingly." Our writer was "agreeably surprised by the singing of the choir, composed of the hospitals nurses, members and employes [sic] of the home." He continues that the contralto and soprano were excellent as was the accompanist and one young man sang a solo of "The Holy City." The one thing lacking he writes was a sounding board as the want of it was noticeable.

The concluding hymn was "America" which was "sung from loyal hearts, by loyal throats, which made the old boys clasps hands as of old and thank the Lord for having a country to suffer for and if needs be die for."

The second letter by the same author and printed in the *Brooklyn Eagle* on July 30, 1899, gave a detailed look at the goings-on at the Home from the time of admission to the burials. Included were sketches of certain images of the Home.

Beginning with the natural scenery of the Conhocton Valley and the "quaint and picturesque Village of Bath" the writer takes the reader to the main entrance of the Home. Here, the traveler is met by a member of the Home Police who is standing at the police station. The policeman is courteous when he asks you to state your business. If you are visiting, he will provide you with all necessary information and, if a guide is needed, will direct you to the police headquarters located in Company B.

Home Police 1898

If seeking admission to the Home, you will be directed to the headquarters building where you will be kindly received by the adjutant. Once your papers are examined and good advice has been offered, you are ordered to the surgeon's, located at the hospital. A physical examination is given and, if not retained in the hospital for medical treatment, you are assigned quarters.

You then report to the captain of the company who, in turns, refers you to the senior corporal (there are two on every floor). You are then assigned a bed and a box which contains a drawer and two partitions. If you are a newcomer, the corporal will escorts you to the quartermaster's where you once again "don the old familiar blue." After the "usual bath" and your civilian "togs" are stowed away, the new admit is free to look around.

Our prolific author next takes us to the parade ground, where the music stand is placed in the center and the grass is kept finely mowed. The grounds are surrounded by an "umbrageous growth of trees" which offer nesting places for a large colony of squirrels. The tameness of such is remarkable as with the robins which will feed off the hands of the old veterans. The writer quips that the robins "have probably read the papers and know that a law has been passed for their protection." The sparrow, he writes keeps a respective distance, seeming to know he is not welcomed.

As you pan to the northeast corner of the parade ground, you will spot a newsstand in the form of kiosk. Here, our guide informs us, is where you can purchase the "leading and misleading papers of the day." The writer tells us on his third day at the Home, (he has been a member for about one year at the time of his writing) here is where some of the celebrities of the Home were pointed out to him. There was the Yellow Kid of Hogan's Alley, Chuck Connors of Mulberry Bend, Ikey Starch from the Swamp, Patsey Jim from Kelsey's Alley, Jimmy Oliver from Paradise Park and the Kerryman. Our writer expresses jubilation in his letter after writing these names, names that reminds him of home.

The Newsstand

Our guide now touches upon the concerts given at 4 p.m. except Saturdays. The Home Band plays a selection of popular airs but when a jig is struck up, he writes, ". . . the old blood rises to the surface and fantastic attempts are made to dance to it, to the great amusement of the onlookers."

We are next introduced to the daily routine which our guide describes as "benevolent discipline." Bugle notes are first heard at six in the morning upon which everyone rises. Beds are then made and after carefully sweeping under and around them, the men are off to "make his toilet." The first bugle sounds for breakfast at 7:15 and the meal, which is a good one he writes, soon follows. Then, if you are not detailed, you are free to do as you please "provided you do it dacent [sic]."

Inspection of quarters and clothing are held every second Tuesday by the Home Inspector and request for articles of need is "cheerfully granted." Wednesday is general bed cleaning day and on Thursday, hot or cold baths are provided and underclothing are changed. On Fridays, windows are cleaned. Saturday, he warns, beware of the man with the mop.

Sunday everyone would "prink up," some attending church in town, presided over by Reverend Father Griffin. Others attended the Home chapel to hear the Reverend J.J. Arnaud. Sunday evening, weather permitting, was dress parade which was largely attended by the citizens of Bath. (Here our writer mentions that the bicycle girl is very much in evidence.) The boys, he writes, do not have the elastic step of '61 but they do their level best. When the colors are paraded to the tune of "Rally Round the Flag", it is difficult to restrain the boys from singing it.

The display of Corps badges is immense and at times, there are reviews for prominent visitors. The latest was for Confederate General Lomax who our author states he had often offered inverted blessings to in the Shenandoah Valley. The band played "Dixie" for the occasion. It must be noted here that the writer offers that he has yet to find a single veteran who bears malice toward their reconstructed Southern brethren.

The essayist sadly goes into funeral details mentioning as many as four burials a day. Upon the death of a member, families or friends are promptly notified. Some have the body sent home while let the body be buried here, often in the request of the deceased be "buried with the boys."

The company of which the former member belonged is notified and all hands promptly dress in their best with white gloves and kepis. A corporal has charge of six pall bearers who proceed to the dead-house and remove the body to the chapel where it is covered with the Stars and Stripes and a handsome wreath of flowers is placed at the head.

The company soon files slowly in to slow music and the service begins. A short history of the deceased is given and appropriate remarks are made by the chaplain. Our recorder notes that he could not recall when he ever heard "Nearer, My God, To Thee" ever sung more sweetly or plaintively.

The body is next raised and carried to the hearse and the slow procession toward the cemetery begins, preceded by the firing party with reversed arms. They travel up the winding road for the final scene. As the body is laid into the ground, every head is uncovered and remains so until the end. The solemn voice of the minister is heard, echoing throughout the valley, followed by three volleys from the firing squad. "Taps" is then sounded. The company files slowly by, thus ending the service.

We next go to the hospital, where our scribe writes "if order is heaven's first law it seems to be so here." He describes the physicians have no easy task, considering there are 155 patients on a daily average. This does not include the countless calls to the barracks, seeing to those unable to make it to sick call.

On the day of his writing, there were eight blind men in the in the ward who curiously seem to be the merriest of all. Ward D was a very sad sight, a place where the imbeciles were placed.

A library and reading room was attached to the hospital, in charge of by James L. Clark of Brooklyn. Mr. Clark read for one or two hours every morning newspaper articles and interesting stories to a large audience.

Now for the gentile lady nurses, above average in beauty, he ponders, "Do the managers of the training school pick out the best looking in order to give the poor sufferers a foretaste of the genuine 'angels,' ever bright and fair, in that better land 'far away on some radiant shore?'"

Pension day is the day of days. Major Howell, the paymaster, has the difficult task of dispensing the greenbacks, assisted by Officer James H. Richardson. Every three months, the pensioners would line up, the crippled seated at the front, and await their pay. Most times, rather than receiving their full pension, men would accept as little as one dollar to last them for three months, and send the remainder home to loved ones.

Court is held every morning except Sunday and is presided over by either the commandant or adjutant. Our correspondent allows that the officers tend to lean on the side of mercy more than not. For the first minor offense, the culprit is told to go on his way and to sin no more. For the incorrigibles with a bad record, they are usually relegated to the "dumps," that is, denied certain privileges or made to perform some light work. Those who refuse their sentence, they receive a dishonorable discharge from the Home. The commandant (Colonel Shepard) displays a sense of humor in some cases. For instance, when one individual was accused of getting drunk after parade, he replied that "he couldn't very well get drunk during parade." He was sent on his way with a suspended sentence. Those who come in hopelessly drunk time and again are ordered to "Snug Harbor" or as the boys refer to "the drying room."

Thanksgiving and Christmas are red letter days. On the latter, all offenses are stricken from the record with good will to all. The "national and rational turkey" is served on Thanksgiving with all the trimmings. The Fourth was celebrated gloriously, the band beginning the day by playing "Hail Columbia" and playing stirring airs throughout the day.

Our source concludes that he wishes all of his Brooklyn friends to know that all inmates are well taken care of and their needs are provided for without stint.

The Soldiers' Home and the village of Bath were in for a rare and honored treat on February 9, 1899, when New York Governor Theodore Roosevelt paid a visit. With the mercury at several degrees below zero, a crowd of about fifty met the special car of the Lackawanna R. R. at 8:00 a.m. The crowd was somewhat disappointed, however, when the distinguished guests stayed inside as the car made its way to the Home.

The governor was escorted into the dining hall, where he delivered a short speech to the veterans. Although he could not compare the small war with Spain to the "Great War", Governor Roosevelt spoke of the honor it was to call these men comrades. He stated that there was a special place in his heart for anything connected with these old soldiers here today that nobody else could hold. The Rough Rider continued, telling his audience that this was his first time away from Albany while the Legislation was in Session, but of all the institutions, he put ahead of the rest the Soldiers' Home.

Governor Roosevelt then received a large round of applause as he began his exit. The Home Band played "America" as he shook hands and spoke with the soldiers, and as he made his way for the door, led by the trustees of the Home. He was then given a full tour of the Home, passing through all the buildings, shaking hands with a smile and calling the men comrades.

The governor was then escorted to the commandant's office in the headquarters building, where he held a conference with the trustees. Following the conference, the trustees conducted their annual meeting, in which every officer of the board and Home was re-elected.

Governor Roosevelt returned to the village, where a public reception was waiting for him. The court house was filled nearly beyond capacity while the Home Band entertained the crowd. A large flag had been draped behind the podium and a portrait of Roosevelt in his Rough Rider uniform graced the platform. When the governor entered the building, the crowd cheered wildly.

After being formally welcomed by Reuben Robie, Governor Roosevelt began his speech. He spoke of the pleasure it was to be there and what an honor it was being made Executive of the State. He spoke of the flag of "the newest nation, of the youngest nation, on the youngest continent . . . being carried in triumph through the islands of the eastern seas." He stated that every American citizen could hold his head a little higher because of what had been accomplished by our soldiers.

At the end of his speech, Roosevelt said that since being elected, he had not had the chance of meeting and thanking the men who were responsible for his present position and he wished to thank every one of them and would strive to show his appreciation.

Governor Roosevelt had been applauded continuously throughout his speech. Before leaving for Albany, he spent thirty minutes shaking hands with all those present, saying how pleased he was with his visit.

Rumors had been circulating for more than a year concerning the management of the Home. Recent newspaper reports stated the purpose of the governor's visit was to investigate these reports. Governor Roosevelt, however, never alluded to these rumors during his visit. In August of 1899 however, Governor Roosevelt called for an official investigation of the Board of Trustees and the management of the Soldiers' Home. Refer to Investigations chapter for details.

Is this Blind Charlie? An 1897 newspaper reported a 'simple-minded inmate' built a shanty in a secluded nook of the Home ground. His passion for singing hymns and playing an immense accordion possibly led to the officers granting permission to build away from the general population.

THE POPULATION PEAKS
1900 - 1909

On March 17, 1900, Colonel Andrew Davidson was appointed commandant, replacing Colonel Shepard. Although the investigation was still in progress it would appear that the board would not function as it should, should Shepard remain. This act prompted Generals Sickles, King and Shoemaker to resign their positions as trustees in protest.

In May of 1900, a memorandum was filed by the governor's office and approved by the assembly relating to the Soldiers' Home. In his memorandum to the Attorney-General, Governor Roosevelt informed him that the "... New York State Soldiers' and Sailors' Home [was] hereby exempted from the management and control of the State Board of Charities and in respect to said institution said Board [were] hereafter only to exercise their constitutional right to visit and inspect." Whether this had anything to do with the investigation is unclear.

Colonel Davidson officially assumed his duties on April 16, 1900, when the new Board of Trustees held their first meeting. In his brief term as commandant, the Home saw many changes and improvements.

Colonel Davidson was a mover and a shaker. In his first

annual report, which covered the second half of the fiscal year, Colonel Davidson pointed out that a gain of over 150 members had been realized since the previous year. This brought the average number of inmates up to 1,483. Citing that the population would continually increase, he stressed the importance of a new barracks capable of housing an additional 300 members to help relieve the impending crowded condition of the Home come winter.

Other recommendations made were for a study room added onto the chapel for the chaplains, addition to the headquarters building for a cashier's office, a new guard house at the bridge, carriage house and stable for headquarters, and repairs, alterations and addition to steam and electric light plant.

Work was still being performed on the new assembly hall, as ventilation and a warming system were being installed. An appropriation of $10,000 was made for improvements but when bids were opened, it was found that they exceeded the funds. The plans were modified by the state architect and bids were again asked for, to be carried over to the following year.

Dr. Burleson had resigned on July 1, 1900, after ten years of service at the Home. He was temporarily replaced by Dr. A. P. Shellman. Dr. T. C. Crance was made assistant-surgeon. Dr. Oran W. Smith was chosen from a list of three veterans certified by the State Civil Service Commission to become (permanent) surgeon. Dr. Smith began his duties on October 1, 1900. He reiterated his predecessor's recommendation of improving the circulation of air and ventilation by means of electric fans.

Also in 1900, Spanish-American (Span-Am) War veterans were being received for treatment at the hospital. The Soldiers' Home had been built specifically for Civil War veterans, and while these Span-Am War veterans were not eligible for full admittance, they were eligible to receive treatment at the hospital.

Three new houses were erected for the inspector, chaplain and engineer at a combined cost of $6,000, and an addition was built on to the mess hall and kitchen.

Soldiers' and Sailors' Home
Bath, N. Y., December 21, 1901
To the President of the New York State Board of Health, Albany, N.Y., 7:
Sir—I and others who are somewhat interested in the matter are anxious to know if there is a general law throughout the state forbidding persons to inhabit and sleep in cellars, or does such a law only appertain to New York city? If there is such a law. will you kindly inform me where and how a copy of such law can be obtained. The reason I ask for such information is this: There are now at the Soldiers and sailors' home at this place in the neighborhood of 200 veteran soldiers and sailors of the late civil war now compelled to sleep in the cellars under the barracks, which are mostly built on made ground and are damp and unhealthy; also a number of sick men who are compelled to sleep in the cellars of the hospital, the place being overcrowded. Hoping to receive an answer to this, you will permit me to subscribe myself
    Yours respectfully
    Mrs. A. C. ACKERMAN

Bath, N. Y., December 30, 1901
Daniel Lewis, Commissioner:
Dear Sir—I have the honor to report the number of men sleeping in cellars at the New York state soldiers and sailors' home as follows:
In the hospital 12
Company A building 13
Company B building 25
Company C building 10
Company D building 14

Company E building 18
Company F building 15
Company H building 3
Company I building 40

In all of the cellars the floors are cement, are dry, and side walls whitewashed. Ventilation is very poor in all the buildings except Companies H and I. The hospital basement, in my opinion, is unfit for occupation. This is the only unsanitary condition that I find. In Company I there are 40 beds clean and perfect, making a very handsome basement dormitory. The home has proper accommodations for about 1600 inmates, while today there were present 1706. The only suggestion I could make would be extra buildings for the relief of this congestion.

I am, very respectfully,

G. C. McNETT

Albany, N. Y., January 4, 1902

Hon. Benjamin B. Odell, Jr., Governor of the State of New York, Albany, N. Y.:

Dear Sir—On December 24, 1901, this Department received a communication from Mrs. A. C. Ackerman of Bath, Steuben county, N. Y., calling attention to alleged unsanitary conditions existing at the Soldiers and sailors' home at that place, claiming that many of the inmates were compelled to sleep in the cellars, which are mostly built on made ground; also that a number of the sick men were sleeping in the cellars of the hospital building, the place being overcrowded. In view of the complaint made by Mrs. A. C. Ackerman, the attention of Dr. G. C. McNett, the health officer of Bath, was called to the matter with instructions to investigate as to the alleged unsanitary conditions and overcrowding of the buildings, and to report the result to this Department. For your information I enclose herewith a copy of the complaint made by Mrs. A. C. Ackerman, also a copy of the report made upon investigation of

same by Dr. G. C. McNett.
Very respectfully
DANIEL LEWIS
Commissioner of Health

In late March or early April, The Reverend Arnaud passed away after a brief illness. His position was temporarily filled by the Reverend Edward B. Furbish, who began his duties on May 17, 1902. Also elected was the Reverend John F. Farrell, who was to be the new Catholic chaplain. Colonel Davidson welcomed these two men and felt they would be of great benefit, not only in spiritual matters of the men but also in connection with the management and discipline of the Home.

At the annual meeting of the Board of Trustees, held on February 13, 1902, permission was granted to the Right Reverend Bernard J. McQuaid, Bishop of Rochester, to erect a house for the Catholic chaplain with a chapel attached. The building was allowed to be built on the Home grounds, conveniently located near the hospital.

An agreement was signed in May between the trustees and the contractors, and the Holy Trinity Chapel was to be built and completed by September 15, 1902, at a cost of $3,680.46. The parish was established on July 1, 1902, and was blessed by the Reverend Farrell, the first pastor. In his annual report, Colonel Davidson gave recognition to the Reverend Bishop McQuaid for the erection of the chapel at his own expense.

Except for minor details regarding ventilation and heating, the assembly hall was finally completed and being used. With a seating capacity of 1,200, it was often used for housing the overflow of new inmates.

Companies H and I, Assembly Hall

As for the repercussions of tying into the existing ducts, mentioned in 1898, the following were just some of the reasons for problems. There was no uniformity between the old and new conduit running from the boiler-house to the principal buildings. A great amount of coal was being consumed trying to heat these buildings. The ductwork ranged in size from a 4-inch sewer pipe to a 14-inch brick trench covered with half a tile. It also ran from 18 inches underground to five feet.

Some of the ducts were old and in very poor condition, and when a leak occurred, it was hard to discern where the leak existed. Another problem was the covering of the pipes. Those with less protective covering lost a large amount of heat, thus resulting in insufficient heating. One other problem was that the ducts did not travel a level course. As the ducts continued from one building to another, the pipes had to make ninety-degree upward turns and travel overhead across the basement of the buildings. This created a trap, obstructing the flow of steam.

Chief Engineer C. C. Cornwell recommended a general overhauling of the heating system at a proposed cost of $32,450.00. Unfortunately, other work seemed to have been a priority and only patchwork had been done on the system until new conduit could be installed.

A larger boiler-house had been built and two new boilers were added. However, three old boilers were removed, leaving the heating capacity insufficient for the additional buildings.

The New York State Soldiers Home

Mr. Cornwell reported that a new chimney was erected also. This may be the present-day 125' chimney. However, the access door used for cleaning contains the following data: Erected by H. R. Heinicke, Inc. N.Y.C. There is what looks like Italian writing on a small plate which gives the date October 3, 1909, and the word Macello and another illegible word.

Dr. Warren L. Babcock, previously an assistant physician at the St. Lawrence Hospital for the Insane, was appointed Surgeon of the Home and assumed his duties on April 1, 1902.

Boiler Plant and Laundry

In his report, Dr. Babcock mentioned that the convalescent barracks, when completed, would be a much-needed relief to the old veterans. Two of the three floors would accommodate an additional 200 men. This would double the present hospital capacity. Under the present conditions, men were sleeping in the basements of the barracks, which would bring on a recurrence of acute rheumatic and other chronic diseases.

Dr. Babcock also recommended that an enclosed corridor should connect the second floor of the new barracks to the hospital. He explained that this passageway would also serve as a sun corridor. During the past three winters, an additional ward in the basement needed to be opened to alleviate the crowded conditions. With a

Convalescent Barracks /Company L

passageway opened up, the overflow of patients could be roomed on the second floor of the new barracks.

Another recommendation was for elevators in the new barracks. Dr. Babcock had noted that the new three-story convalescent barracks would ultimately need them, so he felt it would be best to install them as soon as possible. He had noticed that on several occasions, patients, due to discomforts from their ailments, were unable to make it to the mess hall. In order to rectify this, Dr. Babcock suggested that elevators be installed. He further recommended moving the more feeble and crippled patients to the new barracks, which had its own kitchen and other facilities. He believed much better care could be provided this way.

Dr. Babcock also pointed out the need for a new morgue. The condition of the present morgue, he cited, was unsanitary and insufficient and had been condemned by sanitarians and undertakers for several years. The old morgue had been built when the population did not exceed a few hundred. The death rate now had exceeded over 120 a year for the past four years and a morgue with refrigeration was recommended. Dr. Babcock suggested a small building containing an ice refrigerator capable of holding six to eight bodies at a time. Also, a room for embalming and autopsies and another for laying out the bodies for viewing were thought needed.

Dr. Babcock also recommended that the former dresser's room be altered slightly and used as a laboratory. The doctor felt that if a high standard of medical care and treatment were to be maintained, then it was pertinent to the hospital to have a facility where the examination of blood, sputa and other body fluids could be conducted.

Also in his report, Dr. Babcock mentioned an isolation pavilion built during the summer. He stated that it was very helpful in safeguarding the Home from contagious diseases. He mentioned that during the past three months, 33 men who had come from areas infected with small-pox had been isolated for a period of two weeks. He also made note that all newly admitted patients and members returning from furlough were vaccinated, beginning July 1, 1902.

Dr. Babcock also called for a new means of transporting the sick and disabled from the barracks to the hospital.

Other changes in the medical staff throughout the year were as follows: Drs. Thomas Hart Cunningham and Michael J. Thornton were appointed assistant-surgeons on May 22, and August 14, 1902, respectively. Colonel Davidson had heartily approved the many changes Dr. Babcock introduced in his department.

Before his untimely death on November 10, 1902, Commandant Davidson made requests for appropriations for a number of new projects and improvements. In his report, he pointed out the need for a new bakery, a second-hand store, tailoring and repair shops, a house of detention, the enlargement of the hospital kitchen, electric ceiling fans for several wards in the hospital, fill and grading around buildings, and a new cemetery. He also requested a carriage house and stable to protect horses, wagons, carts, and implements from the elements. Also, general repairs to the engineers department and other buildings were requested as deemed necessary.

Davidson further recommended the purchase of 153.75 acres of the Faucett farm, located southwest of the Home, at the cost of $6,918.75, or $45.00 an acre. With only twenty-five acres of open woodland, the remainder was suitable for farming purposes. This does not appear to have been approved. The annual inventory for succeeding years does not show any such increase in real estate.

Colonel Joseph E. Ewell was elected commandant of the Soldiers' Home on December 8, 1902 and entered upon his duties January 1, 1903. The new commandant wasted no time in asking for appropriations. Along with all that his predecessor had asked for, Colonel Ewell also requested money for a metallic drying room in the main laundry, plumbing and fixtures in Barracks A, B, and C, an addition to the hospital kitchen for a dish-room and cold storage, and also $18,625 for the engineers department.

The new commandant also requested $2,000 for ten acres of the Longwell Farm adjacent to the cemetery. This was approved. The purchase was made and was reflected in 1905 Annual Inventory.

In his report, Colonel Ewell also noted that there were about 50 cases of tuberculosis present. He wrote that an isolation pavilion with the capacity to accommodate 60 patients would cost $25,000. He made a request for $5,000 to convert Barracks C annex into a tuberculosis pavilion.

According to Master Mechanic Thomas Fogarty, the electric plant now ran non-stop for 22 hours a day. The lighting for the new convalescent barracks, or Company L, would tax the already overloaded plant even more when construction was completed unless improvements and upgrades were made.

Mr. Fogarty noted the following as just a few of the improvements made during 1903. A new roof had been put on one of the cow barns, seventeen ward and hall tables had been made and put into place and 142 feet of tables had been installed in the dining room. Seven thousand feet of cement walk had been put down and more would be laid as weather permitted.

Greenhouse circa 1905

A new greenhouse had been erected and was ready for use and the "new eating house" (restaurant) had been established at a cost of $1,650. Since the officers and staff paid for their rations at the mess hall, this was probably for their benefit.

Dr. Babcock reported that admissions to the hospital had increased 12.5 per cent over the last year, bringing the total admissions for the year up to 681.

Also reported was the conversion of the two upper floors of the convalescent barracks into an annex to the hospital. This created 13 small wards containing 12-15 beds each, increasing accommodations by 170 beds. This made it possible to remove 104 beds from the basements of several barracks to the lower floor of the convalescent barracks.

The isolation pavilion had proved a wise move. During the past year, fifty-nine men had been isolated from a period of twelve days to four weeks. Among the patients isolated were cases of erysipelas, an infectious skin disease, and men from smallpox communities.

Smallpox had been prevalent in Bath for some time and in July of 1903 all members of the Home were vaccinated.

The electric ceiling fans were finally installed in the hospital and the corridor connecting the hospital and barracks was built. A new skylight was also installed in the operating room.

Among the recommendations were again the building of a new morgue and a tuberculosis pavilion. Additional bathing facilities in the hospital were considered an important requirement. With the increase of patients, no provision had been made in the new barracks for baths. The bathing facilities of the old hospital were unable to handle the large number of patients now at the facility.

A larger kitchen area and an additional washing machine were considered essential, as well. The present kitchen and washing machine were sufficient to provide for 200 patients but with the increase of patients, new provisions were needed.

As for the medical staff, Dr. Thornton resigned on May 31, 1903, and Dr. Clayton K. Haskell was appointed assistant-surgeon on June 15, 1903. Dr. Cunningham, due to ill-health, resigned on September 30, 1903, and was replaced by Dr. Lawrence J. Gerold on November 23, 1903.

The 1903 Annual Inventory states that the worth of all buildings, real estate, cottages, offices, farm and all miscellaneous items for that year amounted to $569,324.96.

The Home now had in its possession 77 buildings. Colonel Ewell noted that the $4,000 annual appropriation for repairs was totally inadequate. The buildings were suffering and he recommended an additional $6,350 for the engineers department just to bring the buildings up to satisfactory condition. The constant repair and upgrading necessary to maintain the aging buildings, some of which were a quarter century old, seemed an endless task. One hundred and seventy-eight inmates were detailed weekly to perform unpaid labor on the grounds, in the mess hall, and in the hospital. In addition, 228 inmates were set to work doing clerical work at a pay of five to seven and a half dollars a month. Special details were also chosen to perform tasks such as unloading flour, picking peas or apples.

Colonel Ewell pointed out in his report that with the members performing such tasks, a large amount of money was being saved on labor. However, twenty per cent of the approximate 2,000 members were in the hospital. Thus, in time, age and infirmities would increase the labor cost of the Home.

On May 6, 1904, the headlines in the *Steuben Courier* read "The End of the Canteen at Soldiers' Home in Sight." Commandant Ewell was notified in an addendum attached to the appropriation bill that no funds [would] be made available to any institution where a canteen was maintained for the sale of malt or spirituous liquor. Since the federal government paid $100 per capita for the entire membership in the Home, or $180,000-200,000 annually, it was decided to comply with the order rather than appeal. The board decided to sell all beer and

The New York State Soldiers Home

ale on hand and the doors were closed on July 1, 1904.

The board did not let the matter rest however. Minutes from the meetings show that the board was constantly urging Congress to restore the canteen. On June 30, 1908, a bill before Congress to restore the canteen was defeated by a large majority.

On May 12, 1904, Mr. Drummer received an increase in pay and was now earning $75 a month. Fred McConnell's, bookkeeper to the treasurer, pay was raised to $75 a month. Lyman Balcom, assistant-cashier, was earning $85 per month. Balcom replaced Wm. E. Howell, who resigned in early August, 1905, as Cashier of the Home.

The activities planned for the 25th anniversary of the Decoration Day services at the Home were cancelled due to rain. As in the past, a ceremony was to have been held at the Home, followed by a second service held in the village. The graves in the cemetery were still decorated with small flags, though.

Work throughout the year included completion of the ventilation system in every barracks. This was a much needed improvement, as energy was lost when windows were opened for fresh air. The cold draft was also the cause of many colds and ailments, which proved fatal to men of advanced years.

A new building for the electric lighting plant had been built and a new 75 K. W. and a 50 K. W. direct connected unit were installed, along with a new switchboard.

Dr. Haskell replaced Dr. Babcock, who had resigned. Improvements had been made in the hospital, as well. The interior of the old hospital had been painted and the walls of the main corridor on the second floor had been wainscoted. Steel ceilings replaced the plaster in Ward I and old Ward E had been converted into a smoking room for the convalescents. Also, the laboratory for clinical work had been established.

A call was again made for a pavilion for patients suffering from tuberculosis. By September 30, 1904, twenty-nine men were in the latter stages of the disease and another thirty men about the grounds were in the early stages. Dr. Haskell attributed 13 per cent of the deaths that year to the disease, ten per cent the year before that, and nine per cent for the year 1901-02 (fiscal year). Dr. Haskell did not agree with converting Company C annex into an isolation pavilion. He pointed out that a kitchen, bath, and showers would need to be installed and that would again create a crowded, unsanitary condition for the men. He recommended building a pavilion, with all the necessities provided, capable of accommodating 60 patients.

A call was made for civilian orderlies. Although some old soldiers still performed this duty, their aging bodies, Dr. Haskell noted, were unable to keep up with the arduous tasks. He felt that the need to employ young, robust civilians was most urgent in keeping the hospital and wards as clean as a "well-regulated" hospital should be.

Dr. Haskell also recommended a sliding awning for the skylight in the operating room. The discomfort was very distracting during the summer months while operations were being performed. Also, he asked that new floors be laid in the two drug rooms, the clinical laboratory, and the main hospital corridor. His report also mentioned a soldier who was not a member of the Home, dying from a stab wound.

The medical staff was once again transformed when Dr. Willis E. Merriman, Jr., was appointed to fill the vacancy created when Dr. Haskell took the job as surgeon. Dr. Merriman resigned shortly thereafter to take another position in the State services. He was replaced by Dr. Haase, who was appointed in August. Dr. Haskell praised his assistants and nurses in his report as well.

By 1905, the cemetery had been expanded to 20 acres and contained one thousand evergreens. A permanent fence had been erected around the three outer edges of the additional acreage, giving the cemetery a cul de sac feature. As of

September 30, 1905, 1,950 soldiers had been interred here; as many members lived at the Home at this time.

The grounds were now intersected by 23,750 feet of drives and lanes, 13,320 feet of gravel walks, 7,740 feet of cement walks and 3,480 feet of stone walks. The ornamental grounds, including the cemetery, covered 50 acres. The lawns were broken by shrubbery and trees, and 77 flowerbeds were laid out and filled with flowers and plants.

Thirty-eight iron vases were distributed about the grounds, and the greenhouses produced 70,000 plants annually for bedding. Sixty-five thousand plants were used for bedding and 5,000 for vases. Cut flowers were furnished for Chapel services and funerals and all other occasions which required them.

Fountain in front of Greenhouse

The libraries now contained 10,000 volumes of books. Leading newspapers and magazines were also provided. One general library was located in Company G and the other was located in the hospital.

The water supplied to the Home now came from two 4-inch artesian wells, 103 feet deep. The wells had a capacity of 2,000,000 gallons of water a day while surrounding springs provided another 50,000 gallons. A cement floor had been laid in the reservoir during the past fiscal year with valves installed for easy cleaning.

The old, outdated plumbing of the toilets in Barracks A, B, and C was finally removed and modern plumbing was installed, a much-needed improvement. Another improvement which brought much satisfaction to all was that cold, warm, and hot water was now being supplied to every toilet room.

Also, a full supply of hot water was now supplied to the main bathroom.

Another major improvement made was the installation of the Parsons System of Forced Draft and Furnace Construction. This was intended to burn a cheaper grade of fuel yet be more efficient. Conduit at last was being laid out to certain buildings. This was a time-consuming task but work was proceeding. A carriage house and stable were also constructed over the year.

A new morgue was finally constructed at a cost of $1,800. (Space in an old barn had been previously used to store the deceased while awaiting burial.) He had also mentioned in his report that the addition to the hospital kitchen for a dish-washing apparatus and a cold-storage area was a much-needed improvement.

Morgue

Among the recommendations made by Dr. Haskell was the location of a new well west of the outhouse. The present well, which supplied water to the isolation pavilion, was located on lower ground and was being contaminated. He also asked that the old reading room in the hospital be converted into a separate ward for patients suffering from delirium. The patients would become noisy and this was a cause of great distress to the others.

Dr. Haskell also requested again an additional washing machine for the hospital, a screened verandah for Ward G, the dementia ward, so the patients could enjoy the sun and fresh air. He recommended making the proper alterations to the window weights in the convalescent barracks. Since the building was completed, the windows never opened and closed properly.

Dr. Haskell repeated his request for an isolation pavilion and civilian orderlies. He also asked that his steward, Mr. Backus, the charge nurse, receive a raise. It was reported that he had received the same pay when the hospital was one third its size. Dr. Haskell also mentioned that two seriously ill Spanish-American War veterans, not members of the Home, died shortly after applying for treatment

Carl H. Richter, acting bandmaster since September of 1904, was appointed permanently to that position from the civil service list on September 1, 1905.

Many repairs were made throughout 1906, as was the case in the past. It appeared that more patchwork was being done than rebuilding. The new forced draft system installed a year earlier proved a wise decision, however. After a full year of service, a total saving of $12,134.78 was realized.

Another improvement was the installation of a Jeffery ash elevator powered by steam. This would replace the hand-operated system run by the inmates. The elevator was used to hoist the ashes up out of the fire room.

In his report, Dr. Haskell noted that the much-needed washing machine had been purchased over the past year (this would not be installed until 1907). The water-closets and lavatories in the old hospital had been painted, as well, and a cement runway had been installed for the wheelchair-bound patients.

Dr. Haskell pointed out that fire escapes should be installed outside the employees' sleeping quarters over the kitchen and outside Wards K and L. He suggested that these be made of iron bars. He also recommended a verandah similar to that on Ward I for both Wards D and G. The matrons' suite, he felt, should also be altered to allow for extra sleeping room for the nurses.

Another necessity mentioned was a combination autoclave, hot and cold water instrument sterilizer with a large receptacle for the boiling of basins. The present sterilizer was too small to handle the increasing workload. A request for civilian orderlies, a tuberculosis pavilion and an awning for the operating room was again made. This would be installed in 1911.

On a sad note, Dr. Haskell wrote that Dr. Gerold had died on March 15, 1906. He was described as a "conscientious, willing and able medical advisor." His death was mourned by all on the staff. His position was filled by Dr. Spencer L. Higgins.

Captain Reed A. Pierce, an inmate of the Home, was appointed as Chief of Police on April 13, 1906. Captain Pierce, age 59 or 60, had been a member of the Home for nearly three years. He was admitted from Buffalo and served in Company K, 8th N.Y. Heavy Artillery.

At the quarterly meeting in August, the subject of maintaining a Home Agency in New York City was brought up. The subject was referred to the Classification Commission. Also, Adjutant Morgan requested an increase of salary to $1,500 which was tabled. At the monthly meeting in May of 1907, an increase in salary for the inspector was approved.

A peak population of the Soldiers' Home had been reached when, on February 1, 1907, the greatest number of members present was 2,143. The daily average was 1,905, which was also the all-time high. Of the 1,812 men present on September 30, 1907, 1,753 were pensioners.

In his annual report, Colonel Ewell mentioned that the library, which had grown to over 12,000 volumes of assorted books, newspapers and magazines, was a very popular diversion for the men. One hundred and seventy-five books were signed out daily. Two reading rooms, located in the library and the hospital, were also supplied with the local papers and magazines.

The band now consisted of fifteen members, and outside concerts were given six days a week during the summer season.

The New York State Soldiers Home

As the weather turned colder, one concert a week was given in the amusement hall and two concerts a week were given at the hospital. Music was also provided at all funerals and upon request for special occasions. Interestingly, when the band performed inside during the winter months, they would reorganize as an orchestra.

Soldiers' Home Band circa 1908

Colonel Ewell also made note that the large amusement hall was used daily as a club and conversation room. Besides concerts various programs were frequently given to entertain the men here.

For the past several years, much talk had surrounded the firefighting system. According to Engineer Cornwell's report, the most satisfactory firefighting equipment (standpipes and fire hoses) had been installed in the convalescent barracks, headquarters building and the quartermaster's store over the past year. Also, a shelter had been built to house it near the officer's quarters and a new hose cart was added to the equipment of the general fire service.

Mr. Cornwell mentioned, however, that the equipment in the other buildings was totally insufficient and should be changed. He wrote that the present equipment in the large buildings consisted of 1 ¼ inch or 1 ½ standpipe and a rack with a 1-inch cotton or linen hose with a 3/16-inch or 1/4-inch nozzle. In most cases, there was only one per floor and these were usually located at the extreme end of the building. These hoses had been stored in this condition for the past 12 years and he felt that they could not be depended on. Most of his recommendations that year were for firefighting equipment.

Among his other requests, Mr. Cornwell recommended constructing an extension to the present coal pocket under the railroad switch, ninety feet long, fifteen feet wide and ten feet deep. This would increase the holding capacity by 300 tons. Currently, the storage was capable of holding only 200 tons, which would not last six days if the weather turned extremely cold.

One interesting request was for $300 for a small fully-equipped hook and ladder truck. He cited the reason for this as the men being too old and feeble to handle and up-end the large wooden ladders.

Another request was to install transformers and main lines to the farm buildings and also wire and place fixtures in said buildings. This would eliminate the kerosene lanterns now being used. He also recommended replacing the 176 incandescent lamps in the dining hall with ten long-burning, direct current arc lamps.

In the surgeon's department, little improvements were made. Provision was finally made for the awning for the skylight. The matron's ward was rearranged to afford additional sleeping quarters for the nurses, and a means was provided to isolate the noisy and delirious patients.

Unfortunately, the call for fire escapes, verandahs, civilian orderlies and a tuberculosis pavilion was being made again. Also, another call for elevators in the convalescent barracks was again made, along with the employment of people to operate it. Also mentioned was the water supply for the

The New York State Soldiers Home

quarantine pavilion.

Other minor improvements needed were new flooring in the two drug rooms and in the clinical laboratory, and replacement of broken tiling in water sections in different areas.

Assistant-Surgeon Dr. S. L. Higgins resigned in November of 1906 to accept an appointment as assistant-surgeon in the U.S. Navy. His position was filled by Dr. E. C. Foster. Dr. Haase resigned in the spring of 1907 to pursue a course of post-graduate study abroad. Dr. R. C. Hill was appointed to his position.

On September 28, 1907, the board approved salary increases for various positions of the Home, ranging from $1.50 to $5.00 a month. In December, the board recommended an increase of salary to the assistant-quartermaster to $100 a month. This was referred to the Fiscal Supervisor.

It appeared that 1908 was a very busy year. Prior to the Home's receiving their federal aid in the form of $100 per member per year, the government required evidence of proper maintenance, care and compliance of all laws requiring pensions. After brief visits during April and in September of 1908 General Newton M. Curtis, Assistant Inspector-General of the Board of Managers, NHDVS, assured the government that all was well. In his report, General Curtis remarked that the general management of the Home was well conducted.

The Home was also inspected on separate occasions by Henry L. Lechtrecher, Inspector for the State Board of Charities; by the Honorable William R. Stewart, President; by Dr. Stephen Smith, Vice-President; and by the Honorable Horace McGuire, Commissioner of the State Board of Charities. There was no mention of the purpose or outcome of their visits, however.

Colonel Ewell made a rare entry in his report when he described the Fourth of July observation. The day began at 6:00 p.m. with reveille, followed by a cannonade salute and then music provided by the Home Band, who he mentions as still maintaining their high standards. At 10:00 a.m. at the amusement hall, a program of music, recitals and songs was held. A baseball game followed, then a concert. At 8:30 p.m., a grand display of fireworks was given, followed by the playing of taps.

The new bakery building and oven that Colonel Davidson requested in 1902 was finally furnished at a cost of $11,000. Besides the bakery, a new piggery was constructed at a cost of $3,000; the annual inventory for 1908 lists 2 boars, 12, breeding sows, 81 hogs, 139 shoats, and 120 fall pigs. A potato peeler had been installed in the mess hall, large lights replaced the small lanterns in the basement of Barracks H and I, and an addition had been built onto the rear of the second-hand store.

Other improvements listed were new floors and steps in the main kitchen and the repair of stone pillars and coping in the cellar way. Repairs were made to the slate and tin roofs on many of the barracks and cottages. Painting was done throughout the buildings and grounds. Not just for cosmetic purposes; it protected many of the wooden features. The Catholic Chapel was painted inside and out. The spring-house on the hill was repaired, as well as repair work performed on the corridors. Overall, a general maintenance program had been developed over the years and repair work had become a routine process.

In his first Florist's Report, Mr. Drummer submitted that the ornamental ground now covered 55 acres. The lawns and drives were all bordered with shade trees and shrubs. The seven-acre parade ground, or plaza, was laid out with walks and flowerbeds, and the American flag floated from a staff which rose 110 feet in the air.

The plaza (parade grounds) contained 150 lawn benches, on which the old veterans could rest under the shade trees. Eighty-one flowerbeds decorated the grounds, and 31 large iron vases now graced the Home, four of which were connected with water attachments and gave the effect of vase and fountain.

The 4,066 ornamental trees were broken down as follows: 31 varieties of deciduous trees, 10 varieties of coniferous trees and 2,225 decorative shrubs of about 40 varieties. (Mr. Drummer had propagated a rare line of ferns, palms, shrubs and flowers.)

Around the twenty-acre cemetery, 1,500 evergreens formed a natural enclosure and made for a picturesque background to the Home grounds. There were now 2,420 graves as of October 1, 1908. Most were properly marked with headstones, while wooden markers were emplaced for those awaiting their markers. On Decoration Day, each grave was marked with a flag. The grass was cut short during the summer and the drives and walks were properly trimmed. Flowers were also provided for each funeral and all chapel services.

Inside the Greenhouse

Dr. Haskell gave, in his report, the average age of the patients in the hospital as 70.896; the average age of those who died was 70.084. Of note was the considerable drop in visits to sick call throughout the year. In 1908, 19,564 veterans reported to sick call, while the previous year, 26,458 veterans reported. No reason was given for this, but the following year, the average number of visits for the year rose to 22,773.

The hospital department finally received their awning for the skylight over the operating room. Standard size fire hoses replaced the previously inferior hoses and doorways were cut into the wards where they were previously non-existent. A new water supply was finally provided for the quarantine pavilion and provision was made to the ". . . evil construction of window weights and wells."

A repeated call was made again for fire escapes, verandahs, elevator, tuberculosis pavilion, steam sterilizer and civilian orderlies. Also, requests were made for new furniture for the employees' room, steel ceilings for the second floor of the old hospital building, and painting the interior of both hospital buildings. New floors were also recommended for the two drug rooms and the clinical laboratory.

Dr. Haskell wrote that the medical staff remained the same; however, he noted that the matron, Miss Mayer, resigned due to ill health.

In 1908, we see the first Chaplain's Report. In the Protestant Chaplain's Report, Chaplain Furbish wrote that the sacrament of the Lord's Supper had been administered every other month, beginning with October in the evening of the second Sabbath. The sacrament of baptism was administered to all who desired it and by the denomination of their choice.

Sabbath services were held in the forenoon at 10:00 a.m. and at 3:00 p.m. in the hospital. A prayer meeting was held in the evening at 7 o'clock except on communion Sabbaths. Singing for the services in the hospital was provided by the choirs of the churches in Bath, joined by the chapel choir.

There was also a daily reading of the scriptures in the chapel from 10:15 to 11:15 in the forenoon. Weekly prayer meetings were held on Tuesday and Thursday evenings at 7 o'clock, and from 10 until 12 o'clock, the chaplain could be seen in his study.

Chaplain Furbish presided over 127 funerals for the year with the chapel choir providing the appropriate music. He also made rounds of the infirm at the hospital and the barracks. The chaplain was assisted by a committee of seven members of the Home, selected by their "brethren."

The Reverend Farrell related in his report that his work had been pleasant and agreeable. Religious services were held every Sunday at 8:30 a.m. and 3:00 p.m. in the chapel and at 9:45 a.m. in the hospital reading room. On week days, daily services were held in the private chapel attached to the chaplain's residence.

He, too, made daily visits to the hospital and wrote that "...it has been a source of much consolation to witness the spirit of piety and resignation in the last moments of those who contributed so largely to the preservation of the Union." During the past year, 67 of his "flock" had passed away. Of these, 57 were buried in the Home cemetery.

Nurses and Chapel Choir

Each chaplain complimented the other in the work they performed and only positive words were recorded in these reports.

Captain P. J. O'Connor resigned as quartermaster and George P. Watson filled the vacancy on February 1, 1908.

An interesting side-note is that on April 1, 1908, the commandant authorized the barber $1 for shaving the deceased members of the Home. The money was to be paid out of the deceased member's pension.

In the annual report for 1909, the Board of Trustees expressed great dissatisfaction with the appropriations for the past few years. They cited that buildings were not kept in sufficient repair; in most cases there was a deficiency in equipment. The increasing age and infirmities of the members made it necessary to hire more civilian employees.

The board now suggested that civilian men or women should be hired to replace the approximate fifty resident waiters. The age of the existing waiters, who were residents of the Home, limited their performance. The duties they were tasked with were deemed near inhumane treatment. The board referred to other Homes as having made this change, largely with women substitutes. Should this recommendation be accepted, then a building would also be required to house such new employees and appropriations were asked for such.

Company captains and policemen had applied for an increase of pay from $12.50 a month to $15. It is unknown, however, if this had been approved.

Upon describing the present conditions at the Home, Colonel Ewell mentioned the funerals. One Home company acted as an escort at each funeral while music was provided by the Home choir and band. The casket was draped with the American flag and flowers were furnished from the greenhouse. Two services were held; the first in the chapel, the second at the grave. This was followed by the firing of a parting salute and the playing of taps. Of the 184 interments that year, 132 were in the Protestant section and fifty-two were in the Catholic section. There were 2,575 burials, all properly marked, by September 30, 1909.

In his report, Mr. Watson listed the improvements made throughout the fiscal year. He mentioned a water supply pipe which furnished water to the cow barn. Also, individual water basins and eight additional stations were installed, increasing the capacity to thirty-eight cows. A hot water heating system was installed in the piggery, which now furnished enough hot water to the receptacles used and also, for heating the breeding section of the building.

An old house, once used by employees, was placed upon a cement foundation beside the cow barn and was now used as a milk house. A modern ariator was installed, which removed the animal heat from the milk, lowering the temperature to near 50 degrees. A large cement water tank inside the house then cooled the milk to the desired temperature.

Among the needs listed were a new silo and corn-house. The fencing about the farm was also listed in very poor condition. Repairs throughout the past years were evidenced by areas where two and three posts supported the fencing.

Mr. Watson also recommended that electric lights replace the oil lanterns still in use in the farm buildings. It was pointed out that the farm carried no insurance. Because the cow barn and piggery were located on the hill, a fire would be devastating, as there was very little water pressure.

Another item he mentioned was the failure of the cabbage crop. The oat and potato crops fared well, but because the cabbage garden was in a low area, there was no drainage. Heavy rains and the river flooding its banks kept the garden submerged. (This was probably near today's ball field.) One suggestion was to create one large garden plot, opposed to working several smaller ones.

An extra horse would be useful also. Thus, the two present horses could be rotated when needed, and a three-horse team would be very helpful on the steep hills of the farm. A new manure spreader, farming tools, a wagon for the garden department and one for hauling ice in the winter were also recommended. Overall, Mr. Watson stated that the farm had produced satisfactory results for the past year.

In the industrial department, a saw bench was listed as being added to the carpenter's shop. A great deal of work was accomplished due to the addition. If the other machinery requested was approved, this would allow for many of the repairs and improvements to be done on the grounds at one-third less than to contract it out. (There is no list of the other machinery requested.)

The shoe shop did a great many repairs throughout the year. It was noted that many of the shoes were returned with the uppers cut or altered, for relief of corns, etc. It was also noted that many of the shoes, bought from the prison system, appeared not to have been worn. It was thought that perhaps the shoes were too hard on the feet. It was recommended that shoes with softer uppers be supplied or that shoes be bought on the open market at prison prices.

The second-hand store overhauled a large number of uniforms and put them in good condition, along with making towels.

In the last week of October, the Home Band reorganized into an orchestra with sixteen musicians listed. Just as the previous year, concerts would be held once a week in the amusement hall and at the hospital.

On November 1, 1909, a moving picture plant was installed in the assembly hall by Mr. Drummer. Entertainment was one of the many undertakings the florist was charged with and he oversaw the project with zeal. Families and relatives of employees enjoyed the feature films free of charge, while non-employees paid the nominal fee of ten cents.

Mr. Drummer had also noted in his report that, with the aid of the quartermaster, one hundred 5" by 7" photographs had been taken, finished and mounted by his department. These were to be used as the New York State Soldiers' and Sailors' Home exhibit at the State Fair, which occupied a space in the new building erected for exhibits from State institutions.

The library continued to be a popular pastime for the inmates so on May 1, 1909, Colonel Ewell authorized $2,500 to be expended from the Post Funds for books. On June 30, the board directed that the balance of the Abby S. Hornell's bequest be used for library purposes.

Dr. Haskell repeated several requests for what seemed the most basic essentials. Civilian orderlies, elevators and fire escapes were still not forthcoming. Again, a steam sterilizer, steel ceilings in the hospital and upgrading the employees' quarters were requested.

During the last legislation, however, $15,000 was finally

appropriated for a segregated annex for tubercular patients on the third floor of the convalescent barracks and adding new equipment to the hospital department. This was due mainly through the effort of the Honorable J. L. Miller, assemblyman from this district and chairman of the Soldiers' Home committee in the Legislature. Because the tuberculosis pavilion was still in the planning stage, the only practical solution to housing the increase in patients was to build a corridor to Barracks A and set hospital beds up there.

The average age of the patients as of September 30, 1909, was 72.85. To better facilitate transporting sick and injured men from the barracks to the hospital, the purchase of an "easy-riding" covered ambulance was recommended. A Roentgen Ray Outfit was also requested for diagnostic purposes. A larger hot water tank, more bathtubs, and lockers for patients' personal belongings were also requested.

Other requests were for airshafts and skylights in the various wards, a new dish-washing machine for the hospital kitchen, additions of recovery rooms, and covered food containers to fit on conveyors. This was to provide hot meals to the patients in the hospital wards.

A new operating room was considered essential due to the increase in the number of patients. The sterile environment was being now encroached upon by the cases of unclean nature. A steam disinfector and automatic flushers were also needed in the wards containing the demented patients.

An alcoholic ward was first mentioned in this report and was intended to keep alcoholics separated from the general hospital population. The hospital and convalescent barracks now contained 27 separate wards. The installation of telephones was considered a must in order to maintain control of every department. Dr. Haskell also mentioned "one destitute Spanish-American War veteran" who died soon after being admitted to the Home hospital.

Changes in the hospital included Dr. E. C. Foster

resigning in November 1908, to take up private practice. Dr. Alexander L. Smith replaced Foster as assistant-surgeon. Mrs. L. A. Weller took charge of the housekeeper's department.

Dr. Raymond C. Hill is also mentioned in this report as being in a supporting role. Curiously, both Smith and Hill made a request for a separate dining room. Trustee Robacher offered the following resolution at the October meeting that: "At the expiration of one year after the death of a member, all sums of $2 or less standing to his credit be transferred from the posthumous fund to the post fund. A memorandum of said transfer be put in the jacket of the deceased." After being passed, the cashier was then directed to do so.

The hospital and convalescent barracks now contained 27 separate wards. The installation of telephones was considered a must in order to maintain control of every department.

THE DECLINE
1910 - 1919

The needs of the Home, such as clothing, food and other necessities, were bought in conjunction with sixteen other State Institutions. They were under strict specifications, which insured satisfactory quality. Nearly 7,000 pounds of sugar were used a month, along with 150 barrels of flour. Butter, about 7,000 pounds a month, was also consumed. These items, along with forty-five to fifty other, were purchased on a monthly basis from various firms.

One entry which stands out in the annual report for 1910 was the statement that Isaac T. Cross, a member of the Home, was appointed superintendent of the dining hall on March 8, 1910. This was the first time the position was listed.

On July 1, 1910, the board recommended the purchase of 20 acres of the Longwell Farm, at a cost not to exceed $20 an acre. This acreage may have been intended for more cemetery space or for vegetable gardens. However, the annual inventory does not show any increase in acreage, so the purchase was probably not approved.

Among the official visitors for the year was Corporal Tanner, who spent August 30 and 31 at the Home. He addressed the men on the evening of the 31st at the amusement hall.

Chief Engineer Cornwell again called for a complete system overhaul of conduit to nearly every building. Coal consumption could be cut down considerably, once these improvements were made. Among other recommendations was a call for a light hook and ladder truck, fully equipped, costing $300.00.

Mr. Drummer, now listed as Superintendent of Grounds, reported that for entertainment, daily concerts were given between four and five p.m. during the summer, totaling 109 band concerts. From December, 1909, to September 30, 1910, 41 moving pictures were shown. Six lectures, 29 concerts, and one minstrel show were given at the amusement hall. (Drummer probably meant the Assembly Hall, where more seating was provided.) The appeal of the moving picture plant made it necessary to rearrange the seating, increasing accommodations from 1,200 members to 1,600.

Henry L. Drummer

Of the 3,761 men who died at the Home, as of September 30, 1910, 2,742 had been interred in the cemetery.

Surgeon Haskell submitted in his report that the average age of patients under treatment as of September 30, 1910, was 72.93, as opposed to 72.85 a year earlier. The average age of those who died was 73.139, against 71.805 the preceding year.

The substitution of civilian employees for soldiers' help had reached a point where there were now forty-seven civilians and fifty-five soldiers caring for over 410 patients in the hospital. With the addition of women substitutes in the dining hall, 133 civilians were employed at the Home by December 1910.

After five years, fire escapes had finally been placed outside wards K and L and the employees' sleeping quarters over the hospital kitchen. Steel ceilings had replaced the plaster on the entire second floor of the old hospital building. A new hand ambulance of modern pattern was purchased for $150.00.

The third floor of Company A had been converted into sixteen bedrooms for use by the civilians. These were furnished with bathing and toilet facilities, new and used furniture, and a general assembly area.

Recovery rooms had been installed in nine of the sick wards. These contained one bed, a nurse's table and chair, and a window which commanded a view of the entire ward. New bath tubs had been furnished in seven of the sick wards, and three additional bathrooms were installed in the convalescent barracks.

Ward 7 was rearranged to provide for treatment of the alcoholic patients. Two wards on the third floor of the convalescent barracks had been converted into one large sick room for the segregation of advanced tubercular patients. This new ward was provided with its own kitchen and dining facility. The remainder of the floor was for the care of the less advanced cases. Ward 22 had been converted into a dining-room and was connected to the kitchen by a dumb-waiter. A separate dish-washing apparatus was used for all patients on this floor.

Dr. Haskell boasted as the greatest accomplishment a glass-enclosed solarium. Well lighted and heated, this addition had a separate entrance, making complete segregation of tubercular and non-tubercular patients possible.

While some requests were finally met, Dr. Haskell made repeated calls for others. One was for the installation of elevators. This was considered most essential. Telephones to connect the twenty-seven wards of the two barracks were also considered an important necessity.

One new request was for a corridor connecting the convalescent barracks to Company A. Due to the growing number of patients, more bed space would be needed in the near future and the only logical choice would be in this direction.

Changes in the hospital staff occurred. Dr. Albert C. Snell resigned as ophthalmologist on December 1, 1909, and was replaced by Dr. Leonard Jones of Rochester. Mr. Donald Backus who was in charge of the nurses and attendants resigned in February of 1910 after six years. He was succeeded by Mr. James Fagan. While praising the nursing staff and hospital employees, Dr. Haskell also mentioned the clerical staff as well.

On March 1, 1910, the board moved to re-instate Thomas Fogarty as master-mechanic. However, his reinstatement was not approved by the Fiscal Supervisor. Fogarty's salary was increased however, from $50 a month to $75.

The board also recommended the extension of the building used as a public restaurant and dormitory. No reason is given.

A petition was signed by all officers of the Home, asking for full maintenance of their families or a 25% increase in their salary. The board adopted a resolution on April 30, 1910, recommending a 25% salary increase and referred it to the Fiscal Supervisor.

Another request for a salary increase was made by Dr. Haskell on behalf of his nurses. This was referred to the Classification Commission.

On August 31, the board recommended substitutes for the firemen, enabling them to take vacations. This was a wise move considering fires were always a present danger. On

November 10 for example, a fire broke out in the old hospital, beginning in the refrigerator room near the kitchen. It was quickly extinguished however, and the damage was slight.

On June 30, 1911, another milestone was reached in the history of the Soldiers' Home. Governor John Alden Dix made an amendment to Chapter 577, Section 1 under section 64 of chapter 48 of the Laws of 1909. Effective immediately, a law was enacted that every honorably discharged soldier or sailor who had served during the Spanish-American War or the insurrection of the Philippines was now eligible for admission to the Home, providing he met the criteria outlined in the Rules and Regulations.

As the aging Civil War veterans began to die out the Rules of Admission were revised once again. By 1917, Spanish-American War veterans, veterans who received wounds, sickness or disability incurred during time of service would be eligible for admittance. The rules were again revised on April 13, 1922 to include those who served in the insurrection of the Philippines and during the Great War. This was to become effective immediately. NYS Guardsmen were also admitted to the Soldiers' Home around this time.

Pursuant to the provisions under Chapter 92 of the Laws of 1910, the State Commissioner of Health would, when requested by the Fiscal Supervisor of State Charities, inspect the sanitary conditions of institutions, reporting to the Fiscal Supervisor.

On June 26, 1911, an inspector made a visit to the Home, and it would appear that a very thorough inspection was made. Inspection of the various areas and concerns of the hospital (total capacity of 444) included the operating room, nursing (eighteen male nurses were employed), medical attendance, quarantine and disinfections, pathological equipment, dispensary, dead house (morgue), laundry, food and drugs and other provisions, storage facilities, laborers, clothing, bedding and grounds.

All appeared to have passed with very satisfactory results. Eleven inspections were made throughout the previous year by the following: the Inspector-General of the National Home; Miss Florence R. Corbett, a dietary inspector; and members of the State Board of Charities, the State Department of Health, the Department of Agriculture, and the Legislative Committee on Soldiers' Homes.

According to the quartermaster Thomas F. Brown, a drought early in the year had had a huge impact on the oat crop. The yield for the season was only 450 bushels, as opposed to 1,100 bushels the previous year. The vegetables, however, did not suffer and an ample supply was laid upon the tables when in season. New farm implements purchased during the year were a corn planter and a potato planter and digger, which were used with great results.

Another call had been made for electric lights for the farm buildings to reduce the liability of fire. A motor was also requested to provide necessary power for cutting silage, threshing wheat and other chores which civilians were now hired to perform.

In the engineer department, Mr. Cornwell stated that more work on the boiler house had been done. This was a continuation of the past number of years. Unfortunately, funds were not enough to completely overhaul the boilers. Again, the conduit to all the major buildings was said to be worsening and repairs or replacement was an absolute necessity.

Mr. Drummer included in his report more details of the entertainment given at the Home. One hundred and four moving pictures were shown over the course of the year, and baseball games were becoming more common at the Home. On Flag-Day, 2,500 flags were

Flag Day at the Soldiers' Home

displayed upon the grounds, and a fine display of fireworks was offered. On Memorial Day, 2,834 flags were placed on the same number of graves in the Home cemetery.

A road machine and power sprayer were received, and by December 1, 1911, it was expected that 3,427 square feet of cement walks would have been laid and 3,224 running feet of drives re-graded.

Dr. Haskell resigned on February 28, 1911, and was replaced by Dr. R. C. Hill. In his report, Dr. Hill mentioned that other institutions of similar nature had greater surgeon-to-patient ratios than here. The Johnson City, Tennessee, Home, he cited, had an average population of 183 patients with four physicians. The Marion, Indiana, Home also had an average population of 211 patients with a staff of five physicians. Here in Bath, he concluded, the Home had an average of 438 patients with only three physicians. For this reason Dr. Hill requested that another surgeon be added to the staff. He also requested an additional assistant-surgeon or medical intern.

One repeated call made was for rubber matting, a yard wide, to be placed down the center of the hallway of the hospital. This would not only eliminate the wear on the floor but it would also cut down on the noise level. It was also thought it would make walking safer for the older veterans.

Entrance of Hospital Circa 1912

One new request was to combine the hospital laundry with the main laundry. Not only would this be economically wise but it would also allow for yet more bed space for an ever-growing patient population.

Another request was for construction of a porch on Ward 7 with wire netting. The netting would be a safeguard for the alcoholic and partially demented patients wanting to go out for fresh air or to sun themselves.

Dr. Sanford H. Kinne was appointed assistant-surgeon on March 4, 1911. Nine attendants, two waitresses, one assistant cook and one nurse had also been added to the civilian workforce. By September 30, 1911, the hospital employees consisted of 56 civilians and 46 soldiers.

On February 20, 1911, the citizens of Bath petitioned Congress to prohibit the sales of intoxicating liquors to within one and a half miles of the Soldiers' Home. This was declined as being cited as unconstitutional.

By September 30, 1912, forty-four Spanish-American War veterans were listed on the books. Reading various reports, it is safe to say that there was much animosity between the groups of Civil War veterans and the Span-Am War veterans. The aging Civil War veterans believed, correctly, that the Soldiers' Home had been built for them. Even with the admission of the Span-Am veterans, the Soldiers' Home was seeing a decrease in membership. Colonel Ewell wrote in his report that age was not the only factor for this; larger pensions had made it possible for former members to care for themselves outside the Home. A decrease in the percentage of deaths was realized, he noted, thanks to improved civic conditions in the town of Bath.

Colonel Ewell also acknowledged Mrs. M. B. Fairbanks of Brooklyn for donating a statuette, with pedestal, of General Rogers "administering the oath. It was displayed in the main hall of the hospital along with eight new pictures.

The farm and garden production for the year was very satisfactory. Seldom did the quartermaster give details concerning events in this department. For the year 1912, however, we learn that the net profit was $6,091.02, which was nearly double that of the previous year. The garden had produced large quantities of a variety of vegetables, which were relished by the members of the Home.

Thirty-one cows were averaging 800 gallons of milk per annum, which was an increase of 79 gallons per cow from the preceding year. The pork production was by far the most profitable at the Home. An increase of 16,000 pounds of fresh and salt pork was realized from the last year's nearly 32,000 pounds.

Additions and improvements on the farm consisted of another work horse, a manure spreader, a cement silo (the second one), and a forty-gallon chemical engine for fighting fires.

Mr. Brown asked for a 24x40 foot addition to be built onto the piggery at an estimated cost of $1,050. Other requests made were for a 36x62 foot addition to the vegetable cellar, costing $3,350. The existing facility was inadequate for the season's supply of potatoes. Also, a storage barn was recommended for the hay and straw. Roofs for the loading platforms were also considered essential.

Mr. Cornwell reports that the most important work performed during the previous year was the resetting of boilers 6, 7, 8 and 9. He also wrote that a contract had been made for repairing, painting, and generally overhauling the line of poles carrying the electric wires.

Another call for a new upgraded conduit system was made. Here, Mr. Cornwell recommended that a conduit five feet wide and seven feet high (inside dimensions) be installed from the boiler house to and through Barracks B, C, D, E, the Mess Hall, H and I, terminating at the assembly hall. The steam and return lines could then be properly installed.

Mr. Drummer reported that 104 moving pictures, accompanied by orchestra concerts, were shown over the course of the year. Ten special programs which coincided with the holidays were also given for the benefit of the members.

The greenhouses, covered by 10,000 square feet of glass,

had produced 75,000 plants. The ornamental ground now covered fifty-five acres and included 23,700 feet of drive and 24,500 feet of walks.

By Decoration Day, 1912, the cemetery contained 2,960 graves, all decorated with small American flags.

In his report, Mr. Drummer requested $500.00 to repair the three ponds in the cemetery. These ponds were used in times of heavy rain to prevent washing out the drives and grounds. They also helped prevent the hospital from flooding. He requested another $500.00 for re-grading the old section of the cemetery, which consisted of about four acres. The boxes in this area were giving way and the graves and head-stones were "scutting." He also requested $1,000.00 to rebuild River Drive.

Dr. Hill reported that the average age of patients under treatment was 72, and over the course of the year, 3,611 "surgical dressings" were performed in the surgery.

Dr. Jones, the ophthalmologist who specialized in diseases of the eyes, ears, nose and throat, visited the Home the first Thursday of each month. It was reported that Dr. Jones had treated 340 patients over the previous year. He had performed major and minor surgery, particularly extraction of senile cataracts. A large share of his work was the examination of the aging veterans for eyeglasses.

Repairs and improvements made consisted of new skylights in the main hall, operating room and pharmacy. Also, twenty oscillating fans were installed in the various wards. Five hundred and eighty-six yards of rubber and fibre matting had been purchased for the corridors and stairways, and 36 new rugs had been placed in bathrooms.

Fourteen galvanized iron food trays with tin compartments replaced the wooden trays previously used for transporting food from the kitchen to the patients unable to leave their beds. This was a great improvement, as now the food could be covered and served warm.

Other improvements were electric heaters for keeping

plates and special diets warm in the various wards, a potato peeler in the vegetable cellar, a new kitchen range and a sink with hot and cold running water in the hospital restaurant. A foot rest 125 feet long, made of iron pipe, was installed on the front porch and eighteen new rocking chairs replaced the old benches on the porch. These improvements were received with great pleasure by the patients.

Again, requests were made for telephones, elevators, lockers, awnings and a porch with wire netting for the alcoholic ward.

Key personnel changes took place in the hospital staff. Dr. Alex L. Smith, the assistant-surgeon, resigned on July 13, 1912, to take up private practice. He was succeeded by Dr. John D. Tierney who was appointed July 19, 1912. He resigned to resume private practice on September 19, 1912 and was replaced by Dr. Arthur F. Hinman, September 24, 1912.

On March 30, 1912, the salary of head surgeon was increased to $2,000 with maintenance not to exceed $2,500 per annum. On May 31, 1912, seventeen nurses petitioned for a raise in salary.

The Reverend Furbish resigned on February 28, 1912, and the Reverend S. F. Frazier was appointed to fill the vacancy on June 1, 1912.

May 25, 1913, began a string of misfortune which plagued the Home. Five horses were lost when a fire destroyed the 50x80 feet horse and grain barn. One horse had been rescued, suffering serious burns. All contents of the barn were lost. The milk house was also damaged considerably and deemed useless. No cause was discovered for the blaze. When the workers had secured the barn for the night, everything had seemed intact. Damages were totaled at $6,000, for which there was no insurance. This caused an increase in expenses, as farming implements had to be replaced. No funds were made available to replace the horses, so team labor had to be hired to carry on the farm work. Mr. Brown reported that without the chemical engine, the cow barn would have also been lost.

Many of the vegetable gardens suffered tremendously throughout the growing season. A late drought and then a killing frost on June 10, 1913, and an early frost on September 10, 1913, occurred, which caused considerable damage. Also, a severe hailstorm with heavy winds on July 13, 1913, wreaked havoc on the field crops. The oat crops suffered the worst, being a complete loss.

The farm did report some good news, however. The herd of cattle on the farm was tested for tuberculosis by the Department of Agriculture. Of the 25 head, sixteen had proven to be reactors and were slaughtered and properly disposed of. However, the farm would be indemnified by the department for these cows, and grade Holsteins replaced those slaughtered. Milk production increased to an average of 893 gallons of milk per cow.

Although the weather set back the value of the gardens, the milk and pork production did help the farm show a profit for the year. Pork production was up, again amounting to 50,000 pounds. Remarkably, the farm did realize a net profit of $2,067.32 for the year. Unfortunately, the following year would see another setback on the farm.

An addition of a cement wading pool near the piggery, which could be drained and cleaned anytime, greatly improved sanitary conditions for the nearly 300 pigs on the farm.

Mr. Brown requested another 40-gallon chemical engine be purchased and placed on the farm. Also, he again called attention to the necessity of a 36x62 addition to the vegetable cellar. The excess winter vegetables and potatoes had to be stored in the old condemned headquarters barn, where there was possibility of their freezing.

The weather had also taken its toll on the ornamental grounds, as well, according to Mr. Drummer. The frost in June had destroyed a large number of flower beds. The hail storm in July also did considerable damage to the flower beds. About

100 panes of glass in the greenhouses were smashed by hailstones measuring up to one and a half inch in diameter. Trees and shrubs also suffered broken limbs and branches, damage that only careful pruning would rectify.

Mr. Drummer also expressed in his report his sincere appreciation to Mrs. Genevieve Day Hayes for her contribution in seven of the ten special programs for the year. Also, thanks were given to Mrs. Leon Thompson, Misses Irene and Pauline Grant, Professor B. Frank Mayer, and members of the home orchestra for their fine solos throughout the year.

As in the past, Mr. Drummer made a request for funds to continue the improvements and grading around the Home and cemetery. His task was very great indeed. Rains and the oft times swollen river would cause considerable damage to the grounds, and he worked constantly to remedy the situation.

The hospital saw a dramatic increase in patient admissions in 1913. Nearly 1,500 patients were admitted throughout the year, compared to 931 the previous year, the average age being 73. The average age of the 199 patients who died in the hospital throughout the year was 74.

Dr. Hill reported that a regular inspection of the buildings and grounds was made by the surgeon or assistant surgeon. All members and civilian employees were vaccinated on admission when necessary, and garbage was removed daily and not allowed to accumulate.

Throughout the year, Dr. Jones, the ophthalmologist, saw an average of 13 patients a month. This was less than half the number of the preceding year. The 156 visits to the clinic included six surgical operations.

Among improvements in the hospital was the replacement of the old sinks with new white enamel sinks of the latest pattern.

Seven more civilian employees had been substituted for twelve veteran orderlies, making 65 civilians and 35 orderlies in the hospital department.

As to personnel changes in the hospital staff, Dr. Paul E. Betowski was appointed assistant-surgeon on October 5, 1912. He replaced Dr. Sanford H. Kinne, who had resigned.

The Reverend Farrell resigned on December 1, 1912 and was replaced by the Reverend John J. O'Donoghue.

Although the chaplain's report was often brief and redundant, Chaplain Frazier did write that his parish had greatly increased. Although the population was decreasing, admittance to the hospital and the death rate of the members increased. As a result, many members probably felt comfort in the ministering of the chaplains.

Reverend Frazier also reported that 179 members of his congregation had died over the year and of these, 63 were taken away.

The Reverend O'Donoghue reported his usual routine for the year. He also gave the average attendance as follows: Sunday mornings, 275; Sunday afternoons, 100; Lenten devotions, 200; and weekdays, 75. Of the 45 of his congregation who died, twenty-nine were buried in the Home cemetery.

What may be one of the first calls as to what to do with the Soldiers' Home was related in the State Board of Charities' annual report. The report stated that, due to the rapidly decreasing membership of the Home, it would be unwise to spend any more money on the Home except for the maintenance of the members and upkeep of the buildings. However, it went on to say that with the growth of the state's population, the Home could be, in the near future, used as training school, custodial asylum or some similar facility. This would be the subject of a long, hard debate in the next decade.

Another item of interest occurred when Bath's Town Supervisor John H. Bowlby met with the Board of Trustees at their quarterly meeting on March 31, 1913. Because Belfast Street, with its many saloons, had been the source of many court cases in Bath, Mr. Bowlby suggested that a court system and police in and for the Home be created. This would allow the village and town courts to save on the expense of local court costs, which were high. After a lengthy discussion, the board agreed with Mr. Bowlby's suggestion. Assemblyman and member of the board, Robert Bush of Horseheads, agreed to introduce a bill creating a tribunal with the same powers as a justice or police justice. An adequate number of police officers would be added and would have jurisdiction to act on cases of

Belfast Street Circa 1905

misdemeanors only when members of the Home were involved.

Among the acknowledgements for the year was one to the W. G. Mitchell Camp, N.Y.C., Sons of Veterans, for a gift of fifteen pounds of chocolate candy.

On Sunday morning, January 25, 1914, fire destroyed barracks H and I. The origin of the blaze was not determined but it was considered to have started in the rear basement. The entire building, which housed 370 veterans, was quickly consumed. Except for cots, mattresses, bedding and other miscellaneous items thrown out the windows, the entire contents of the building were lost. Fortunately, no one was seriously injured, except Albert Lane, of Campbell Hose, who was struck on the head by a brick. He remained at his post until the fire was finally extinguished.

The loss of the building and personal property totaled

$50,000. There was no insurance, but the building was replaced in 1918. (It is odd to note that, in the annual report, only $5,500 was for the members' personal losses. There was no mention as to where the inmates were housed, and no other money was requested to rebuild the barracks until 1916.)

On May 24, 1914, president of the Board of Trustees General Clinton D. MacDougal died in Paris, France. He was succeeded by Colonel Joseph A. Goulden. A memoriam had been inserted into the annual report by Goulden, eulogizing MacDougal. The same would be done for Goulden a year later.

Companies H and I on Fire, 1914

The farm and garden reported a loss of $946.45 for the year ending 1914. This debit was due to the purchase of $1,500 worth of farm horses, replacing those lost the previous year. Also, $1,577 was paid to replace cows that tested positive for tuberculosis and were condemned by the Department of Agriculture.

The herd was again tested in August of 1914, and five more cows were found to be reactors. These cows were slaughtered and disposed of under the supervision of the State Department of Agriculture. The farm would again be reimbursed for their loss of these cows.

The average production of milk per cow was up again, averaging 904 gallons of milk. This was an increase of eleven gallons per cow over the past year's production.

The pork production for the year was only 15,374 pounds due to an outbreak of hog cholera. This was nearly a 35,000 pound loss from the year before. Two hundred and five pigs and swine were lost to this disease and added a $3,500 deficit to the department.

It is thought the carrier for the outbreak was a full-blooded Mulefoot boar which was added to the herd in November of 1913. When the boar died the following January, an autopsy was performed but by this time the disease had already affected the herd.

After a thorough examination, every surviving hog and pig received a serum treatment, which seemed to halt the disease. A feeding platform added to the piggery was installed so that it could be properly cleaned and kept in a sanitary condition. It was thought that within the year, pork production would again flourish.

A temporary horse barn had been constructed to replace the one lost the previous year, and the milk house had been repaired. It was recommended that the milk house be enlarged to provide room for the chemical engine and that the building be heated to prevent freezing of the equipment.

It was also suggested that the construction of the permanent horse and grain barn begin at the earliest time possible. The temporary building was too small to store grain, implements and other devices needed to be kept out of the weather.

One other recommendation was that of moving the farmer's cottage nearer to where the farm help was housed. They were located on the farm itself, about a quarter mile distant from the Home.

The garden had produced during the year an adequate amount of vegetation to sustain the members, now totaling approximately 1,500. Nothing more was reported as far as the garden was concerned.

Mr. Drummer, in his report, wrote that the 104 moving pictures provided for the members were received from the Mutual Film Exchange of 71 West Twenty-third Street, New York City. The cost for these was $473.20 for the year.

In the grounds department, Mr. Drummer reported that 10,000 tulip bulbs had been bedded about the grounds for spring flowering and 76,000 plants had been grown and used in bedding and in filling the numerous vases stationed on the grounds. An apple orchard consisting of 400 trees was located southwest of the Home. The orchard had been pruned and sprayed, and Mr. Drummer mentioned that it formed a floral backdrop to the hill located behind it.

As for funerals, Mr. Drummer wrote that civilian employees dug and filled all the graves. For the past year, he reported that "... 127 graves [had] been dug out and filled, at a cost of 150 days or $255.00." Four citizen employees, clad in full khaki uniform, the same as the United States Army, acted as pall-bearers at a cost of $204.00 for the year. The graves were properly marked with a headstone bearing the name, company and regiment of the soldier or sailor, or by a marker bearing the number of the cemetery record, which was kept in the cemetery office.

One of Mr. Drummer's recommendations was the purchase of a twelve-ton steamroller at a cost of $3,000. He mentioned the many automobiles and the fine State roads which allow more visitors on State grounds, stressing that this purchase would be a wise investment. The cost of renting a steam roller was 7-10 dollars a day; an investment in such a piece of equipment would surely pay for itself, not to mention the cost of labor. He also pointed out that when repairs on roads were needed, it was hard to acquire this equipment on short notice.

In his report, Dr. Hill mentioned the average age of those who had died throughout the year as 77. He also wrote that nine more civilian employees were added to the department. There were now 77 civilian employees and 26 soldier orderlies. Every employee was now regularly instructed in the location and use of fire apparatus.

A change in the hospital staff occurred. Dr. William A.

Andrews was appointed as assistant-surgeon on May 15, 1914, in place of Dr. Hinman, who had resigned the day before.

One major improvement mentioned was that all hospital wards, toilets, and bathrooms, the reading room, smoking room, main hall, verandah and window casings and sashes on the hospital front had been repainted. All floors in these areas had been re-varnished.

Calls for an additional assistant surgeon or medical intern were made again, along with a telephone system, lockers, wire netting and more rubber matting for the hallways.

The Reverend Frazier died on December 1, 1913, and the Reverend Clarence Eugene Sutton was appointed on January 3, 1914, to fill the vacancy. In his report, the Reverend Sutton wrote that he was allowed a "missionary grant," which enabled him to provide Bibles to those unable to afford them.

On May 3, 1915, president of the Board of Trustees Colonel Joseph A. Goulden died in Philadelphia, Pa., at the age of 71. Vice-President George B. Loud filled in as acting president. Trustee William H. Nichols, secretary of the Board of Trustees, died on June 21, 1915.

In his report, Colonel Ewell asked for an additional $2,000 to apply towards the previous $4,000 awarded to replace the farm house, which had burnt. The previous amount awarded was not sufficient to house the farmer and his family.

In his report, Mr. Brown allowed that even after an unfavorable season, the garden had produced an abundance of green vegetables. Milk production was high and pork production was making a tremendous comeback.

The preventative measures taken in caring for the herd of swine seemed to have paid off, as an addition to the piggery was again asked for. The horse and grain barn, which had been lost in the fire, was now being replaced. It was expected to be completed ahead of schedule. The milk house addition was also being worked on, as well as an addition to the old ice house for additional storage.

Credit should be given to the men who had charge of this and other departments. Although faced with setbacks, they were able to remedy each situation and prevent continual episodes of the same.

Mr. Cornwell entered in his report that the elevators in convalescent barracks had finally been installed (after a wait of twelve years) at a cost of about $4,000. They were not yet running, however, because the A.C. wires were not ready.

Mr. Cornwell also wrote that bids were now being asked for a sanitary bubble fountain on every floor of every barrack and in every ward of the hospital (forty-two in all).

Mr. Drummer gave his usual report for the year, relating work done about the grounds. However, one item which stands out is that fifteen basketball games were played in the Assembly Hall during the year. He again requested appropriations for a twelve-ton steam roller.

Dr. Hill's report did not mention anything out of the ordinary for the year. He did state that seven more civilian attendants have been substituted for sixteen Home orderlies, bringing the number up to 81 civilians, as opposed to 19 soldiers. Another call for an intercommunicating telephone system was made; also stated was the apparent need for an x-ray apparatus.

Except for minor time changes in services and number of deaths, nothing new was reported in the Chaplains' Reports.

After twelve years of service as commandant, Colonel Ewell turned in his resignation, effective May 31, 1916. This may have been the reason for the changes in the reports. He was succeeded by Colonel Samuel M. Morgan, who had been adjutant since July of 1909.

It is interesting to note that the annual reports now showed that the fiscal year ran from July 1 to June 30. The Superintendent of the Grounds' Report (Mr. Drummer's) was now entirely omitted from the reports.

Colonel Morgan does not give us much information concerning the affairs of the Home. He does, however, make a request for $3,524.00 for a retirement fund. This was the first mention of this fund in the reports. Colonel Morgan also asked for $53,550 to rebuild Barracks H and I.

The farm and garden again fell victim to the wrath of Mother Nature when on June 17, 1916 the Conhocton River overflowed its banks. Nearly fourteen acres of the Home gardens lay under water, in some places up to eight feet deep. Some areas of the gardens had to be re-seeded, to no avail. Certain items such as onions would need to be purchased on the open market.

Down by the River

Although the report covered only nine months, the average milk production per cow was expected to reach 944 gallons for the entire year. Pork production was still satisfactory and was expected to supply a sufficient amount of fresh pork for the ensuing year.

Improvements and repairs made throughout the year were as follows: addition to old icehouse for storage purpose, repairs to slaughterhouse, including new roof and floor, addition to vegetable cellar and milk-house, construction of new horse and grain barn, new floor with drainage in meat room at storehouse, electric flat irons installed in tailor shop, guards and ribbon feeds for mangles at main and hospital laundries, drain installed at garden near bridge to carry off excess water into river, and new awnings for officers' cottages and guardhouse.

In the engineers department, Mr. Cornwell had resigned as engineer, and Chester A. Williams was appointed to take his place on September 1, 1916. Under the direction of

Mr. Williams, the boilers and heating systems were cleaned and overhauled. This led to substantial savings in coal consumption.

Dr. Hill's report was quite short and to the point. In it, he wrote that there were but twelve nurses on duty, a number which was completely inadequate. During the previous nine months, 1,224 patients had been treated.

Dr. Hill believed the department needed at least 20 nurses in order to take care of work satisfactorily. He complained that the department had been unable to maintain a full quota of nurses, and five more had resigned their posts the past year for more lucrative positions. There had been several responses to the advertisements for nurses, but they came to nothing because of the small salaries offered. Dr. Hill believed that this "deplorable condition" could only be remedied by a salary increase.

Dr. Hill also wrote that the new electric elevator had never worked properly and needed immediate attention. He also made another appeal for an appropriation of $2,100 for an intercommunicating telephone system and an x-ray machine.

Dr. Jones was now seeing patients on the first and third Thursdays of each month.

The Span-Am War veterans formed their fraternity, the Milton R. Wheeler Camp, No. 103, on April 4, 1916. The camp utilized Annex C as a meeting place, which had been formerly used as a gymnasium and since been abandoned. While their membership was small at first, they did what they could to improve their standing with their fellow veterans and staff at the Home.

The Home baseball team had organized with William Pedit as captain and Mr. Van Keuran as manager. After May 15, 1916, the team was open for games against all on-comers; the veterans spectators anxiously awaiting the exhibitions.

Governor Whitman had visited the Soldiers' Home during the week of May 5 much to the pleasure of the men. The camp fell out by company around the band stand and listened to stirring speeches praising the services of the veterans and their dedication to the Union. The governor stated that "every decent man and woman appreciated what we had done and nothing could ever fully repay that debt."

On June 30, 1916, orders for 2,000 copies of By-Laws, Rules and Regulations were reduced to 1,000 copies, as most members could not read.

On November 20, 1916, a potential disaster was averted. Shortly after 10 a.m. the fire whistle sounded. Smoke was seen rising from Company A and the Home Company responded quickly. They were unable to subdue the flames, so a call was put out to Bath, and their fire fighters responded in record time and the fire was doused in short order. The flames were contained to one end of the attic but the three floors below were damaged by water. Several fire fighters were injured but were expected to recover. The men of Company A were relocated to the library, while forty men were quartered in the annex of Company C. By supper time, all was quiet.

By 1917, over 14,000 veterans had passed through the Home. The average daily number of residents had now dropped to 1,091, down from 1,208 the year before. The three societies at the Home, Barry Post 248, G.A.R.; Encampment No. 150, Union Veteran Legion; and Milton R. Wheeler Camp continued to flourish, contributing much to the patriotic sentiment of the Home. As in previous years, Decoration Day services were held under the auspices of Barry Post 248. The ceremony was held at the cemetery, where nearly 4,000 graves had been decorated with flags, and banks of flowers were heaped around the monument. The men then formed into battalion formation and marched to the assembly hall. Here, an address was given by the Honorable Clayton R. Lusk of Cortland.

On Flag Day, the Ladies Drill Corps, Daughters of Veterans of Rochester, gave an exhibition drill, which was very much enjoyed by the members of the Home.

Mr. Fred McConnell was appointed quartermaster on February 1, 1917, in place of Mr. Brown, who had resigned. Besides the inventory, his report shows a profit of $1,883.20 for the year.

Mr. Williams wasted no time getting to work. It appears that his main concern was the cleaning and repairing the traps on all the steam lines. He also placed in service those which were previously out. This made it possible to return to the boiler house condensation from all the steam lines. Condensation, he explained contained considerable heat and deposits no scaling. This meant considerable savings in fuel.

Mr. Williams then had all the boilers thoroughly cleaned, removing all possible scale. The largest amount removed from one boiler was 2,400 pounds. He also changed the method of firing leading to yet more savings.

He also reported that curbing was placed around three springs and pipe lines were laid connecting them with the springhouse, thus leading off to the reservoir (which was cleaned). This resulted in daily supply of 50,000 gallons of water without the use of a pumping system.

Ten new radiators were installed in barracks D, E and F, replacing broken ones. Also, a new heating system was installed in Annex C. The automatic pumping apparatus to return water of condensation, which had never worked properly, was now in operation.

In his final report, Dr. Hill gave the usual information. The average age of those who died in the hospital was 75, and Dr. Jones was back to visiting the hospital department one day a month.

Dr. Hill now asked for $6,100, not only for an x-ray apparatus and telephone system but for painting the toiletrooms, main hall, dining rooms, tin roofs, porches and other exterior woodwork. He also requested the floors in the hospital be varnished. Also mentioned is that fire drills were held twice a month.

On July 20, 1917, Dr. Hill was granted an indefinite leave of absence to accept a commission for service to the United State government. He would be discharged from the service and again assume the position as chief surgeon on February 15, 1919.

Dr. Betowski assumed Dr. Hill's position as surgeon but on August 31, 1917, he, too, would be granted a leave of absence to accept a commission in the U.S. Army. Tragically, Dr. Betowski was killed in France on July 2, 1918 while discharging his duties.

Dr. Andrews became acting chief surgeon upon Dr. Betowski's departure and Dr. Frank C. Shaut was appointed assistant surgeon.

The Reverend Sutton stated in his report that he regularly visited the patients in the hospital and that "[t]he work done in the silent wards of the hospital must of necessity ever remain unknown."

It appears that $20,000 of the $53,550 authorized to rebuild Companies H and I had been appropriated for such. However, no report was given as to what was being done.

Hospital Ward

The farm and garden report showed an unusually large profit for the year but no explanation was given for this. Mr. Williams reported that a pole line was installed to carry electric feeders to the farm buildings. It was expected that the barns and farm house would be lighted with electricity by the end of summer.

The heating system in the hospital had been thoroughly

overhauled the past year. Mr. Williams wrote that these improvements in the hospital and convalescent barracks afforded a comfortable temperature during the coldest months. Since 1914-15, a savings of over 5,300 gross tons of buckwheat coal had been realized by the cleaning, repairs and improvements made.

In the Surgeon's Report, Dr. Andrews mentioned that the demands of the war were felt here, with many changes occurring. The medical staff was short one member, and the nursing and attendant organization consisted of only seventeen members. (Dr. Andrews was probably referring to the changes in the medical staff when he mentioned the demands of the war.) He did state, however, that the service provided had been satisfactory and the general health throughout the camp had been good overall. Also, he mentioned the sanitary conditions about the grounds as satisfactory.

Encampment No. 150, Union Veteran Legion is no longer listed in the annual report. The Fourth of July was observed by an order of exercises commencing at 6 a.m., with reveille, a cannonade salute and music by the band. The Steuben County Pomona Grange held their annual meeting at the Home on the Fourth as well.

A patriotic address was given by Mr. F.L. Strivings of Castile. At 2 p.m. At 3 p.m. the Daughters of Veterans of Rochester, gave an exhibition drill under direction of the Honorable Peter Sheridan.

Dr. Hill once again became chief surgeon when Dr. Andrews resigned on February 12, 1919. In his report, Dr. Hill speaks of the general health of the camp as being good despite an influenza epidemic during the previous fall.

Contrary to Dr. Andrews' report the previous year, Dr. Hill writes the physical condition of hospital buildings and equipment show deterioration. The toilet room floors were in need of repair, especially in the annex and new urinals were badly needed as well.

All the floors required re-varnishing and the beds needed repainting. He also called for replacement of the gutters which were missing or pulling away from the roofs. He noted that the brick work required re-pointing, the operating room repaired (not stated what repairs were needed), and the painting of all roofs. He did mention that the sanitary condition of the mess hall and kitchen was satisfactory.

He also called special attention to the urgent need of a special room for surgical dressing. A daily average of 28 cases is handled in the operating room which was not good practice as there was always a chance of contamination.

Hospital and Convalescent Barracks

Another call was also made for $2,300 for an X-ray apparatus and laboratory equipment.

The department was inspected in May of 1919 by Colonel Miller, inspector of the National Homes and in June, 1919, by H.L. Lechtrecker of the State Charities Commission.

Because the annual report for the year 1919 was lacking at the time of this writing, not much information can be given concerning repairs and improvements.

We do know however, that the Home was again facing a time of crisis. Newspapers reported much criticism which derived from present and former members of the Home, their relatives, past employees and residents from in and around the village of Bath.

In December of 1919, Governor Alfred E. Smith appointed Lieutenant-Governor Harry C. Walker as Commissioner of the Moreland Act. Walker was empowered with full authority to subpoena and examine witnesses concerning the allegations. The ensuing investigation is covered under the chapter Investigations.

Walker's investigation revealed that when a veteran is admitted to the Home, he is first examined at the hospital. He is then either admitted into the hospital or assigned to a company and given a bed in the barracks.

The barracks are situated so they resemble large dormitories. The beds are side by side and are, for the most part, "comfortable and commodious." Mr. Walker does mention however, that the arrangement of the fire escapes in some of the barracks is dangerous and should be remedied.

The barracks fall under the charge of a captain, who is selected from the members by the commandant. The captains, who are assigned a separate room for office purposes is responsible for the condition of the members and their barracks.

Able-bodied members are required to do detail work, under the charge of the adjutant. The captain furnishes the adjutant with a list of men who are available to work. The detail last a week and consist of light-duty tasks as sweeping and mopping, waiting on tables in the mess hall, peeling potatoes or other food prep work, working in the mattress factory, "pulling hair" and other light work the men are capable of doing.

Any member unable to perform these tasks could obtain a certificate from the surgeon exempting him from duty. (It was noted by Mr. Walker that many of the members were unaware of this regulation. The men would hire a substitute, paying them an average of $1.50 to $2 a week.)

The hospital was under the immediate supervision of the surgeon-in-chief. There were now two assistant surgeons but back during the Great War (not officially known as World War I yet) only one was employed. There was also one head nurse, several assistant nurses and attendants. As Dr. Hill had pointed out, like other similar institutions, it was difficult securing the proper staffing, especially since the war.

The mess hall, which had been subject to so much criticism, was actually found to be satisfactory in quality and quantity. During the late war however, rationing or conservation was being practiced. A large number of meals being served to the veterans consisted of corn-meal mush with molasses or other type of syrup, which was cause for consternation. This had been discontinued when the war ended however.

Another subject for complaint was the style of how the meals were prepared and served. Oft times, the potatoes were served hard, uncooked or unpalatable. Although some fault lie with the steam kettle, the cook or operators were often blamed. The potatoes were also served in bowls, stacked atop one another. Obviously, the bottom dish was served, looking less appealing than the top. The meat was served in the same manner. These were considered miner complaints and easily remedied.

Sigmund Huber on Right

THE END OF AN ERA
1920 - 1929

On September 1, 1920, Colonel Morgan resigned and Colonel John C. Fremont Tillson was appointed his successor. The Home had less than 800 members and only two patriotic societies, Barry Post 248 and Wheeler Camp No. 103, existed.

The annual report for the year 1920 is very vague. More than $20,000 had been spent towards the rebuilding of Companies H and I. However, there was no detailed report of progress given.

Colonel Tillson with Bernice circa 1925

The net profit for the farm and garden is far below previous years. The reason may be due to the cost of labor increase by over $2,000 since 1918. The rapidly declining membership of the Home meant more hired help was needed.

Dr. Hill, having returned as surgeon, reports that the average age of the infirmed is 78 and the average age of death is 75 ½ years. Weekly inspections of the buildings and grounds are continued but the doctor notes that the buildings are showing continual signs of deterioration. He also comments on, as in other State institutions, the difficulty of securing employees of all grades, which greatly hampered the services given to the feeble veterans of the Home.

Changes in the medical staff consisted of Dr. B. B. Israel of the Harlem Hospital, replacing Dr. M. H. Cole as assistant-surgeon on April 20, 1920. Dr. Cole had taken ill and returned home to Newfane. Dr. Israel resigned on November 7, 1920.

Among his requests was an x-ray apparatus which would cost $2,000, a new operating room he list as very much needed and special room equipped for surgical dressings. Dr. Hill also mentions in his report a visit by Colonel J. E. Miller, Inspector-General of the National Homes and Mr. H. L. Lechtrecker of the State Charities Commission in May of 1920.

The Reverend Sutton gave in his report that he had been taken by a serious illness during the winter. However, Sunday services were presided over by the Reverend and Mrs. Grant McChesney. The Reverend David Evans, D. D., pastor of the Centenary M. E. Church of Bath, conducted all Protestant funeral arrangements during that period. The Bath Baptist Church choir and soloists of the village were also mentioned as offering assistance over the course of the year.

Again, the information given in the annual report is sparse. Although the average population had dropped by nearly 200 members from the previous year, it appears that $29,098.86 had been spent towards rebuilding Barracks H and I. Another $3,000 was spent on fire protection; however, it does not expand on any details in these areas.

We do know that the year 1921 was mark the beginning of many cutbacks at the Home. At the annual meeting in early February, 1921, it was decided a committee should be sent to Albany in regards to the proposed budget cuts.

As one reporter wrote, "The proposition to cut the appropriation for the band would seem to be a move without consideration for the happiness of the old men who live at the Home, and whose diversions are meager at the most. Nothing has contributed more to the enjoyment of the Home membership, nor to the people who drive many miles every Sunday during the summer to the Home than the music of the band. It has been to the credit of the State that here at the Home has been maintained for many years a band second to none."

Even a bill introduced by Assemblyman Sterling Cole of Steuben County and backed by the American Legion allowing for the admittance of the late World War veterans to the Soldiers' Home did not deter the proposals. It had passed in the Assembly and was now in the Senate. Talks of consolidating the Women's Relief Corps Home at Oxford with the Soldiers' Home in Bath had also no effect.

On March 1, 1921, the State Legislature abolished the positions of second assistant-surgeon and inspector effective July 1, 1921, the start of the new fiscal year. On that date, Dr. J. A. Keown, who was appointed assistant-surgeon on February 26, 1921, resigned. Dr. Wm. H. Armstrong, who was appointed second assistant-surgeon on March 1, 1921, advanced to the position of first assistant-surgeon.

The position of Sanitary Inspector, held by Rozell Seager for the past four years, had also been abolished by the Legislature. Mr. Seager was praised as a "most faithful and efficient officer of the Home."

The farmer, John Pratt, had also been legislated out of his job. His position was turned over to Mr. Drummer and the gardener, Harry VanLoon. William Johnston, the dining hall superintendent, was also out of a job due to the decrease of appropriations.

Perhaps the saddest result of these cutbacks was discontinuation of the afternoon concerts by the Soldiers' Home band. The band would most likely cease to exist as several of the leading members decided to apply for pensions after more than 20 years of continuous service. They were Bandmaster Richter, D.W. Thomas and John Ormsby, cornetists, Leon M. Thompson, clarinetist and William Wiehe, tuba player. (It was thought that these members would form an independent organization and play on contract for movies and on Sunday

Orchestra, 1923

but it was unclear if the pension system would allow this.)

On April 30, 1921, a law was enacted which placed the department commander of the United Spanish War Veterans as a member (ex-officio) of the State Board of Trustees.

The average age of the men in the hospital was now 79 years, three months. The average age of death was 79 years and 9 months. The daily average population in the hospital was 251.

Dr. Hill reported that the general health of the camp was good yet the physical condition of the hospital and equipment showed marked dilapidation. Again, he pointed out the need of repair to the floor in the toilet areas were worn out and new plumbing was badly needed throughout the department. Nearly all the wards and beds required painting and the brickwork needed re-pointing. Almost all the gutters by now have become detached from the buildings or are missing completely.

Dr. Hill also wrote that a new operating room is "very necessary." He also respectfully repeated his request for $2,000 for an x-ray outfit. There was nothing out of the ordinary to report in the chaplain's department.

Curiously, even with the state of affairs of the Home, the 21st Annual Old Folks' Outing was held at the Soldiers' Home. To help carry out the mission of the Association, namely to "foster respect for old age and to increase the happiness of the old people," automobile owners throughout the county were called upon to seek out all folks over the age of 70 and transport them to the Home.

The program began at 10:30 a.m. and members could take their picnic lunch about the beautiful grounds. Ironically, entertainment was to be given by the New York State Soldiers' Home Band, "one of the finest musical organizations in the state."

One interesting tidbit is an act passed by the Laws of New York under Chapter 481 stating that ". . . the board shall have power to organize and maintain a band; . . . to be paid for out of the maintenance funds of the home, not exceeding six thousand dollars per annum."

On April 13, 1922, another milestone was realized when a law was passed allowing every honorably discharged soldiers or sailors who served in the World War to be fully admitted the New York State Soldiers' and Sailors' Home.

Reports of repairs and improvements are again vague. It is unusual that the reports are becoming less informative of the events through the year. We know that another $800 went into Barracks H and I but for what is unclear. With the average daily population less than 500 members, it does not seem to make much sense that $53,000 would be spent on a modern, fireproof building unless the others were in a state of condemnation.

Mr. McConnell reported a loss of $2,820.34 in the farm

and garden department. It is unclear why the value of Home products issued and sold for the year amounted to only $17,869.94 as opposed to the previous year of $27,016.25. The cost of labor had dropped dramatically since the previous from $17,261.52 to a mere $12,324. Even with the new admission policy, the population was waning. Perhaps this contributed to the overall production for the year 1922.

The Surgeons Report is still intact however and Dr. Hill includes much of the same data as in the past. At the date of his report, July 1, 1922, there were 200 Civil War veterans in the hospital and seven Span-Am War veterans. The average age of the Civil War veterans was 81 years while the average age of the Span-Am War veterans was 44. The average age of death was 80 and 56, respectively.

A 1915 Bus

Although there is a decrease in hospital patients, Dr. Hill still calls for more aides and attendants. Many of the infirmed are mental cases and others are bed-ridden, stricken by organic diseases. Repairs to the lighting system and sanitary equipment are now being made along with his request for the x-ray apparatus.

There was nothing new to report in the Chaplains Report.

On May 21, 1923, another law was enacted, enabling the department commander of the American Legion as a trustee (ex-officio) of the State Board of Trustees.

We see only the basic repairs being made now on the buildings. The annual report shows more money is spent on personal service, $147,702.23, than on repairs and alterations to buildings and repair and replacement of mechanical

The New York State Soldiers Home

equipment, which amounted to $11,821.39.

Besides additional fire protection, little else was done to the buildings except the essentials.

In the hospital department, Dr. Hill writes that the x-ray apparatus has finally been purchased and that hospital fire drills are held weekly.

Chaplain Sutton reported that business was as usual except for on Easter Sunday, the choir of the Bath Presbyterian Church sang an Easter Cantata for the patients in the hospital.

Also, at the chapel service on Memorial Sunday morning, Mrs. Sarah J. Loomis of New York City presented a silk flag to the Home; in honor of her father. She expressed her desire to have it stand in the chapel where so many men have worshipped, as a memorial to them.

As for the Catholic Chaplains Report, we see that Arthur E. LeMay is now chaplain. This happened during 1923 but without the report, it is not known what became of Reverend O'Donoghue.

John R. Cotter is now the quartermaster. No explanation is given for this change.

Dr. Hill's report is again very basic. The average age of the patients is 82 and the average age of death is now 81 years, 6 months. The daily average population of the hospital is 163.

The x-ray apparatus with fluoroscope and stereoscope accessories, radiant and ultra-violet lamps and a diathermic cabinet had been added to the hospital equipment. He also reports that the food has been of good quality, of ample quantity and well prepared.

Chaplains Sutton and LeMay both report that they had made frequent and regular visits to the hospital and had availed themselves to the men at all times.

Under the Laws of 1926: Article II, Executive Department the New York State Soldiers' and Sailors' Home came to be known as the State Camp for Veterans. The State Camp continued to fall under the supervision, jurisdiction and control of the division of military and naval affairs in the executive department. The title of superintendent was changed to commandant. The Board of Trustees would now be known as the Board of Visitors. The commandant was to be appointed by the adjutant-general with the approval of the Board of Visitors.

This is the last annual report on hand as of this date and little can be derived from it. As of June 30, 1926, the total number of veterans, present and absent was 231. Of the 207 present, 199 were pensioners. Sixty-nine of which were receiving $72 a month. Only one was receiving $8 a month.

The farm and garden shows a large profit of $3,642.58 but no explanations were given. Dr. Hill gives the same data as in previous years, with no additions or improvements to remark upon. Chaplain Sutton does mention choir of the Bath Presbyterian Church performing their Easter cantata for the third year now.

Between 1878 and 1922 the New York State Soldiers' and Sailors' Home served more than 15,000 New York State veterans as the Rules of Admission applied. A peak population of 2,143 was reached in February of 1907. Increased age and death reduced the ranks and enrollment dropped to 192 by 1928. During this year, the hot topic was what to do with the Home.

The State Camp was now facing a new dilemma, what to do with the Home. Many of the National Homes were full and yet, the State Camp in Bath was nearly defunct. The new barracks built in 1921 had been vacant for several years. Several reasons were offered concerning the lack of membership. Reasons such as no vocational training were offered here, or that compensation was paid to inmate employees of the National Homes. (They were paid at the Bath Home as well but probably not as high a wage.) Also mentioned was that the State of New York was enjoying a time of prosperity. (Commandant Tillson made this last statement and added that the Camp would fill up at the time of financial or industrial depression.)

Most all of New York State wanted the Soldiers' Home transferred over to the federal government. Unfortunately, a small group of disgruntled individuals planned to thwart every attempt of seeing the transfer go through.

New Barracks, Companies H and I

A newspaper report printed in the *Steuben Courier* dated December 7, 1928, related that Attorney-Governor Ottinger was preparing the deed which would convey the Home and property of the State Camp over to the U. S. Government. Ottinger reported that no time would be lost in preparing the papers.

State and National officials had met in Albany just days before and reported that the national authorities had been negligent in providing additional beds for the "invalided veterans." The number of disabled veterans had increased 20% over the past year, which was then 1,700 over the year before. (No exact total of disabled veterans had been given.) Colonel Ward, who represented Governor Smith, stated that the governor requested expediency in the transfer.

The Home was to be transferred to the National Government without conditions. However, some difficulties lay ahead. William Leffingwell had been named Chairman, Special Committee on Soldiers' Home at a recent department convention of the American Legion in Schenectady. Leffingwell had been tasked with investigating and reporting on the transfer of the State Camp to the National Government. The Charles E. Wescott Post of the American Legion was informed by the Honorable Reuben B. Oldfield, Steuben County Clerk that Leffingwell was gathering information and was proceeding to act.

A strongly-worded six-page letter was sent by James T. Rogers, Special Committee dated December 8, 1928 to Leffingwell. (The letter does not specify which special committee.) In his letter, Rogers gave a summary of the actions of the Bath community along with several veteran and civic groups who worked towards securing the transfer of the State Camp.

Cemetery in disrepair, circa 1928

Rogers wrote that the Wescott Post received no request for information or invitation for any hearings. He then informed Leffingwell that the Wescott Post has been in close contact with the Home since the inception of the American Legion.

He also explained that the Wescott Post had "waged several combats" for the betterment of the institution and, being in such close proximity, should logically be the Post to look after the interest of the Legion in this matter.

Rogers continued that information was received at the local legion post was that the population of the National Homes were nearly one-half World War veterans. He relayed that other sources brought to light the fact that the Veterans Bureau was hard-pressed for hospital space. In a thoroughly pre-advertised meeting of the local post in which nearly every member was present, the topic was well discussed. A vote was taken and the Wescott Post was unanimously in favor of the transfer of the institution to the federal government.

Thus, began the crusade to have the Home transferred over to the government. The legionnaires incited the people of Bath to act, pointing out the loss of an important local asset as well as the benefits promised to the all veterans who had served honorably.

A committee was formed and Mr. Bertram, president of the Board of Directors of the CoC, made the following appointments to the committee: chairman was Dr. Walter Woodbury; County Clerk of Steuben County Reuben B. Oldfield, secretary; and Steuben County Sheriff Lynn Kellogg was also appointed to the committee. Other local activists included George J. Collins, Henry M. Hille and Claude R. Smith. The committee then invited Colonel William Schohl, department commander of the American Legion and Major J. Kingsbury of the Veterans Bureau to visit the State Camp. Commandant Tillson, who also sent a strongly worded letter to Commander Leffingwell, escorted the entourage throughout the Home answering questions.

After the visit, Schohl and Kingsbury were confident that there was no opposition to transferring the property to the government. However, when the final discussion took place in Albany and a bill was drawn up specifically stating the transfer was approved and the members would remain at the institution, opposition in the form of certain employees, began to show outrage.

This small group began circulating the stories that the few surviving veterans remaining at the Camp would be sent to the Oxford Veterans' Home should this happen. (This option had been seriously considered by some State leaders.)

The group also called together meetings of the Legion Council in which the Bath post was excluded. At these meetings, efforts were made to pass resolutions, according to Rogers, through the Committee Council, condemning the transfer. It had been found out that certain legionnaires had in fact, personal grievances against the Veterans Bureau, particularly, the Buffalo branch according to Rogers.

Congressman Gale H. Stalker introduced a new bill in which the federal government would accept the property for the Veterans Bureau. Again, there was opposition. Stalker then tried to present a bill directing the Federal Homes Commission to accept the State Camp but protests rang out once again.

Rogers wrote that every Civil War veteran at the Camp and in town were in favor of the transfer. Custer Post, Barry Post and the Veterans of Foreign Wars had all gone on record unanimously in favor of the transfer.

Rogers also made it known that the opposition had sent out 1,000 circular letters and other propaganda when the transfer seemed imminent. They had succeeded in passing through the state convention of the American Legion a resolution condemning the transfer. Rogers wrote that this was but one example of the misrepresentation which had been spread throughout the state.

A meeting of the Seventh District Council of the American Legion was called for and the Wescott Post was not even considered to host the meeting. Rogers made it clear that the Bath post had been completely ignored in all areas concerning the transfer.

In closing, Rogers invited Leffingwell and his committee along with representatives of the state and national American Legion to all information in his possession pertinent to the transfer. He also stated that for the best interest of the state and the best service for the nation would be the transfer of the State Camp.

Rogers had also pointed out one principle reason for securing the transfer was because the Camp was now almost vacant and there were veterans who needed the room and facilities it afforded. He also stressed that the last war was fought by a national army; a state army no longer existed.

On Monday January 7, 1929, the House of

Representatives had, without one dissenting vote, passed the bill introduced by Stalker. Depending on the action of the Senate, which was expected to be favorable, the transfer of the Home and cemetery would be complete. The formal transfer would have to be conducted through the War Department but this would be a mere formality as state and federal authorities all agreed upon the transfer.

According to the *Steuben Advocate* on January 23, 1929, a dispatch in the *Democrat and Chronicle* reported Senator John Knight had stated that there were no intentions of dropping the plans of turning the State Camp for Veterans over to federal government. Other leaders in Albany also voiced their opinions that further legislation may not be necessary. Senator Knight also points out that the small group opposed to the transfer was not sufficiently informed of all the factors involved.

Finally an agreement was reached. The State of New York would lease the State Camp for Veterans to the Board of Managers, National Home for Disabled Veteran Soldiers (NHDVS) for a term not to exceed ten years. This lease specified ". . . that such camp shall be maintained by the lessee during the term of this lease as a camp or home for veterans of the wars of the United States and that the veterans of the Civil War and Spanish-American War, who are inmates of such camp at the time of transfer of possession under this lease, shall be maintained therein by the lessee during the term of this lease."

On April 30, 1929, General George Wood, chairman of the board of National Soldiers' Home; Major P.A. Clune of the state attorney general's office and Adjutant-General Ward was present at the Home to formally secure transfer from state to federal control. Governor-elect of the Home, Captain Robert Bringham signed receipt for the property and at midnight, May 1, after its 50th Anniversary and two years of hard fought legal and legislative negotiations, the New York State Soldiers' and

Sailors' Home was finally transferred from state to federal ownership.

The Camp became known as the Bath Branch, the tenth Home under control of the Board of Managers, National Home for Disabled Volunteer Soldiers. Up to this time, the Home had sheltered 17,181 different men.

Proclamation

After years of gradual decline, Baths' greatest business and architectural asset, the Soldiers' and Sailors' Home has at last been brought back to an active and progressive future. This has taken place principally through the untiring efforts of some of our leading citizens. In order to properly recognize the occasion, a Municipal Celebration will be held on May 1, 1929.

It is particularly requested that between the hours of 3 and 4 o'clock in the afternoon of May 1, 1929 all places of business be closed and that all business operations cease in order that our citizens may join in a hearty demonstration of the rejuvenation of that wonderful institution.

W. R. Campbell,
Mayor

Because the Camp was now a national home, it no longer took in exclusively New York veterans. It had also assumed responsibility of the cemetery where 5,000 veterans were laid to rest as well. Also, it was believed that within three years the Home would grow to 2,500 members. Since the Home was geographically situated to serve Philadelphia, New York, Buffalo, Syracuse, Rochester, Pittsburg and other major cities it was believed to become one of the largest and most important of national homes.

An interesting aside, the first of the federal group of veterans to enter the Home was William Leonard of Johnstown, Pa. Born on Christmas Day in 1871, he witnessed the devastating flood that wiped out the town of Johnstown and took the lives of both his parents. As fate would have it, he had been sent to a friend's house overlooking the town a day before the disaster. Mr. Leonard served in the army as a private with the Supply Company, 146th Infantry from February 5, 1917 until April 13, 1919.

On Thursday, May 30, 1929, the first Decoration Day

under control of the Bath Home Branch was observed. Governor Bringham issued General Order No.4 calling for an extensive program for the special day. All but necessary work was suspended for the duration of the ceremonies. The services began at the sound of a bugle at 9:00 a.m. Members of the Home able to march, employees and visiting organizations formed on the road north of the Headquarters building four abreast. Governor Bringham and staff led the formation followed by the Drum Corps of James A. Hill Post, V.F.W.; massed colors of all organizations; firing party; G.A.R. posts; United Spanish War Veterans Camps; American Legion posts; members of the Home not with the organizations; employees of the Home; Boy Scouts. From there the procession began its march to the cemetery where the monument was once again banked with flowers and plants as in the past. Garlands were hung over the base and flags decorated the graves.

Silas Kimball, commander of Barry Post had charge of the opening ceremony, followed by the singing of "America" by Miss Addis and Mrs. Haley. A prayer was then offered by Reverend C. E. Sutton and Reverend A.A. Le May read Lincoln's Gettysburg Address. A cornet solo was then played followed by the firing squad giving a memorial salute. Taps and then the benediction ended the ceremony.

At the close of the exercises, the procession marched to a place in front of the hospital (Bldg. 29) where another ceremony was carried out for the benefit of the members of the Home unable to attend the ceremony at the cemetery. Seated on the front porch of the hospital, the ailing inmates watched as the procession returned from the cemetery. Another program consisting of orchestra selections, prayers, the Recessional by the Bath Presbyterian Church, reading of General Logan's address; more musical selections and then the benediction.

After the program, all participating organization was invited to join the exercises in the village that afternoon.

Forming at Pulteney Square at 1:30 p.m. the column would march down Liberty Street to the soldier's monument where the address was to be given.

On May 30, 1930 the National Home for Disabled Volunteer Soldiers at Bath held its' ceremonies for Decoration Day. Although the weather conditions were not pleasant the turnout was favorable. Governor Bringham was in charge of the services while the Wescott Post was charged with arraigning the ceremony. Guest speaker of the day was the Honorable Robert F. Thompson, of Canandaigua, Associate Justice of the Fourth Appellate Department of the Supreme Court, State of New York.

At 10:00 a.m. Reverend Arthur A. LeMay, a chaplain at the Home opened the service. The Bath Presbyterian Church choir then offered a beautiful selection as it had in the past ceremonies. Governor Bringham next asked the men of the Home, on behalf of the Legion, if any would like to partake in the program. Those who chose to do so were to meet at the park at 1:30 p.m. Colonel Bringham gave his condolences to the men who were confined to the hospital due to the weather. He then asked Mr. John W. Yost to read the Decoration Day Order. (Three different Orders were used by the Grand Army of the Republic to officially recognized Decoration Day across the country; one for regular services, one for cemeteries and one for public exercises.)

Governor Bringham next asked Justice Edwin C. Smith to introduce the speaker of the day, Judge Thompson. As he addressed the crowd, he promised no long or eloquent speeches but would say that this was a day for memories. He indicated to his chest the badge his father had worn on Decoration Day as commander of old Gordon Granger Post No. 7. He mentioned his father was a veteran of the Civil War and that he had worn the same medal here in 1879 to help dedicate this institute.

Judge Thompson related the tales of the fellow veterans and the hurdles they faced in trying to make this Home a reality. He spoke of James Tanner and Henry Ward Beecher. Also, he spoke of the widow in Columbus, Mississippi, where the idea for Decoration Day was said to originate.

It was a passionate address, punctuated by applause. The members of the church choir then offered another selection. Reverend Clarence Sutton, another chaplain at the Home, offered the benediction. The Home band then played the National Anthem. Following the services, the choir again entertained the crowd as well as those confined to the hospital with more selections.

On June 4, 1930, at the 47th encampment of the Sons of Union Veterans of the Civil War (SUVCW), Harry L. Olney, chairman of the Bath and Oxford Homes' Christmas and Mother's Day Fund Committee reported on conditions at the Home. "No more effective service is performed by our Order than the yearly visits to the Homes," he proclaimed. In his report, he commented that on June 2, he, Carl Hill and past commander Neil D. Cranmer made a trip to the Home to see how their "daddies" were doing since the transfer to federal ownership. He was pleased to announce that since the transfer conditions had improved for the "Boys" and those they were receiving better care than before, according to Captain James T. Brady who has charge of the Grand Army veterans.

They were glad to hear that the commandant had segregated the aging veterans from the younger Spanish War and World War veterans as they were involved in great arguments with the older veterans and it kept them worked up to a point that was not very pleasant.

The commandant made other changes as well, from serving them their meals and allowing more time to eat to fixing lights, making it possible for them to read.

It was noted that there were now 79 Civil War veterans at the Home, 47 in the hospital and 32 in the barracks, 69 Spanish War veterans and 39 World War veterans. On July 30, another 250 Civil War veterans were expected to return to New

York from the National Home in Virginia. These men were native New Yorkers but decided to enter a National Home as opposed to a State Home such as Bath was at the time they entered.

The S.U.V.C.W. had been visiting the Homes at Bath and Oxford for a number of years, distributing gifts and visiting all veterans but because the population was expected to increase at Bath in December by 600 to 1,000 men, it was decided to only buy gifts for the Civil War veterans, from whom they took their namesake.

By 1930, even with the admission of all eligible veterans, enrollment had dropped dramatically. The Veterans Bureau and the National Home had come under harsh criticism for their management of these Homes. To ensure veteran benefits and eliminate confusion in disbursing all benefits, congress authorized President Herbert Hoover to consolidate these two services along with the Bureau of Pensions. Hence, in July of 1930 the United States Veterans Administration was established.

THE VA TAKES CONTROL
1930 - 1954

"UNSAFE, PERSONS USING THIS BRIDGE DO SO AT THEIR OWN RISK."

By June of 1934, the Home had served 25,173 veterans and the cry for repair, rebuilding and expansion was being made. Two veteran hospital facilities had been built in Batavia and Canandaigua in 1933 and yet, the federal government's investment in Bath up to this time had been negligible. Praise had been given to Governor Bringham and his staff for having "worked wonders with this old state property," but its per capita for maintenance was still far below the national average.

Commander Frank Kluck, of the Steuben County American Legion had stated, "We, too, have a Chamber of Commerce, Rotary and Exchange clubs, as well as methods of reaching political Washington." He continued, ". . . we will not let any stone remain unturned to insure that out of the President's four billion dollar relief fund our buddies are provided for at Bath free from the menaces recited in the Legion Committee report."

In a statement to the *Steuben Courier*, Colonel Bringham reported that ". . . the Bath facility serves three

The New York State Soldiers Home

times as many veterans as any other Western New York facility. At present, there are 1,205 veterans cared for and in a few weeks time the total enrollment will be over 1,500 after transfers are effected [sic] from other facilities."

Colonel Bringham would be transferred in April of 1935

Did You Know That:
-The Building comprising the Domiciliary Section of the Vet. Adm. Facility, Bath, New York, are as much as 60 Years Old.
-The roofs are badly in need of repairs.
-The outside walls are cracked in many places.
-The inside walls are badly in need of repainting.
-The ceilings are too high vaulted, so that heating is difficult.
-The floors, are wood, badly worn, dry as tinder, soaked with oil.
-The Stairways are of wood, fast deteriorating, dangerous to use.
-The windows, are loose, sashes all in need of repairs, frames so disjointed, that flies and vermin readily enter, and provide no protection from the elements.
-The surfaces in and out of all Buildings are in badly need of paint.
-The basements draw water from even slight rains, are damp, unhealthy and a menace to health.
-The lighting fixtures, are so high, inadequate and spaced so far apart that reading is almost impossible unless sight is very good.
-The plumbing, is old, outworn and needs to be replaced for the most part.
-The Sanitary facilities are crowded, lack space and are inadequate.
-The Squadrooms hold as many as 65 beds, and often the are increased to 75 beds in one room.
-The Mess Hall is of such distance from some buildings that one gets drenched trying to reach it on a rainy day.
-The Mess Hall roof leaks in more than twenty places and needs renewing.
-The fire escapes are narrow, inadequate and dangerous to use.
-The walks and roads are broken up, dust and germ laden with no provision made for their repair as yet, constituting a dangerous menace to health.
-The Nurses' Quarters will presently be located a quarter of a mile from the new Hospital Building, in a building to be renovated but not made fireproof.
-The Disabled Veteran entering this Facility, takes his life in his own hands crossing a bridge that has been condemned and posted as Unsafe, with no provision made for its replacement.
-The Federal Government has yet to construct a Domiciliary Building in New York State, all have heretofore been constructed by the G.A.R. or the State of New York and turned over to the Federal Government Gratis.

-Hospital Replacement Committee Report

to govern the Pacific Branch. His successor, Colonel John Hadley was being transferred here from that exact place.

A "patient and exhaustive survey of conditions at the Bath Veterans' Home" was conducted by the Hospital Replacement Committee which was formed in early November of 1934. Led by Commander Kluck, the existing hospital was found to be "unsafe, inadequate, obsolete, outworn and a fire hazard of menacing proportions, totally unsuited for the proper care and treatment of the patient load carried." The American Legion pointed out 14 serious conditions which warranted a new hospital and Barracks D, E, and F. (The barracks is thought to have been damaged by fire sometime during 1934.)

Encouraging words were received from Congressman W. Sterling Cole, who wrote from Washington that he had called on the Veterans Administration and had an audience with General Hines and Colonel Tripp. When the subject of the hospital came up both men agreed on the need for a new one at the Bath facility and would try to secure funding from the Public Works Fund for such an endeavor.

"The distinction of being not only one of the first sites for a home for relief and comfort of American Veterans but what is more significant, the community has always been at the forefront as this occasion exemplifies." Excerpt from a speech by President Franklin Roosevelt regarding the Hospital dedication.

It would not be until 1936, after the VA received $25.2 million, its largest construction budget ever, that 97 year old Civil War veteran Orville Nichols, would break ground for a new hospital from his wheelchair on the site where the commandant's quarters once

Ground Breaking, 1936.

stood. Mr. Nichols died in the first week of June, 1939. He was the oldest Civil War veteran living at the Home where he had spent the last 35 years. Three Civil War veterans remained at the Home after his death, the youngest, who had enlisted at the age of 13 as a "drummer boy" was now 89 years of age.

On May 12, 1938, National Hospital Day, the new hospital, built in the Georgian Colonial Revival style, was dedicated. The Bath Chamber of Commerce-sponsored dedication attracted 6,000 visitors, 500 of whom were invited to a banquet. Local veterans, civic and fraternal groups and church organizations, assisted by many local citizens, served on various committees and functions to ensure things went smoothly.

Exterior Southeast New Veterans' Hospital

This new facility stood, not only as a monument to veterans, but also to the founders of the New York State Soldiers' and Sailors' Home and to the people of Bath. The new, six-story hospital, which cost just shy of one million dollars, had a 409-bed capacity. The brightly colored corridors, running north to south, spanned an eighth of a mile. The wards, well-lit and ventilated, were furnished with new chairs, beds and lockers. Four passenger and two freight elevators supplied

The New York State Soldiers Home

visitors and patients access to every floor with ease. The kitchen was furnished with every apparatus needed to provide every type of culinary delight.

There were two state-of-the-art operating rooms, which were provided with every surgical tool known to medical science. No other institution in the country had finer equipment. The hospital had a compliment of medical, surgical and nursing staff that "... are not only a credit to their professions but to the nation."

The official dress for the surgical and medical staff was a blue uniform and officer cap in the fall and winter and white trousers in spring and summer.

On May 22, 1938, Colonel Hadley and his entire staff received scores of visitors at the new hospital. There was not a word of dissatisfaction among them. The following Monday 300 patients were transferred from the old hospital, which had beds for 395, to the new facility. The remaining patients were either discharged and sent home or moved to the barracks.

Medical and Surgical Staff, 1938

Of the original hospital built in the 19th century, the southernmost elevation was used for nurses' quarters. The section located on the northern elevation was converted into an arts and crafts and a print shop while the central part of the building was used for barracks, housing 100 residents until 1961.

The Hospital Replacement Committee now wanted new barracks and improvements to the entire grounds. Congressman Cole, agreeing with the committee's finding from the beginning, reported that the need for a new barracks was imperative. He currently had a bill before the House seeking appropriations for a new building, noting there were at least sixty veterans on the waiting list and the number growing. During the winter, over 150 men had been turned away. In September of 1938, the call for more bed space was heard and ground was broken for a new barracks with a 395 bed capacity. This new building, later known as Section 2 or Nursing Home Care Unit (NHCU), ran east and west, occupying the site of old Barracks D, E and F.

From May, 1929 to May, 1939, the VA experienced many changes. Several of the old wooden buildings had been demolished, while others were repaired or remodeled. A new bakery, sewage disposal plant and supply warehouse had been constructed and utility services had been modernized. The entire farm area, consisting of approximately 200 acres, was entirely reforested with 250,000 young trees. Also, in 1939, a new bridge finally replaced the one condemned several years ago at the main entrance.

Construction of New Barracks circa 1939

In May of 1929, the bed capacity in the domiciliary was 130 but by May of 1939, there was room for 1,067, plus an additional 395 beds when the new barracks were completed.

The domiciliary membership in 1929 was 118 compared to 1,160 in 1939. There were 253 employees in 1929 with a payroll of $283,200. In 1939, the number of employees increased to 405 with a payroll of $492,000. The reason for this increase was noted in the care given to the patient. The medical staff now included 16 doctors, 44 nurses, 56 hospital attendants, five dental personnel, seven technicians and aides, three dieticians, one social service worker, in addition to clerks, stenographers, cooks and mess attendants. In the domiciliary, there were 21 company commanders, sergeants and attendants. The total circulation of the main library was 54,295 books, subscription for 40 magazines and eight daily newspapers including Sunday editions.

Veteran Population				
May 1, 1929		May 1, 1939		
Dom...Hosp.		Dom...Hosp.		
CW	36	48	---	4
USWV	53	21	46	28
WWI	29	18	1,074	333
Other	--	--	---	20

During the S.U.V.C.W. visit at the Home on December, 23, 1940, Captain Brady was found to be the lone survivor of the Grand Army veterans. This was to be the last visit by the S.U.V.C.W. to the Home at Bath. On February 20, 1941, Captain Brady died at the age of 94. He had served with the 186th New York Infantry and was present at Appomattox when Lee surrendered. For many years, he had been affiliated with the Custer Post, G.A.R.

Captain Brady was thought to be the last known Civil War veteran to live at the Soldiers' Home, however, Warren Oxx, the last Civil War veteran of Steuben County entered the Soldiers' Home in November of 1946 and passed away after a brief illness on January 7, 1947 at the age of 99. Mr. Oxx was a prominent lawyer in Hornell and a well-known leader of the G.A.R. Lying about his age; he entered into service in 1862 at the age of 15. He fought in The Wilderness and Cold Harbor battles as a member of the 189th NY Volunteers.

Captain James T. Brady and Warren Oxx

During 1940, the hospital had a capacity for 442 beds.

The New York State Soldiers Home

The Home served a large area as there were yet no VA hospitals in Syracuse or Wilkes-Barre, PA. There were 1,400 beds in the seven sections of the domiciliary, although Companies 3, 4 and 7 were closed due to a low population of about 969 members. It was around this time that the barracks were now being referred to by numbers. Companies A, B, and C, were now known as Company or Section 5, 4, and 3, respectively. As for the buildings, they were now known as Building 35, 34, and 33 respectively. By this time, the headquarters building contained all the offices for the station except for dietetics, laundry and the actual treatment of patients. All paperwork was done in a typing pool.

A friendly rivalry existed between the companies involving who could grow the prettiest victory gardens and who had the best landscaping. Appropriate plaques were awarded for these honors each fall. Vegetable gardens were also cultivated and supplied the general and hospital dining halls with fresh produce.

Prize Winning Garden, Co. A

During this time the gazebo, or bandstand, which had deteriorated throughout the years, was taken down and the six gun battery was scrapped (the barrels were said to have been melted down for the war effort.) Also dismantled were the last two pedestal flower urns which graced the Home after a small boy climbed one and it toppled over, giving him a concussion. Mentioned in an annual survey was that the east tower or spire, on Building 34 had been struck by lightning, shattering the 8 inch square wooden ridge rafter. It was temporarily repaired and shortly thereafter the slate roofs on Companies 33 and 34 were replaced with asphalt; presumably the spires were removed at that time.

When the Second World War broke out many employees were called or volunteered to serve. A service flag hung in the colonel's office with stars representing those serving in the war. There were about 35 stars attached to the flag. The news stand was moved to the main gate and renovated into a guard house. It was manned by security 24 hours a day until it was removed around 1967. As the paper work increased more office space was needed. A double Quonset hut had been erected directly behind the hospital to relieve crowded conditions. Although it was to be temporary, it remained there ten years.

After the war, the staff no longer wore their uniforms, the colonel became known as the manager and the captains were section chiefs.

In 1945, the Physical Medicine Rehabilitation Service (PMR) was introduced to the VA. This was broken down into Corrective Therapy (CT), Physical Therapy (PT), Occupational Therapy (OT) and Blind Rehabilitation. Practicing PMR early, the disabled troops returning from WWII experienced a more rapid recovery, shortened convalescence and faster return to the work force. The Bath VA began with PT in 1946, but within the 2 ½ years grew to include all the services PMR had to offer.

The huge influx of the volunteer movement that followed WWII called for organization. In April of 1946, General Omar Bradley, Administrator since August of 1945, established the Voluntary Service National Advisory Committee. Representatives from the American Legion and Auxiliary, Veterans of Foreign Wars and Auxiliary, the American Red Cross, Disabled American Veterans and the United Service Organization made up this committee. The function of the committee was to help

Gray Ladies 1951

stage planned activities at local hospitals. (The "Gray Ladies," which augmented the American Red Cross were a direct result of WWI, and by 1946, 42 Gray Ladies served at the hospital directly under a full-time Red Cross worker.)

Records show that volunteers were not new to the Soldiers' Home. Civic and military groups donated time and material and had held social events there since 1879. Groups such as Daughters of the American Revolution of Cazenovia, NY and the J.W. Wilkinson Circle of Buffalo, NY donated books and magazines, while Scripture quilts were received from the Woman's Christian Temperance Unions of Hulbertson, Orleans County, NY and Kendall Mills and Malone, NY.

The Veterans Administration Voluntary Service (VAVS) first met in April of 1946. Organized under the Department of Special Services, these "uncompensated" volunteers, often referred to as "the backbone of the VA" and "morale builders", rendered their services to the VA and were utilized in all areas of the hospital and domiciliary. From the nursing division to recreation these thoughtful citizens perpetuated the hopes and dreams of the Soldiers' Home founding fathers. The VAVS Advisory Committee has grown from six in 1946 to 85 today. Today, Bath has 37 active organizations.

Making Poppies

On Oct. 26, 1946, the facility's name was changed to the Bath Veterans Administration Center (VAC). By 1948, the VAC housed 1,400 members.

April 13, 1950 saw the rededication of Union Chapel and in 1953; the Chaplaincy was recognized as a professional service.

Construction of Building 84, located behind Section 2, was completed in 1952 where it hosted a new canteen, post office and print shop. The cost of the building was $54,429.50. The original post store and restaurant were salvaged. A request was made to Congress for a post office on November 18, 1915 but it is not known when the post office was first established at the Home.

The original assembly hall was torn down in 1953. The years, as well as flyovers during WWII, had finally taken its toll on the building. It was deemed less expensive to replace it rather than repair it. The first floor of Company 4 would be used as the recreation center for the next six years.

By mid-June, 1953, the VAC housed 1,650 veterans of four wars. Of these, 1,345 were "members" and the remaining 305 were patients of the hospital. These numbers were broken down as: 56 Span-Am veterans; 1,382 WWI veterans; 172 of WWII; and nine from the Korean conflict. Twenty-nine members were listed as miscellaneous. Their backgrounds included doctors, lawyers, scientists and newspapermen.

Since the Home was first established 75 years ago, all refuse was dumped and covered in an outlying section. By February of 1954, an incinerator was built and a more sanitary means of disposal was provided. A new sewage disposal plant was also in the process of being built to replace the old plant. Contracts had been let to install sprinklers in the barracks and warehouse and the work was expected to begin in the near the future.

Of the sixty buildings now on the grounds, upkeep continued to be a constant chore. The Building and Grounds, Maintenance and Repair section employed 38 men. Carpenters, painters, a tinsmith, a mason, a gardener, cemetery sexton and laborers did much of the minor work. Various divisions put in work–orders on the jobs required and supervisors made recommendations to the engineering officer for future planning. Because of their age, the buildings were painted, both interior and exterior, every four to five years. This was to preserve the painted surfaces and also add to the character of the Home.

In late October, 1954, the VA received word from the General Service Administration that the Center had excess acreage for its use. Sixty acres on the western boundary were offered for sale on a sealed bid basis effective immediately.

By December of 1954, an automatic fire protection system (sprinklers) project was underway at a cost of $80,000. Companies 3-7, the nurse's quarters and the main library would all be protected.

Aerial View, circa 1950

In 1954, the Home celebrated its Diamond Anniversary. Just like the first Memorial Day observance under the federal transfer, this Memorial Day was special as it marked its 25th anniversary under federal control. Again, it was no small affair. The village of Bath treated the somber Day of Remembrance with a parade and program. Flags were displayed and all businesses were closed to properly honor the event. An estimated 7,000 area residents turned out at the Home to pay homage to the fallen veterans of past wars and hostilities.

Representative Sterling Cole, the guest speaker, talked about the significance of this particular Memorial Day as it coincided with the 75th anniversary of the Home. In his speech, he stated, "The sun never sets on the white crosses that mark the graves scattered over the five continents-the islands and the seven seas of the world. To me Memorial Day is also one of the most reverent respectfulness and honor to the memory of those whom each of us may hold dear."

After 75 years in service the Center had grown and flourished; nearly 1,400 members were now being served. WWI veterans made up a large majority of the roll with 87%. WWII and Spanish-American War veterans added to the ranks with 8% and 3% respectively and 2% were peacetime soldiers, discharged from the Armed Forces due to injury or disability incurred in service.

The Bath VA was the only domiciliary in New York at this time and served Pennsylvania and New Jersey as well.

ANOTHER CRISIS AVERTED
1955 - 1979

By 1956, there were beds available for 1,426 veterans and 442 hospital patients. It was estimated that $400,000 would be spent on modifications to the hospital, which would allow more space to be used for the activities required under a modern medical program. Also planned was an increase in the number of beds for the hospital to 472. Six hundred and fifty-six employees with an annual payroll of $3 million were currently working at Bath. Approximately $700,000 was spent in the community through the purchase of supplies and services in areas of concern for the VA.

In the summer of 1956, construction began on three recreational facilities near the main entrance, which were to be used in the new Planned Activities Program for domiciliary patients.

Waiting for Chow 1955

A pitch and putt course consisting of three greens and three tees, two tennis courts and two shuffleboard courts with overhead lighting were to be completed by the fall. A field house and restrooms were also installed. These greatly enriched the lives of the patients as the playing field was open to the public and a wider variety of activities could be accessed by the patients.

On May 30, 1959, a new recreation center and theatre was dedicated. The year coincided with the 80th anniversary of the Home and again, the community turned out in force. Forty schools, veteran, civic, fraternal and recreational organizations participated in the program, featuring a parade and dedication ceremony honoring the nation's heroes.

The modest medical care and services that the Bath VAC provided were not only keeping pace with other facilities, but in many instances also surpassing most in their fields. The professionally staffed, modern and well-equipped hospital was providing the highest quality of care for in-patients while the outpatient dispensary served those in need of a lesser degree of treatment.

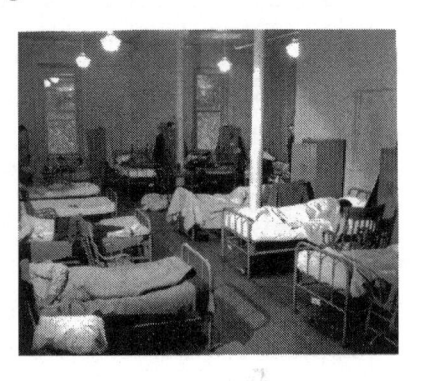

Section 4, 1955

Trained workers managed recreation and other diversionary activities. The recreational services included a library, which had an inventory of over 17,000 volumes in both the general as well as the medical library. Other activities included arts and crafts, bowling, movies and sports. Social activities such as dances, bingo, card games, scenic tours and outings were also available to the veterans.

In 1961, the original hospital, except the southern section, was found to be structurally unsound. The southern section was designated as 29A and remained the nurses' quarters and other staff rooms while the rest of the building was vacated. This arrangement remained in effect until November 1988, when it was again re-designated as a Chemical Dependency Unit.

On January 6, 1964, another era ended when Tom Pender, the last Spanish-American War veteran at the Bath VAC died. He would have been 105 years old on Washington's Birthday. Mr. Pender was a native of Kilkenny, Ireland and lived in Hornell for 15 years until he moved to the VAC in 1957.

He rode with Troop A of the 7th Cavalry on the western plains during the 1880s and fought with Troop H of the same regiment on San Juan Hill during the Spanish-American War, receiving a bayonet wound. He had sailed on every ocean and smoked a corncob pipe until his final days. He had two sons; one who died in childhood; the other during WWI. Mr. Pender was laid to rest at the Bath National Cemetery.

On October 11, 1961, the Most Reverend James E. Kearny, Bishop of the Catholic Diocese of Rochester visited the VAC and offered Mass to the residents. He also blessed the newly refurbished and decorated Catholic chapel. During the past year, funding by the VAC and private donations made renovations to the 59 year old chapel where Father William F. Nolan was the resident chaplain, possible.

In 1963, it was announced that $94,000 was planned for renovation at the facility. Building 34 was slated to undergo complete restoration beginning with sandblasting the entire outside. This would restore the building to its natural color. After sandblasting, the mortar and any defective bricks would be replaced and waterproofed.

Following that, the repair work inside consisted of installing new wiring and fluorescent fixtures throughout the building, refinishing all of the floors, replacing lavatories on the first and second floors, renovation of the heating system, overhaul of elevators and replacement of existing exterior doors.

However, on January 11, 1965, the Steuben County Legislature received word via telephone from Congressman Charles E. Goodell that the VAC was closing down. He had it on "unimpeachable sources" that Bath was just one of 32 VA facilities slated for closing. Immediate concerns were raised over the effects of the closing on the veterans and local community. By 3:00 p.m. on January 13, 1965, the official announcement came from Washington. The Bath VAC would be closing down between May 1 and June 30, 1965 and was ordered to halt admissions. Disbelief and outrage were felt throughout the community. At 3:45 p.m. John Nichols, the VAC director, addressed nearly 500 VA staff and employees in the theater and informed them of the announcement. The crowd was stunned as the rumor was confirmed meaning the loss of over 600 jobs and $3.3 million in payroll.

William Driver, a Rochester native and administrator of the VA facilities, proposed the closing; citing economic reasons, declining veteran population, obsolete buildings, existing Social Service programs and veterans' pensions among the reasons for the decision. The cutback would save the taxpayers $23,500,000 in fiscal year 1966.

Again, true to its nature, the community rallied for the VAC. Letters were sent while protests were planned and pleas to politicians were being made. Local groups and organizations were on the move and they were heard in Washington. On January 21, 1965, 30 congressmen requested a delay in the closings until a review was made. This bought time for those opposed to the closings and ultimately had admissions reinstated three weeks later.

It was reported two days later that Senator Robert F. Kennedy challenged Driver's proposal and undermined the reasons given for the cutbacks. Also, he wanted Driver to justify the so-called "general guidelines" used.
Leading the spearhead on the home front was Edward Humphrey, town of Bath supervisor and Brooks R. Lapp, village utilities superintendent. Together they made plans to meet with RFK in Washington.

Governor Nelson A. Rockefeller also joined the fight to keep the VAC open. On February 12, 1965, he paid a visit to the VAC during a tour promoting the Southern Tier

Expressway and stopped at the facility, meeting with patients and employees. During a short speech, he promised full support from his office in the fight against closing the VAC.

On February 18, 1965, Driver had agreed to a proposal made by Senator Kennedy, which included an evaluation of the VAC. Ten days later, the VA agreed to spend $15,000 for a four week study of the physical plant and space utilization of four facilities, including Bath. On March 16, 1965, a four-man team began its inspection of the Bath facility. The inspection lasted four days, but the results would not be published for a month.

Chester Friedland, RFK, Luther Hoffman

Early in March, Kennedy planned an on-site inspection of his own and on March 29, 1965, arrived at Elmira airport and received a somber reception. The crowd warmed up though as he spoke about the fight to keep the VAC. Kennedy was welcomed in the auditorium of the recreation building at the Bath facility by a standing room only audience. He addressed the crowd stating that he was as "... in favor of economy in government as much as anyone else and could not, in good conscience, be against it" if in fact the shut down in Bath proved to be economically sound.

He also said that when informed of the Washington officials' plans to close the VAs in Bath, Castlepoint and Sunmount, all in New York, the summary of reasons reported for the closings "...made no sense." The decision to close the Bath VA Center is based on "faulty and erroneous" information and "I can't promise you that I can keep it open, but I can promise you that I will fight to keep it open. I need your fortitude and the support of all the people who live in the state." RFK spoke for seven minutes to a standing ovation at the beginning and end of his brief speech.

Fund raisers and rallies from congress and state level on down to individual pleas began to take effect. LBJ was reconsidering the proposal and ordered Driver to make a personal inspection. Driver visited the VAC on April 2, 1965, but remained adamant in his proposal for closure. LBJ then sent in more probes on fact-finding inspections to re-enforce his position.

The inspection team reported their findings on April 14, 1965, announcing that the VAC was in "good condition" and that they were "impressed" with the facility. This gave the activists more hope and they continued to put pressure on Washington. Finally, after more than two months of inspections, discussions and debates LBJ relented. On June 9, 1965, Driver notified Nichols via telegram of the decision to keep the Bath VAC open. The fight was finally over. The people of Bath and the surrounding communities had won a huge victory.

The following month, on July 19, 1965, it was announced that within two weeks, Bath would be receiving 18 patients from the Sunmount VAC, which was one of six VA hospitals and one of two with domiciliary to be closed by the end of September. Ironically, in April of 1966, Driver traveled to South Vietnam to offer support to the troops.

The year 1966 was another of upgrading and improvements. On Wednesday, June 8, 1966, a new cafeteria style service was put into operation in the domiciliary dining room. This cafeteria line was designed to provide better, more pleasant meal service to the veterans and still comply with the VA's emphasis on cost reduction.

Residents were now afforded the opportunity to select his food-hot or cold cereal, fruit juice or fruit, meat or fish. It also permitted a wider variety on the menu and offered longer serving hours because of better utilization of man-hours and better workflow. The use of standardized servings also provided more nutritionally balanced diets and reduced waste. This was all in direct contrast to the family style dining that had normally been used.

The cafeteria line contained two complete stainless steel serving units with heated areas, a refrigerated area, milk dispenser and coffee serving units. An average of six members per minute could now be served on each side. It was purchased for $18,889, with additional money and labor costs for laying quarry tile on the floor, covering the backup wall with sandstone ceramic tile and installation of additional plumbing and electricity.

Behind the serving counter stood a stainless steel pass-through refrigerator, as well as a pass-through warmer. These two items permit the cooks to pass the food from the kitchen to the food service workers on the serving line. A pair of four foot long grills back up the serving area for eggs, pancakes, French toast, etc. to be cooked to order and served directly to the veterans.

On Sunday, June 19, 1966, an open house was held for the new Nursing Home Care Unit on the 4th floor of the hospital. This new, $67,000, 40-bed unit was the second of its kind, the first being built in Buffalo. The "sterile white look" was now replaced with bright colors and two-toned tiled floors. The rooms were broken up into single, double and four bed units and a new $167,000 boiler that was installed.

The Center was now operating a 208-bed hospital, 40-bed Nursing Care Unit and an 800-bed domiciliary. The average patient load that year was 185 patients, with thirty-seven nursing home residents and 740 in the domiciliary.

In the summer of 1967, construction of a connecting corridor was underway linking Sections 4 and 2. Prior to this, Gettysburg Avenue was a thoroughfare, commencing from Veterans Avenue and continuing to the "backyard" of the facility. It continued to the back gate leading out onto Longwell Lane or "Lover's Lane" as it was called. By 1969, the completed corridors connected all of the domiciliary units except Sections 5 and 6.

Funeral Detail, 1960s

On April 30, 1968, a new and expanded canteen was officially opened with a ribbon cutting ceremony in the hospital building. The canteen was equipped with a retail store and a modernized cafeteria that could accommodate three times the number of the previous canteen. It also included the latest in vending machines capable of dispensing complete meals 24 hours a day, seven days a week.

In 1963, VA officials in Washington deemed Sections 3 and 5 "economically inadvisable to repair" but on February 12, 1970, a renovation program was initiated. By July of 1972, the remodeling of Section 5 was complete. There were quarters for 36 residents and on the second floor a Vocational Rehabilitation Program. Section 3 was completed by September of 1974 and was able to house 40 residents. The canteen had been moved to the first floor in 1971 and in 1984, the post office was moved to Building 24. Due to budget issues, the post office ceased to function on station in February, 2001.

On June 22, 1972, the VAC escaped potential disaster when the Conhocton River overflowed its' banks in the worst flood Steuben County had seen since 1946. In the aftermath of

Hurricane Agnes, residents awoke Thursday morning to find water flowing across their lawns on Belfast Street. The earthworks built by Mr. Drummer over eighty years ago helped contain the water from the river temporarily. Bath remained virtually unscathed by the flood thanks to the four lane highway, however, the waters reached the bottom of the train trestle and spilled over the main bridge and River Road, taking with it pavement and leaving the entire baseball field under water. For three days following the flood, the VAC was virtually cut off from the outside community and the Facility was placed in "holiday mode," with some employees unable to go home or report for work.

A press release from the VAC Center dated January 19, 1977, announced that it was readying itself for its 100th anniversary with a ground breaking ceremony to be held in June. It also stated that its short and long-term goals were to maintain the quality service, to improve its level of care and programs for the veteran patients.

A full staff of physicians was now on duty, filling many long-standing vacancies. It was expected that the expanded roles of nursing personnel would insure continuity of improved total care for the hospital patients, domiciliary and nursing home care residents and the growing number of out-patients.

Since there were over 17,000 out-patient visits in 1976, the VAC decided to modernize and expand the Admissions and Out-Patient area to facilitate the expected growth of this program.

The 800-bed domiciliary was now housing veterans from nine northeastern states. One hundred and forty beds were allocated as nursing care beds for those who are unable to meet their self-care needs independently.

During the "recent cold weather winter crisis," the Center converted from natural gas to oil heat. The installation of a $60,000 oil tank facility the previous summer proved to be a tremendous asset. The approval for construction of an estimated one million dollar warehouse to begin later in the year was also announced in the press release.

Salaries for the 700 personnel amounted to $10,339,842 and the total budget was $13.5 million. Plans for construction of a new 200-bed domiciliary to replace the over-crowded and obsolete Section 1 were in its early stages Other engineering projects were geared toward maintaining and updating the 50 buildings and 223 acres at an estimated cost of $200,000. A two year $800,000 contract was already in progress for the updating of the primary electrical distribution system.

To its credit, consultation and medical education was provided through an affiliation with the University of Rochester Medical Center and the Guthrie Clinic at Sayre, Pa. VA-funded research in Problems of the Aging is on-going and the Center has eight student affiliation programs in nursing and other health fields with nearby Colleges and Universities.

At the conclusion of the press release, Center director J.P. Kelly stated that ". . . the desire for improved care will hopefully be met and implemented by the Center's dedicated staff, placing emphasis on the individually chronically ill veteran."

On May 30, 1977, the 98th Memorial Day Services and the Centennial Celebration began a 19-month itinerary of events. After months of hard work and planning, volunteered man-hours and advertising the traditional Memorial Day Parade and Service was at hand. Spectators were urged to arrive early to view the many artifacts exhibited at the special opening of the History Museum. Many of the exhibits were provided courtesy of local community residents. Also, collages and other displays were located throughout the facility, raising questions from the guests and piquing their interest.

During the parade which featured over 45 participating organizations, a "fly over" of small planes from the Hammondsport Flying Club and a squadron of jets from Hancock Air Force Base in Syracuse highlighted the parade. Following the parade, over 40 organizations then placed wreaths in the cemetery in honor of our nation's departed veterans.

On June 13, 1977, exactly 100 years after the laying of the cornerstone, the box which was sealed away inside was opened. At 2:00 p.m. in the Leisure Room of the theatre building, the contents of the square copper box was viewed for the first time by all that attended the ceremony that day.

Other programs throughout the following months were outdoor concerts, special parties, a historical booklet in which a contest was involved, displays and holiday observances.

On Memorial Day, 1978 another spectacular event had been planned. Over 65 units had signed up for the parade on the VA grounds. Bands, floats, color guards, military, fraternal and civic organizations were included in the line of march, highlighted by an air show during the parade. The crowd was also treated to a special exhibit as a re-enactment of a Civil War battle was played out on the Athletic Field. "Mosby's Rangers", a group portraying an authentic southern unit from the war, accompanied by its own Fife and Drum Corps and ladies dressed in proper antebellum attire, clashed with Union troops for nearly a half an hour to the crowd's delight.

The New York State Soldiers Home

List of Articles contained in Cornerstone
Business Cards
$5.00 Certificate of proposed Home.
Ticket admission for Banquet at Opera House
List of members, Votts Post #32, G.A.R.
Press responsibilities, names of reporters.
Proceedings of National Encampment, G.A.R. since the foundation of the Order in 1866 to 1876 inclusive.
Proceedings of the Semi-Annual Encampment of G.A.R.N.Y., Yonkers, 1876.
Proceedings of the Semi-Annual and Annual Encampment of G.A.R.N.Y., Norwich and Albany, 1875-1876.
Pamphlet prepared by General Daniel Sickles
Contributions obtained through effort in aid of New York State Soldiers' and Sailors' Home.
Black and white picture of original three buildings, 2 barracks and Dining Hall.
Silk flag, purple with gold letters, from Thatford Post #3, G.A.R.
White ribbon, Aide de Camp, red ribbon delegate, Semi-Annual Encampment, June 12, 1877, G.A.R.
G.A.R. badge 1534.
Subscription notebook toward establishing a home for disabled soldiers and sailors of the State of New York.
Charters and By-laws of the G.A.R. Soldiers' Home of New York State, 1876.
Copy of the Holy Scriptures, presented by the Steuben County Bible Society.
Newspapers: Western Echo, New York Herald, Grand Army Gazette, Daily Graphic, New York Daily Sun, The World, Brooklyn Daily Union-Argus, Brooklyn Daily Times, Brooklyn Daily Eagle, Brooklyn Review, New York Times, The Evening Post, Wochenblatt der New York States Bertung, Buffalo Daily Courier, New York Tribune, Elmira Daily Advertiser, Steuben Courier, Steuben Farmers Advocate, Elmira Gazette, Rochester Democrat and Chronicle, Rochester Daily Union and Advertiser.
List of Officers of the Village of Bath.
List of Churches in the Village of Bath with names of officiating pastors.
List of Officers of Steuben County.
List of Officers of New York State.
List of Officers of the Davenport Institute for Female Orphans.
Money- Paper: Ten cents, fifty cents, twenty-five cents, one dollar, indented bill of eight dollars, 1/6 of a dollar, 2/3 of a dollar bill, one dollar bill, two dollar bill, four dollar bill, eight dollar bill.
Coins: Indian head penny, three cent piece, five cent piece, nickel, dime, twenty cent coin (with sitting Liberty), quarter, half-dollar, one dollar.
Commemorative coins: Geo. Washington Centennial, Candidate for Pres., Horace Greely, Centennial Art Gallery, Philadelphia, Major George B. McClellan, Abraham Lincoln, Candidate for Pres., Samuel J. Tilden, Benjamin Franklin-George Washington, Candidate for Vice-Pres., William Wheeler, Candidate for Pres., Governor Rutherford B. Hayes.

THE LEGACY CONTINUES
1979 - PRESENT

The past quarter century has also seen its share of changes. In February of 1979, the Recreation Service was established to encourage both individual and groups of veteran patients to discover new interests. Although used as a diversion when the Home was first opened, over the years it has developed into a therapeutic service. Today's activities are planned around the patient's needs. Working at times with Voluntary Services, the program coordinates planned activities such as trips, picnics and a variety of tournaments.

The recreation center is equipped with pool tables, shuffleboard, two TVs, a movie theatre and stage and a bowling alley. This is quite a change from the first amusement hall, which now houses the engineering offices. Also, a new warehouse with a square footage of 13,000 feet was officially opened for use on June 11, 1979. The cost of the new building was $606,215.00.

On Memorial Day in 1982, the annual parade was cancelled for the first time since the Home first opened. Construction and renovation on Building 78 had the Gettysburg Avenue parade route torn up, however memorial ceremonies were held at the National Cemetery beginning a

The New York State Soldiers Home

new tradition at the VA. Having realized that it took four cemetery workers two days to place flags on the gravesites, cemetery officials decided to ask teachers at the Dana L. Lyons School if students would be interested in participating in the annual event. A precedent was set when fifth grade students eagerly agreed and after a short briefing, the students placed nearly 10,000 flags on the veterans' graves.

Haverling fifth grader Laura Jenkins. 1996

In 1983, the domiciliary mission of the VA was to provide quality healthcare to all veterans, while this was to provide quality healthcare and housing to veterans in need. A Chemical Dependency Unit (CDU) was also created and housed in the Section 3. Its staff developed a forty-two day rehabilitation program based on the principles of Alcoholics Anonymous for the treatment of drug and alcohol abuse.

On October 25, 1983, the Ambulatory Care Extension in the hospital was dedicated. Over 500 community residents, patients, VIPs and staff were present for the program. Six newspapers, two TV stations and all of the area radio stations covered the event. The existing first floor was renovated to improve space utilization. The two story addition, projecting from the face of the original building, extended the entire length of the building. This expansion allowed for reconfiguration of the facility. The pharmacy, dental and x-ray clinics occupied the north end with Information Resource Management (IRM) utilizing the floor beneath and Life Support was located at the southern end. This extension provided better access to out-patient clients.

In September of 1984, on POW/MIA Recognition Day, a special Rose Garden was dedicated in conjunction with the

Disabled American Veterans (DAV). Ten rose bushes were donated to initiate the garden and every year thereafter five to ten rose bushes have been planted. Over 200 personal invitations were sent to former POWs and their families as well as to the families of MIAs in the area. The attendance was favorable for this emotional event. A Memorial Garden for employees is also on the grounds where perennials are planted in memory of the deceased.

Rose Garden

Also in 1984, a new greenhouse was erected by the old sludge house located on the northeast corner of the grounds near the railroad spur. The original greenhouse, located on Argonne Avenue was demolished around 1970 after it was deemed beyond repair in 1967.

The lovely flowerbeds, though not as plentiful as in the past, were maintained by 2-3 Incentive Therapy Program workers. Five thousand plants were put in around the flagpole and patient's rooms were also provided with plants from the greenhouse. The greenhouse program was under the direction of Recreation Services and supported by outside donations. Unfortunately, it was discontinued in 2006 and these projects are now maintained by the VA's ground crew.

In 1984, the Sobriety Maintenance Unit (SMU) was developed and housed in Section 5 along with the CDU Program. The SMU provides a supportive atmosphere for residents recovering from Drug and Alcohol dependency.

On May 16, 1986, a new 208-bed domiciliary was dedicated. Located between the dining hall and recreation center, it replaced the old Section 1, which was torn down in 1983 because of the excessive cost for its renovation. The new building provides a state of the art wheelchair and handicapped accessible residence for domiciliary patient care and ensures patient privacy by having an adjoining bathroom for every two patient bedrooms. Also included are spaces for the Art Therapy Clinic, Graphic Arts – Print Shop, Kinesiotherapy Clinic, Doctor and Nursing Clinic Space, and the Domiciliary Operations Administrative offices.

With the opening of the new Section 1, the 2,500 member Federal Credit Union office was moved into Building 18, the old shower house. Chartered in 1949 for VA employees, their spouses and children it was originally housed in Building 44.

Section 1

The Credit Union at the VAMC was closed in February of 2006. In June of 1987, new chimes were installed in Union Chapel, replacing the "Burr Bells." The Burr Bells were a result of a $300 dollar donation from Samuel and Sara Burr in 1920. The new chimes sound on the hour from 8 a.m. to 6 p.m. and briefly on the quarter hour. On national holidays, they also play patriotic music.

The station newsletter *CENTERPIECE* was revived in July of 1987 with the full support of Director Mel Gore. Vocational Rehabilitation Specialist, James Derosiers, editor of the monthly newsletter, highlighted station events, accomplishments and outstanding employees. The publication continued until the Winter Edition 96/97.

On October 30, 1987, the rededication ceremony for the Nursing Home Care Unit, complete with color guards and patriotic music, took place. The $8 million renovation project lasted more than two years and was officially opened by 100 year old William Fisher, Bath VA's oldest patient, assisted by Congressman Amory Houghton with the ribbon cutting.

This 140-bed unit had gone through major alterations and in 1969, the East Wing of the third floor was converted into

The New York State Soldiers Home

an Ambulatory Nursing Care Unit, designed for those who required a greater degree of medical and nursing assistance.

The East Wing of the second floor was organized as a Behavioral Health Care Unit, which consisted of a multidisciplinary group comprised of representatives from Social Work, Nursing and Psychology Services. The West Wing of the second floor served as an Admission Unit, where patients were evaluated for proper placement. In July of 1972, the Ambulatory Nursing Unit was converted into a 140-bed Nursing Home Care Unit. On July 1, 2000, the Bath VA received their first married couple when Doris Kenefick joined her husband Tom as a resident of the nursing home.

In the May 1988 issue of *CENTERPIECE*, renovations where announced for Sections 3, 4, 5. The third floor Annex in the hospital was also going to be renovated to make room for an O.T. Clinic, MAS offices, a barbershop and a nursing classroom. The second floor of the Building 42 was completely remodeled to allow for expansion of the Bicentennial Museum. The canteen retail store in Section 3 was renovated in conjunction with the installation of new fixtures in the canteen.

The Bath VA participated in "Project Extend" under the organizational efforts of William Kastner, Director of Steuben County Veterans Service Agency, utilizing donations from the American Legion. This enabled the Bath National Cemetery to acquire a six-acre parcel of land and develop it for 6,500 additional gravesites. Construction of a new administration building for Cemetery Service was also completed.

On June 30, 1988, the Bath National Cemetery became the final resting place of 28 casualties of the War of 1812. The remains of the American soldiers were discovered in Ft. Erie, Ontario the summer before

Repatriation Ceremony 1988

by construction workers. Testing in a Toronto laboratory confirmed them to be Americans.

A repatriation ceremony, which included Thomas Niles, U.S. Ambassador to Canada, 150 Canadian and 50 American soldiers and the Army's elite ceremonial unit, the Old Guard from Arlington National Cemetery, was held in Ft. Erie. The caskets were then placed in hearses and driven across the Peace Bridge. The New York State Police honor guard escorted the procession to Bath. After a moving ceremony at the Bath National Cemetery, the remains were finally laid to rest with full military honors.

In October 1988, Ronald Reagan signed legislation creating the Department of Veteran Affairs and on March 15, 1989, a ceremony marked the beginning of the Department, as it became a cabinet level post. The Department of Veteran Affairs was broken down into three programs, Veterans Health Services and Research Department, the Veterans Benefits Administration and the National Cemetery System.

In August of 1993, the northern and center part of Building 29 was demolished. It had been condemned in 1961 and the entire building was vacated except the southern elevation, which was designated Building 29A. This remained nurses' and staff quarters and had 20 rooms available. In September of 1988, the last staff member left Building 29A and it was re-designated as a Chemical Dependency Unit, a component of the Psychology Service. Today it houses the upholstery shop and Historical Museum.

The mission of the domiciliary changed in April 1995 to substance and alcohol abuse and vocational rehabilitation. Since it no longer housed long term care patients, the length of a stay for treatment is four to six months.

On April 19, 1996, the psychiatric ward located in the hospital moved from the Bath VA to the Canandaigua VA ending important psych care at Bath. A new greenhouse was also erected in 1996 and was to be used as an additional dimension of patient therapy.

In 1997, the number of available beds rose to 220, while Sections 3, 5 and 6 were closed and that space was allocated for other Medical Center usage. The CDU Program was disbanded, the short term Substance Abuse Residential Treatment Programs (SARRTP) were enhanced at the Buffalo and Albany VA facilities and a Psychiatric Residential Rehabilitation Treatment Program (PRRTP) was instituted at the Canandaigua VA.

In 1971, the VA hospitals in Bath, Batavia, Buffalo, Canandaigua and Erie, PA were consolidated into VA Regional Medical District #6. At this time, there were 37 districts throughout the country making up 15 Regions. In 1997, the VA was again reorganized and the Veterans Integrated Systems Networks (VISN) came into being. Out of the 22 Networks, Bath belongs to VISN2 which includes the five major Medical Centers at Albany, Buffalo/ Batavia, Canandaigua and Syracuse and twenty-five Community-based Outpatient Clinics located throughout Upstate New York including the Finger Lakes Region and the Southern Tier. Today we are known as VA Health Care Network Upstate New York at Bath and one of just 42 VA's with a domiciliary. The Bath VA provides Primary and Secondary Services in an in-patient and out-patient setting. In-patient care includes acute medicine as well as a 160 bed Nursing Home Care Unit and a 220 bed Domiciliary.

On March 25, 1999, a great honor was bestowed upon one of our patients here at the VA. Guy Bennett Sr., a 103 year old veteran from Wayland, New York, was honored in a special ceremony sponsored by the French government. Mr. Bennett was named Chevalier of the National Order of the Legion of Honor, France's highest award. The award is handed out to military personnel and civilians alike for meritorious service. Created by Napoleon Bonaparte in 1802, the award was presented to Mr. Bennett by Mr. Richard Duque, of the French Consul General.

Mr. Bennett entered the Army on November 28, 1917 and served in France during WWI as a mechanic. He was discharged on June 28, 1919 and returned home to Wayland where he began a car dealership. Mr. Bennett was perhaps the last WWI vet to stay at the Bath VA.

On January 23, 2004, in a simple ceremony marking the 125th Anniversary of the Bath VAMC, Senator John (Randy) Kuhl and Assemblyman James Bacalles presented a joint resolution endorsed by the full NYS Legislature honoring the dedication of its staff. The VA now has 650 employees and serves more than 12,000 area veterans.

On Saturday, May 21, 2005, the Bath VA once again made headlines when 866 buglers, trumpeters, trombone and tuba players set a new world record for "longest distance playing a single piece of music."

At the Woodlawn National Cemetery in Elmira, high school student and descendant of Civil War General Daniel Butterfield, Hannah Sollecito of Baldwinsville, NY began the EchoTaps relay. After the first four notes, the call was repeated by founder of "Bugles Across America" Tom Day, on the bugle used to play "Taps" at the funeral of President William McKinley. Spaced at 200 foot intervals, the attempt took the instrumentalists two hours and 20,784 notes to cover the 41.5 mile distance to the Bath. The final bugler George Taylor, who has played "Taps" for nearly ten thousand funeral services, played solemnly near the monument of the Bath National Cemetery.

To the Cemetery

The epic conclusion was the entire entourage assembling at the VA grounds and playing the melody en masse. This event was done in conjunction with "Bugles Across America" and sponsored by its Finger Lakes Chapter. Tom

Day, of Berwin, Illinois, carries on a personal crusade to supplement the 500 buglers in the U.S. to raise awareness for the need of brass musicians to play "Taps" at military funerals and other memorial observances.

Grand Finale EchoTaps 2006

Although long-term care at the Bath facility began to phase out during the 1990's and rehabilitation and recovery was becoming a more prominent feature, the staff has learned to adjust and still maintain their quality of care for veterans.

Once a place for the elderly, disabled or indigent soldiers to come and live out their final years, the VAMC has now become outpatient oriented. Disease prevention, patient education, early detection and treatment of illnesses and easier access all provide better quality care for the veterans and improved customer service and satisfaction at a more cost-effective rate.

In the Domiciliary Care Program, the veteran is offered a wide variety of services that can be used to enhance his or her life skills. The program has evolved and developed into a 4-6 month Residential Substance Abuse Treatment Program with a focus on relapse prevention and Vocational Rehabilitation Services. It is a therapeutic environment providing active residential rehabilitation directed towards the development of skills necessary for return to independent community based living.

Clinical intervention builds on the strengths of the veteran, enhances quality of life experiences and maximizes potential for independent functioning. The staff in the domiciliary believes that the patient is the center of the planning process and expects the veteran to take an active role in their treatment. They provide each patient with individualized services designed to meet their treatment goals, needs and objectives.

Treatment is provided on an interdisciplinary team model. Each patient is assigned to a treatment team, with a case-manager, Addiction Therapist and a Vocational Rehab Specialist who follow them throughout their 4-6 month stay. Services offered in the dom setting include medical care, Behavioral Health Services, Substance Abuse Services, and Vocational Rehabilitation Services.

Behavioral Health Care staff, working in the dom setting, provides many educational groups on various topics. These include Anger Management, Assertive Communication, Diabetic Support, Discharge Transition, Women's Support, Grief and Loss, Stress and How to Manage Change, Self Esteem Building and life skills classes on Budgeting, Safety, and Nutrition.

Vocational Rehabilitation Services include assessment and testing, referral, general vocational education groups, pre-vocational training, vocational goal setting, work hardening and vocational preparation. A Patient Computer Lab is also available and GED preparation classes are offered in the Bath community. Most patients are encouraged to participate in work incentive therapy assignments, which build and maintain acceptable work habits.

When appropriate, some veterans are assigned to Contract Work Therapy (CWT). This is meant to assist veterans in gaining skills to ready them for competitive employment. Recreational staff provide Leisure Education (appropriate use of leisure time), Tai Chi Classes, Golf, Tennis and a Creative Decision-Making Group. Also, each patient is assigned to the Health Fitness Center and encouraged to work with the Recreational staff on developing a therapeutic exercise program. Nursing staff in the Dom provide Men's Health groups, Hepatitis Education, Hypertension Education, and Sleep Hygiene Education. Dom Care is available to all eligible veterans who are able to ambulate distances, are independent in activities of daily living (ADLs), free of active substance abuse withdrawal, psychiatrically stable and capable of benefiting from domiciliary care.

There is no denying that the Bath VA has become an integral part of the community. The VA Volunteer Services, which turned 60 in April of 2006, reported in Fiscal Year 2005, 541 volunteers donated 42,896 hours. Cash donations and gifts for the same time period totaled $213, 603.51. These figures speak volumes for the community and their gratitude, compassion and respect for the veterans who have served proudly.

These resources were utilized in the following projects and activities: Holiday Gift Program, Christmas Day Program, National Salute to Hospitalized Veterans, Re-Creation Variety Show, AMVET Because We Care Day, Mini Stand Downs, Superbowl Parties, Women Veterans Wellness Program, Veterans Day Program, Volunteer Awards Program and 127 consecutive years of paying homage on Memorial Day.

The VAVS has also partnered with the Southern Tier Hospice to certify 10 VA volunteers as Palliative Care/Hospice workers to assist veterans in the community and within the local facility. Bath is one of the very few in the VA system to do this. In return, the VA has given back to the community which it serves. Bath, Prattsburg, Corning, Avoca, Painted Post, Canisteo, Hammondsport, and Savona are but a few of the places VA employees have volunteered; donating their time, dollars, and material. In 2002, the VA began participating in Relay for Life and by 2003 over $5,000 had been raised for this worthy cause. They have supported the local CROP Walk for over 10 years and been a major contributor for Care and Share at Christmas. The VA Employees Association has also donated to the Turtle Beach fundraiser for many years. School tours are conducted several times a year; allowing students to tour the facility and learn about Nursing, Radiology, Dental, Audiology, etc.

The VA has had major food drives for the Turning Point in Bath, contributing not only food but hundreds of dollars too. They conduct a supply drive in August to help children who do not have the paper, pens, pencils, crayons, notebooks and backpacks to start school and the Hazardous Materials Team and Fire Department have responded to numerous calls for mutual aid within the community.

Today, when you travel across the Conhocton Bridge onto Veterans Avenue, it is lined with the Stars and Stripes, which blend into the century old ash, oak, black walnut and maple trees. The ball field and athletic fields are well kept and groomed. Yellow ribbons adorn the trees in support of our troops. The high bluffs to the left show prominent outcroppings of rocks through the scattered trees that cling to their sides. Ahead, upon the high ground, through a sparsely wooded area, you can make out the hospital, with its prominence enhanced by the tree-covered hillside used as its backdrop. Rounding the bend to the right onto Gettysburg Avenue, it is evident that our predecessors had looked ahead to the future. While the Home was originally built for the men who wore the "Union Blue" an unknown force compelled them to build an everlasting shrine to our veterans. The campus-like facility is laid out to be both appealing to the eye and yet accommodating to the veterans it serves.

The buildings had been constructed using state-of-the-art design that, in its day, was second to none. No expense was spared. This in itself is testament to the gratitude the people of yesteryear felt for our veterans who had fought for their liberty and freedoms.

Inside the perimeter of these buildings is the parade ground. A gazebo has replaced the old bandstand and an inviting copse of pine trees at the southern end adds just the right amount of contrast to the open expanse of green lawn. The symmetrical sidewalks, flower boxes, and shrubbery surrounding the flagpole are beautifully manicured, evidence of the pride of the grounds keepers who maintain them. The cannons, which once fired in salute, are gone. Their wooden features long deteriorated in the harsh elements of the New York climate. When there were but the barrels remaining, obelisks were stationed on the four corners of the flag pole and the barrels mounted atop. And then they were scrapped aid the war effort of WWII.

Gone are the guard houses, water fountains, flower vases and newsstand that graced the grounds. One hundred year old maples leave evidence of old walkways; two-toned brickwork on buildings shows where additions were made. At the north end of the parade ground stand the three original buildings, having weathered the test of time. You may notice small changes in the features of the buildings; the spires are missing, slate roofs replaced by asphalt, windows have been bricked and verandas removed. but the buildings are, never the less the same.

What began as an expression of gratitude from a proud band of brothers has now turned into a thriving and vital part of the community. While the fate of our country today is unclear, one thing is sure; our service members deserve all the Bath VAMC has to offer. They served to ensure this country remains free. We must do our part to ensure the Bath VAMC remains operational for the next 125 years.

The New York State Soldiers Home

INVESTIGATIONS

At the quarterly meeting of the Board of Trustees on June 8, 1883, the first major investigation was called for to look into the management of the Soldiers' Home. Charges of neglect, ill-treatment of inmates, insufficient rations, and the misconduct of past and present board members, became public via the newspapers. Upon the motion of Trustee Hosea H. Rockwell, five members of the board were appointed to investigate these allegations. President Slocum appointed H. H. Rockwell as Chairman, Wm. F. Rogers, I. F. Quimby, B. B. Taggert, and John Palmer as the committee.

Shortly thereafter, the "scandalous affair" erupted when the *Buffalo Sunday News* printed an interview with Trustee Wheeler, conducted by William N. Cruttenden. Wheeler had just recently been appointed as trustee and had attended only one quarterly meeting prior to the interview. He now asserted that the treatment of the inmates was "simply damnable."

(Wheeler is listed to having been appointed by the governor on June 5, 1885. He was replaced by John F. Little on August 12, 1885. Wheeler would later be called to the stand during the ensuing investigation to answer these allegations.)

Wheeler also alleged that the complaints of the soldiers had been the talk of the town for more than a year. He felt it was his duty, when he first received his appointment as trustee, to bring these matters before the board and the state. He also claimed that the financial mismanagement and irregularity were far greater than believed. Mr. Wheeler further charged that the administration of the Home had discharged inmates who had worked for the Democratic ticket within two weeks after the election.

These allegations pitted newspaper against newspaper. Stories of the notoriety of the Soldiers' Home conflicted with editorials of support. While returning from California after visiting his gravely ill son, Superintendent Pitcher was stunned when a well-circulated newspaper in Chicago carried a story denouncing the Home as "A Second Andersonville in New York" and branding the commandant a "tyrant."

One paper supporting the Soldiers' Home was the *Steuben Courier*. In the June 15, 1883, edition, the editor denounced the Elmira *Sunday Tidings* for writing a "most outrageous and disgraceful article." The *Sunday Tidings* had charged, among other things, that "the affairs of the Home were a seething mass of corruption and jobbery, whereby a few men were enriching themselves at the expense of the State." The editorial in the *Steuben Courier* went on to state that the accused trustees were "prominent citizens of unblemished character."

The *Steuben Courier* also reprinted segments of the *Sunday News* interview in the issue of June 22, 1883, reporting the charges and complaints as "radically untrue" and so considered by 99 out of 100 citizens. They described Superintendent Pitcher as a perfect gentleman and a humane man who possessed remarkable administrative capacity, sound judgment, and rugged integrity. They ventured to say that any mismanagement under his administration was absolutely impossible.

As for his character, they stated that before General Pitcher's appointment as Superintendent, the Home was a great nuisance to Bath. Under his control, however, the Home became an institution in which the whole town took pride. The *Steuben Courier* also provided Consolidated Ration Returns for the second quarter of 1883 to disprove the lack of food asserted by Wheeler.

As for the charges of medical malpractice against Dr. Dolson, claiming he forced patients out to perform manual labor, the reporters called upon Dr. Dolson. He denied the charges. One incident had been reported, the death of an inmate after being ordered out to pick stones. The doctor stated it was not an uncommon occurrence for an old man or woman to drop dead suddenly from apoplexy or paralysis.

Another charge was that the doctor was negligent of his duties and was seldom at his post. Dr. Dolson vehemently denied these charges, claiming he had never missed a day since his appointment in March of 1882. He also stated that he spent 2-3 hours in the morning making his rounds and would often return in the evening for cases requiring more attentive care. He further stated that he was connected by telephone to the Home and could be summoned at any time. Incidentally, the first telephone call made from Bath was to Hornellsville on August 25, 1882, by Dr. Dolson. The doctor also remarked that he made arrangements with another competent doctor in the case of his being away during the afternoon, should an emergency arise.

The charge made that every worker for the Democratic ticket was discharged after the November election in 1882 was disproved by a statement from the Adjutant, Robert H. Gansevoort. He produced records showing that only two inmates were discharged from the Home between November 7 and December 16, 1882, one for repeated intoxication and bringing liquor on the Home grounds (his third offense) and the other upon his own request.

Many prominent citizens and soldiers alike were outraged at the charges, and numerous letters of support by the townspeople and inmates were offered. A full-scale investigation was now underway. On June 27, 1883, a notice was placed in the *Steuben Farmers Advocate* under the heading "Soldiers' Home Matters." This notice instructed all persons having grievances against any members, past or present, of the Board of Trustees or employees of the Soldiers' Home, to put them down in writing and submit them to the investigating committee. The said committee would then meet on July 10, 1883, at the Home Headquarters and hold sessions until the investigation was complete. It would then post its findings in the *Steuben Farmers Advocate.* In the same article it was reported that a Buffalo newspaper wrote that posts of the Grand Army of the Republic, Dept. of New York, should hold their own investigation in regard to the charges of cruelty and lack of food.

At 10:00 a.m. on the appointed day, the Board of Trustees met at the Home. They were joined by the subcommittee of the Council of Administration of the G.A.R., which had been appointed at the June encampment. Their members included H. Clay Hall of Little Falls, Chairman; Major T. L. Poole of Syracuse; and H. J. Swift of Cuba. President Slocum called the meeting to order, and after the regular order of business, he advised the board that Trustee Wheeler had raised the point that the Board of Trustees did not have the power to summon and swear witnesses. (President Slocum had previously sent a letter to Mr. Letchworth, President of the State Board of Charities, asking if they wished to conduct the investigation.)

The State Board happened to be in session in Albany and would respond in a few hours. Slocum had discovered, however, in Chapter 699 of the Laws of 1871 that the Board of Trustees did in fact possess the same powers as the State Board of Charities, but felt the public would prefer the State Board conduct the investigation to avoid conflict. The Board unanimously agreed with his position. For some reason Wheeler, at this point, blurted out that he only preferred charges against a member of the Board of Trustees but not against General Pitcher. He also defied anyone to say he did. Trustee Palmer then produced evidence that Wheeler had drawn up three affidavits which were sworn to by inmate John Cowan. Wheeler contended that inmates were constantly coming to him with charges but he would not do anything unless they swore to them.

Comrade Hall, of the G.A.R. Committee, then asked that his committee be authorized to conduct a secret investigation. General Rogers thought it necessary that at least one member of the board should be present. President Slocum, however, decided it would be inconsiderate of the board to authorize a secret investigation after inviting the State Board of Charities to conduct the investigation.

Mr. Hall responded, stating that the reason for the secret investigation was that it was reported that certain inmates were afraid to testify against the management of the

Home. General Quimby retorted that several inmates were not afraid to sign affidavits and publish them in newspapers.

At this point, Superintendent Pitcher asked to be heard. He said he hoped that action could be taken at once, as he was anxious to clear his reputation. He recounted the newspaper article which had branded him a "tyrant" and how it was reprinted in the *Police Gazette* one week previously. He demanded to know the character of the affidavits and the witnesses thereof. Pitcher spoke of the demoralized state into which the Home had fallen and also wished that his "reputation might be cleared of the shadow cast upon it."

Mr. Hall relayed the message of his committee to agree to go along with whatever the board decided. Trustee Rockwell moved that the request of Mr. Hall be laid upon the table until word was received by the State Board of Charities. Generals Slocum and Rogers then offered resolutions which were combined and adopted as follows: that the request of the Committee of the G.A.R. should be tabled until such time as it was received from the State. In the meantime, the committee was invited to examine all books and papers pertaining to the Home and have full access to the hospital, mess halls and buildings, and to meet any of the inmates they so desired. The board then recessed until 4:00 p.m.

At 4:00 p.m. the board reconvened. President Slocum read a dispatch from the State Board which stated they would send their decision as soon as it was reached. President Slocum then read Chapter 699 of the Laws of 1871 and expressed his opinion that even though the Board of Trustees had the power to conduct an investigation, he doubted it had the ability to give the power to a committee. He then moved to have a resolution made, declaring the five-man investigation committee rescinded and stating that the board should, as a board, conduct the investigation if the State Board failed to respond. The resolution was adopted. General Quimby then made the motion to adjourn the meeting until 9:00 a.m. the following morning, at which time if no word was received by the State, the investigation should commence. The motion was passed, and the meeting was adjourned until Wednesday morning.

On Wednesday morning, July 11, 1883, at 9:00 a.m. the board met with all trustees present. With the minutes of the previous day read and accepted, Trustee Rockwell made a motion that Mr. H. A. Corell be appointed stenographer. The motion passed. President Slocum then announced that he had received a telegram from Mr. Letchworth, dated July 10, 1883, saying, "Committee appointed, undetermined when they will organize. Will telegraph you again during Wednesday. W. P. Letchworth." Another telegram was received the same day stating, "Committee of this board will soon visit Soldiers' Home and if the condition of the institution, and nature of the charges against it seem to demand, an investigation will be made. James O. Fanning, Ass't Secretary."

The question now was whether the board should proceed with the investigation. A motion made by General Quimby to proceed was passed. It was then decided that President Slocum would have control of the proceedings and ask the questions first. The board members would then be allowed to ask questions of the witnesses. An intensive 3-day investigation thus ensued.

It was decided to address the charges of cruelty first. The first witness to take the stand was John Cowan, the first appointed pastor of the Home and librarian. Cowan, who claimed he had served with the 6th New York Heavy Artillery. He also produced a certificate of ordination dated January 27, 1864, from the Church of Pilgrims, City of Brooklyn.

Cowan was admitted to the Home in April of 1879. His notoriety was well known at the Home and in town alike. It became obvious that he was somewhat an agitator. Cowan had signed no fewer than three affidavits against the management and officers of the Home. These affidavits mentioned everything from cruel and inhumane treatment of inmates, threats and harassment by the officers, poor food and improper clothing. By the time the board was through with Cowan, it was obvious that many of the charges were fabricated or embellished, to say the least.

Right from the onset of questioning, Cowan contradicted himself on almost every answer he gave. The dates he gave for the time he entered the service, his discharge, and the time he entered the Home were all conflicting. He stated he was a minister, ordained in Boston, and also had a daughter in New York City. Upon being asked if he ever spent time in a State penitentiary he replied, "Only as a visitor."

Cowan was asked to describe what he knew about the death of an inmate named Tuit. Cowan had sworn that Tuit was ordered out one morning to pick stones on or about the 28th day of June, 1883. According to Cowan, when Tuit protested, claiming to be too sick to go, he was "forced out" by Sergeant Emery by the use of threats; an offense which could lead to a dishonorable discharge. Tuit had to be helped in later that day and taken to the hospital, where he died at 2:00 p.m. the following day. Cowan claimed the man received no medical attention whatsoever.

In another affidavit, Cowan swore that Trustees Robie and Howell tried to coerce him into signing a petition stating that the men were well cared for and had plenty to eat, and that General Pitcher was a good and faithful officer. Cowan claimed that when he refused to sign he was threatened with discharge.

A third affidavit by Cowan stated that another man, of a weak mind, was coerced into signing the same petition. When questioned about any other charges, Cowan referred to the clothing as being inadequate. He stated that 500 overcoats had been stored in the attic of Company B for the previous two years and had not been issued. He also mentioned that the socks were too small and of poor quality.

The issue of the food was brought up next. The quality and quantity had improved, he stated, since the affidavits were filed, but it was only then that they did. Cowan complained that the men received the "refuse" of the meat. He explained that the quartermaster and his family received the first cut, the general (Pitcher) and his family the second cut, next the steward and family, the farmer and family, the musician and family, the first officer's table and finally the second officer's table. What remained were the neck, ribs and legs, which went to the men. Cowan also complained the coffee was not full strength.

Cowan cited many other incidents and occurrences which were damaging to the reputation of the Home. He then produced a certificate with roughly 282 signatures attesting to his character. Cowan stated that the paper was circulated on July 7, 1883. (Robert H. Gansevoort, Adjutant of the Home, later compared the list to the records of the Home. He found that, of the men who supposedly signed, 25 were dead, 40 had been discharged, 30 had been dropped from the rolls or deserted, 37 had been summarily discharged and one was in the Willard Asylum, making a total of 138 names. Cowan claimed he did not see every individual sign his own name.)

Trustee Palmer now asked to present sworn testimony and a transcript of the penal system. The first was a letter from Major Chas. H. Palmer, of the N. Y. 6th Artillery. In his letter, the major said that Cowan's service record was bad. He wrote that Cowan would get drunk and steal and had also been court-martialed in Petersburg, Virginia. Major Palmer also stated that Cowan had been arrested since for some offense in New York City and was not to be believed under oath.

A second letter written by Colonel Stephen Baker was presented. He had reiterated the contents of Major Palmer's letter, emphasizing that Cowan had stolen Major Palmer's boots, had been tried and found guilty. He further stated that at the close of the war, Cowan had traveled to England and collected money for freedmen through fraudulent letters. Colonel Baker concluded that most veterans of the outfit felt that Cowan was a disgrace to the regiment and the Christian church and he hoped that he (Cowan) would meet his just desserts.

Another letter, written by G. W. Van Buren, editor of *The Union Volunteer*, was presented as testimony against Cowan. Here, the writer described how Cowan had tried to defraud the government for a pension for "stricture of Urethra" from an explosion. After two examinations, the doctor declared it was a result of venereal disease. The editor also mentioned that Cowan had tried to pass a bogus U. S. $1,000 bond, for which he was tried and convicted and sent to the Albany penitentiary.

The Record of Commitment to the Albany penitentiary was then presented, showing that Cowan had been convicted of conspiracy. Cowan was sentenced to two years in the penitentiary and fined $1,000. A sworn transcript from the

First Baptist Church of Boston, Mass., was also produced. This showed Cowan being "disfellowshiped" on account of his confinement.

At this point Cowan, wanting to rebut the evidence of his conduct in his regiment, ask to call upon seven witnesses who were residents of the Home and had served with him. (In the opening questions, Cowan stated that there was no one at the Home who had served with him.) Four inmates named in the transcript came forward to speak on behalf of Cowan. The only testimony they gave was that they had never observed Cowan under the influence of alcohol or ever heard of his being court-martialed.

The next accuser to be called on and sworn was James Turner, who also authored three affidavits. Turner, who came from the Blackwell's Island Alms House, had been an inmate of the Home since February 4, 1879. Turner stated that he had witnessed Sergeant Worth, of Company A, violently drag from his bed an inmate, Jacob Cramer, who was in a sick and dying condition, and forced him to walk around the buildings. This had resulted, Turner claimed, in the death of Cramer the following day. (Sergeant Worth had since vacated the Home.)

The second affidavit signed was in regard to Turner's having been fined five dollars and confined to "the limits" for 60 days. Turner claimed that this was retaliation for working for the Democratic Party on behalf of Captain Little. Trustees Robie and Little were opponents during the election. (Turner admitted to not being present for roll-call the night of the election, which is in violation of the rules.)

The final affidavit was in regard to the death of Philip Tuit. All three affidavits had again been drawn up by Wheeler.

Upon examination, Turner admitted to missing roll-call numerous times, but he believed that last sentence was not for missing roll-call but for working for Captain Little. However, upon further examination, it was found that, for employment at the Home, Turner was assigned as letter-writer. His duties were to write letters and assist in pension applications for the fee of $5 a month. It was also understood that he was not to charge for this service as he was already being paid by the Home. It was later found out that he was taking payment or tips for his services. He also gave the same story related to

Tuit's death as Cowan had. (Cramer's death could not be proven to have occurred through mistreatment.)

The next inmate to have an affidavit published was Felix Duffy, who entered the Home on March 15, 1879, from King County Alms House. Duffy had been assigned the Home Guard, earning ten cents a day, for nearly three years until his suspension in February of 1883 for disobeying a direct order. While on the stand he had also claimed that mistreatment of Tuit had caused his early demise.

Dr. Dolson was finally asked to the stand. After stating that the hospital was in the best possible order, he then began to answer questions in reference to Tuit's death. He testified to having no knowledge of Tuit's activities the day before his death; however, when he arrived on the morning of April 26, 1883, and examined Tuit, he stated it was apparent that death was imminent. When asked the cause of death, Dolson responded that it was apoplexy.

He was then asked about making the men go outside to work. He stated that General Pitcher and he had decided the best thing was for the men to go outside for fresh air, although they should not be forced to work. He claimed that General Pitcher stated that when a man asked to be excused from picking stones, it would be better to "err on the side of mercy."

Frank Krause, the ward-master, next took the stand and swore that Tuit was admitted to the hospital between 6:00 and 7:00 a.m., and Dr. Dolson was informed of his condition within ten minutes.

Charles K. Emery, sergeant of Company C, testified next. Tuit had been in his company and he denied the charges made that Tuit begged not to go out. He also stated that Tuit had come from town the night before his death in an intoxicated condition. The morning of his death, while the company was at chow, Emery was informed that Tuit had taken sick. Emery sent for a stretcher from the hospital and helped carried Tuit there. Emery also testified that when General Pitcher appointed him, he was instructed to be kind when dealing with the men, that they were not to be forced to work but should be encouraged to go outside for exercise.

The proceedings continued as inmates and past employees were called and recalled during the intense questioning of the witnesses. Other charges made were minor compared to the previous charges. Coffee, while of good quality, was not of sufficient strength. There was a shortage of potatoes during the winter of '82-82, and for a short time, a shortage of meat. Two reasons were given for this: one, the inefficiency of the cook, since removed; and two, no complaints were ever made to call attention to the problem.

The case of mismanagement and theft of goods was next addressed. The charge that Trustee Robie had entered into contracts with the Home for the purpose of profit was next addressed. Wheeler felt that Robie, who was part owner of J. & J. C. Robie's, a local store in Bath, used his position as a board member to drum up business with the Home. This was considered an extreme conflict of interest as it could be perceived as a manipulation of Home funds for personal use.

Quartermaster Leavens bought articles and supplies for consumption on the open market, and neither he nor Robie felt a wrong was being committed in the business dealings. When supplies were low, Leavens would make inquiries on the open market and make purchases, usually the lowest prices. Some of the goods were purchased from J. & J. C. Robie's, only about $1,200 worth over the past five years. However, after an examination of the vouchers and receipts, it was shown that discretion had been used when making all purchases. Not all business had gone to J. & J. C. Robie's.

The charges preferred by Wheeler against Quartermaster Leavens were that Leavens, while manager of the purchase and sale of supplies, "[had] been and now [was] wasteful, incompetent and extravagant . . . .That he [had] taken supplies from said Home and given them to his friends without accounting and he also furnished the inmates with rations that were inferior in quality." Wheeler also claimed, according to witnesses, that Leavens willfully gave away a hat and boots to certain employees.

Again, witnesses were called and scrutinized. According to the testimonies given, not all was as it appeared. Those testifying against Leavens seemed to harbor ill-feelings towards him because he was not a veteran. Although they were correct in what they had testified to, the full circumstances did not come out until this investigation.

On Saturday morning at 9:00, the Board of Trustees reconvened once again. President Slocum then addressed the board and related his feelings toward the previous investigation. He stated that he believed the Home was honestly and economically managed and the inmates were kindly treated. General Slocum then offered that each charge should be heard and a resolution voted on separately. He also recommended a complete transcript of the investigation should be published for the benefit of the public. These suggestions were unanimously accepted by the board.

The first resolution was that it was the judgment of the board that the charges against the management originated in personal and political differences and antagonisms among the residents of Bath. (This goes back to 1879, when the State Attorney-General rendered an opinion in favor of the inmates having the right to vote in all elections. The town did not feel their best interest would be well-served at the hands of the inmates.)

The second resolution passed was that the allegations of cruelty were unsustain and unfounded. The board also felt that Superintendent Pitcher was kind, generous, and lenient in his treatment of the inmates, and the Home owed him a debt of gratitude.

The third resolution resolved concerned the charge against Jonathon Robie. Investigation showed that the charge stemmed from a technicality. The vouchers provided proved that his store merely acted as an agent in securing goods for the Home and that he did not capitalize on these transactions.

Fourth, the evidence against Leavens proved him guilty. However, the vegetables given away were of a surplus that would have gone to waste soon. Also, the boots, five pairs in all, had been worn and repaired and had cost the Home no money whatsoever. The hat was a sample sent to him at no cost either. These items were given away with the full knowledge of General Pitcher. It was also noted that he was hated by most inmates and his job was made much more difficult because of it. The board also felt that, for the meager wages paid for his position, a better man could not be had.

The fifth resolution voted on was what to do with the three main accusers, John Cowan, James Turner and Felix Duffy. Of all those who testified against the management, these three men had their affidavits printed in newspapers. Because of their instigation, a dark cloud had temporarily hung over the Soldiers' Home. Their affidavits were found to be false, their credibility and character questionable. It was decided through a vote to summarily expel them from the Home. Of the witnesses who had signed affidavits against the management, or had them written for them by Wheeler, not one was found to hold any water.

The report of the Council of Administration to General Reynolds, Dept. Commander, was that the only fault of General Pitcher was that perhaps he was too kind in his position as superintendent. They did report, however, that two cases of mistreatment were found. One was committed by a Sergeant Worth, who had since left the Home and the other by James Turner himself. Their recommendation was to have their report printed immediately and sent to every post in the state, as well as the press. An interesting side note is that James Turner, upon being discharged, was being returned to the Home in a drunken state, whereupon he rolled out of the back of a wagon. He sustained internal injuries and a hip injury. Unable to travel, he was hospitalized until his death on July 20, 1883. He was buried in the Home cemetery.

Investigation of 1900

On August 19 and November 9, 1899, the State Board of Charities received communications from Governor Theodore Roosevelt regarding various charges and countercharges made in regard to the management of the New York State Soldiers' and Sailors' Home. Governor Roosevelt felt that these charges warranted an investigation. A committee was formed, co-chaired by Commissioners Harvey W. Putnam and Eugene A. Philbin. They were accompanied by Commissioner Peter Walrath. The governor also desired that a representative from the State Comptroller's office and one from the Attorney-General's staff attend. Deputy Comptroller Gilman and Deputy

Attorney-General John C. Coyne filled these positions respectively.

On November 27, 1899, the trustees of the Home and other interested parties were notified of the investigation and informed that their co-operation would be appreciated. After sending out proper notice, seventeen hearings were held in Bath, Albany and Buffalo between December 5, 1899, and February 28, 1900.

The first hearing was held in Bath and the ground rules were laid out. The governor wished the hearings to be closed until after he received the final report. This was protested by Monroe Wheeler of Hammondsport, who represented the four trustees making the charges, and John F. Little, Esq., who represented Superintendent Shepard, the accused. Both felt that the media would report the proceedings more accurately should they be allowed in. Initially overruled, the governor would later rescind his order upon request of the committee, when a leak to the press was discovered during the investigation. Articles began to appear in the papers condemning Shepard and accusing the investigating committee of "whitewashing" Shepard's character. (It appeared that the local press showed an "unfriendly attitude" toward Colonel Shepard and hoped the investigation committee would refrain from making a favorable report on his behalf.) The press was later admitted during the defense hearings of the proceedings.

Later, on the afternoon of December 5, formal charges were drawn up and signed by Trustees Smith, Campbell, Finch, Sutherland and Cleary. Attached to the charges were the names of 34 witnesses, along with a statement saying more witnesses might be called. Eighteen charges had been filed against the Commandant.

The committee decided that those who presented the strongest case against Shepard should be cross-examined in the most scrutinizing manner. To preserve the integrity of the Home, all charges were to be proved beyond a reasonable doubt. Because certain charges were similar in nature it was decided that they should be heard concurrently. Due to the distance of locations of the hearings, three sessions a day were held. The committee would then meet at night, hoping to wrap up the inquiry as quickly as possible.

Charges VII, X, XI, XV, XIII, XVI, XVII and XVIII were summarily disposed of. After testimony was given and responded to for each, it was found that there was no ground for the charges being made.

Charges I and II, considered the most serious, were the first to be heard. Several witnesses testified as to the alteration of the telephone bills and shipping bills. Erasure marks were shown to prove this but Colonel Shepard explained that the bills in their original state gave the impression that the services were for his own benefit. He claimed to have made the alterations to halt the continuation of the state being charged for services rendered to him.

As to the third charge, the disposition of fines, Colonel Shepard gave an accurate accounting of all fines imposed. Upon one audit made, the books showed that the account was indebted to him. (Trustee Smith testified that he did not accuse Shepard of misapplication.)

Colonel Shepard, in answering to charge number four, concerning the recovery of unpaid wages proved that he had advanced the salaries of four workers authorized by the State out of his own pocket. These employees left before their terms had expired and Shepard was entitled to the wages once received by the state.

Charge V could not be proved. Colonel Shepard did admit to purchasing a case of champagne with the $30 a month grocery allowance. However, there was no stipulation that the money be used specifically for groceries, and Colonel Shepard had purchased the champagne for entertaining semi-official guests, including the trustees.

In Charge VI, the employing of the Home laundry for his personal use, the committee felt that there was no wrongdoing on the part of Colonel Shepard. It appeared to them that the trustees were more concerned that the superintendent continued to use the laundry after being told it was prohibited. The committee decided that the trustees did not have the power to give such an order; only the board could. Since the board did not, there was no reason to sustain the charge.

Many versions were given in regards to charge IX, alleging Colonel Shepard entertained guests at the Union Chapel, plying them with champagne and playing a phonograph. The committee again felt that Colonel Shepard was the most plausible witness in this case. Dr. Burleson was the chief witness in this case and appeared biased against the superintendent. His testimony against the Colonel Shepard was contradicted by many of the other witnesses. Chaplains Arnaud and Griffin gave testimony on behalf of Colonel Shepard who, as a deist, had encouraged his staff to attend weekly services as he had done for the past two years and had exhibited a strong respect for every individual's convictions.

As to the charges of XII and XIIa, Colonel Shepard's excessive use of liquor and behavior on the parade ground in July of 1899, the committee again ruled in favor of the superintendent. Trustee Campbell was unable to state positively as to whether the Colonel Shepard was under the influence to a degree of incapacity or not. Many of the witnesses present that day on the parade ground testified on behalf of the superintendent. It was also noted, and Colonel Shepard had admitted it himself, that he was a nervous and excitable individual. This could be perceived by some as being intoxicated. Again, insufficient evidence was given to sustain the charges made in reference to his behavior at the depot.

In conclusion, the investigating committee discovered that much animosity existed between the superintendent and several of the trustees, especially Smith and Campbell. It seemed that the latter two's biggest concerns lay with the welfare of the town, not the Home. Remarks made by these two during the investigation reflected poorly upon them. One such statement concerned Belfast Street, the main approach to the

Home. Fourteen saloons lined both sides of the street outside the main entrance and were viewed as a nuisance and a menace to discipline. Colonel Shepard introduced into the Legislature a bill to have the saloons shut down. Trustees King, Shoemaker and Sutherland were for the resolution, while Campbell, Cleary and Smith voted against it. Their reason was that being citizens of Bath, they had to protect the interest of the town against such action. Removing the saloons, they reasoned, would force the inmates to travel to town to imbibe in the spirits that could not be obtained at the Home.

Smith had gone to great length to bring a case against Shepard. In early summer of 1899, Smith employed the services of Monroe Wheeler, who had taken a number of statements from witnesses who would later testify against Colonel Shepard. The credibility of the accusers, however, overshadowed the investigation. Close attention was now being paid to the board. Because of remarks made during the hearing it appeared the trustees had a personal vendetta against Colonel Shepard. Had the superintendent been more subservient to the trustees, the committee felt, no charges would have been filed.

Colonel Shepard's character was defended by three long-standing members of the board, Trustees Sickles, Kings and Shoemaker. Referred to as "the big three" by Smith, these men had resigned their appointments as trustees before their term had expired. The remaining board members were also replaced except Smith. Mr. Smith was allowed to stay on till his term expired in November of 1904. Dr. Burleson resigned his position on July 1, 1900, and was replaced by Dr. Oran W. Smith, chosen from a list of three veterans certified to the State Civil Service Commission.

Although the committee praised Colonel Shepard for his performance as manager of the Home while under duress, he was still relieved of his duties. On March 17, 1900, Colonel Andrew Davidson, a man of high meritorious record, was elected the new Superintendent. While highly protested by General Sickles, the appointment stood, as the committee felt that the Home's welfare would not be threatened by the competency of the new Superintendent. Colonel Davidson assumed his duties in April 16 of 1900. No appeal or further testimonies were filed.

Investigation of 1919

On August 12, 1919, amidst rumors again concerning the management of the Soldiers' Home, the Board of Trustees requested an investigation of the institution. Newspapers around the state had printed articles of severe criticism reported by present and former members and employees of the Home, as well as residents residing in and about the village of Bath.

Perhaps the most damaging allegations were made by George W. Peck, a trustee appointed in the spring of 1919. According to the official report, Peck's attitude toward the management was well known, although it is uncertain as to why he was dissatisfied. Because of this, statements, letters, and affidavits were forwarded to him by the afore-mentioned complainants. He, in turn, reported these to the newspapers.

In December of 1919, Lieutenant-Governor Harry C. Walker, along with Cortland A. Wilber of Binghamton acting as counsel and A. G. Palmer of Binghamton as accountant, began his investigation. The hearings took place at the Soldiers' Home, in the village of Bath, the city of Elmira, and in the city of Syracuse. These men mingled freely at the Home and chatted with the members and were able to gain a first-hand account of the feeling towards the management. Nearly 1,800 pages of evidence would be recorded.

The *Steuben Courier* reported on January 2, 1920, that Walker had examined all officials of the Soldiers' Home and was satisfied with their integrity and the character in which they ran their respective departments. (This would be somewhat contradictive to the final report Mr. Walker submitted to the governor.)

Next, Mr. Walker began looking into the rumors that had been circulating for several months concerning the hospital, barracks, post funds, pension funds and food. The most serious of the charges was the handling of the patients by the nurses and attendants in the hospital. Ailing, hospitalized veterans, bedridden, or unable to manage their own financial affairs, often relied on the cashier to safeguard their pensions. Theft, not only by other members, but hospital staff as well, was allegedly common.

In the second week of February, 1920, Mr. Walker began questioning Dr. Hill extensively as to the complaints made by former inmates. The complaints ranged from forcing patients to take icy baths, surrendering personal property, tipping, favoritism and indifference. One former inmate, Harry Force, testified that feeble members had been treated cruelly and their money taken from them by attendants. Dr. Hill denied any knowledge of such incidents and testified that Force had been discharged from the Home for being absent without leave and for carelessness in his duties.

During the year, the population fluctuated between 850-1000 veterans, a majority of which fought for the Union. Nearly all of these Civil War veterans received pensions, ranging from $6 to $50 per month. Mr. Walker also includes that about one-third of the members are constantly in the hospital. With the average age of the members being seventy-six, one-third of the approximately one thousand residents were permanent members of the hospital. Dr. Hill reported that the staff was badly undermanned and the patients were not given the necessary care required. The surgeon and his assistants were required to make their daily rounds in the wards and barracks, but only occasionally did so.

Upon being admitted to the hospital, the patient had to give up his money and valuables for safekeeping. Unfortunately, convincing evidence proved that a more effective system was needed in securing and safeguarding a patient's valuables when turned in.

The pension fund was instituted for the benefit of the members of the Home, which most members had little complaint about. However, patients who were bed-ridden or unable to handle their finances were unhappy with the system. From a list drawn up by the surgeon in charge, a nurse would accompany the patient to the cashier to receive his allowance of two dollars per week. The nurse would then take charge of the cash and accompany him to Venuto's store; formerly the canteen. The patient was allowed to choose his items, such as fruits, cigars, cakes, candies, and pies. When the purchase was made, the nurse would then make note of how money was spent. The remainder would be held by the nurse and deducted from the following week's allowance. For example, if the patient spent 75 cents at the store, he would receive 75 cents the following week for his allowance, thus totaling $2. Although strong objections were made by some of the patients as to this practice, the system continued. The nurse would often have in his or her possession $25-$35 to keep track of. This responsibility, coupled with their other duties, could easily lead to a patient being shorted on his allowance.

Other misfortunes the patients allegedly encountered were the nurses demanding tips from the patients and even forcibly taking money from them. Several serious charges had been made by the residents, and upon deep investigation, it was proved that unscrupulous acts might have been committed by the hospital staff. All this had been strenuously denied by the surgeon in charge.

The Home did have witnesses who spoke up on behalf of the institution. William G. Crum, better known as "Billy," testified that he had been a member of the Home for 35 years.

Mr. Crum spoke very highly of "his home" and said he had received nothing but the kindest and most considerate treatment in all his time here. Other members testified to the same effect.

Assemblyman Sterling Cole spoke up for the Home also. Cole, who had sponsored a bill to admit veterans of the late war to the Home (Governor Smith vetoed the bill), stated that for the past thirty years, this had been a real home for the veterans and this was the reason he had introduced such a bill.

Even the Charles E. Wescott Post, American Legion of Bath, got into the action. The post sent out a letter to every legion post in the state, declaring that most of the testimony given in the hearing was false. Wescott Post requested that all other posts assist in getting the public to suspend judgment until the hearing was complete. The names of eleven current or past employees of the Home hospital were affixed to the letter.

Another area examined was the post funds, which date back presumably to 1896, when the canteen was first in service. When the canteen was discontinued, the building was leased by the trustees to a man named F. S. Venuto, who converted it into a store, a restaurant, and a hotel. The rent, fifty dollars a month, was deposited into the Post Fund. Funds were also generated by leasing another building for the sale of newspapers and periodicals. These funds were then deposited into banks designated by the Board of Trustees, the interest on which was credited to the fund.

Originally, these funds were used to provide entertainment for the members, such as books and magazines, and to defray the cost of the moving pictures. However, many other expenses were absorbed by the post funds. When the farm house had burned several years before, funds had been used to offset the costs of rebuilding that were not covered by the appropriated amount.

The post funds also covered the expense of the commandant's coachman at $10 a month, cigars and merchandise bills for the trustees' meetings at $4 to $5 a month, premiums on burglary insurance at $19 per annum, premiums on the bond for cashier Lyman H. Balcom at $25 per annum, premiums on highway robbery insurance at $75 per annum, and premiums for insurance on the store and band instruments at $64.60 per annum. There were also expenses for a female singer in the choir, two members of the band, and a janitor for the amusement hall, all of whom received a monthly wage of $2.00 each.

Mr. Walker claimed that it was not within the trustees' power, however, to rent buildings belonging to the State unless the money was turned over to the State Treasury. While the use of the post funds would be considered admirable if gotten legally, Mr. Walker condemned the existence of the funds. As it stood, Mr. Walker maintained that the State already provided for the needs and comforts of the members, and the mere existence of the post fund, their management, and their disposition should be censured.

These two funds, combined with the Posthumous Fund and Transportation Fund, had grown into a great sum of money. Ultimately, the trustees were charged with exercising poor judgment when depositing these funds. It appeared that sheer indifference had resulted in a low return of interest paid on these accounts. The funds were deposited at the Farmers' and Mechanics' Bank of Bath, where only two per cent interest was paid, and in two Buffalo banks, where it drew an interest rate of three and a half per cent. (On June 9, 1887, the Board of Trustees passed a resolution designating the Farmers' and Mechanics Bank as a depository of all funds of the members.)

Another example of mismanagement occurred during the Liberty Loan Campaigns. Special efforts were made to have members subscribe for Liberty Bonds and pay for them out of their pensions. The trustees invested $10,000 in the bonds and when payment was due, money was withdrawn out of the surplus funds held in the two Buffalo banks. This transaction, along with others, had depleted these two accounts. The result was that all pensions were deposited into the Farmers and Mechanics Bank at two per cent interest.

Around February, 1919, the account had exceeded the requisite amount and the finance committee finally moved to have banks submit bids for the money. This resulted in the Farmers' and Mechanics' Bank agreeing to pay four and a half per cent interest.

Originally, the Post Fund was authorized by law as a legal source of revenue but under inspection by the Fiscal Supervisor, it was deemed that the present status of the fund's income was illegal. A large portion of the Post Fund was from interest earned by the Pension Fund. Earning money from property owned by the Home was not considered ethical. While some of the revenue did go toward the entertainment of the members, a good portion also went toward frills for the board. Cigars, a lady singer for the choir, a janitor for the assembly hall, a coachman for the commandant, and an assortment of insurance policies were not deemed permissible or acceptable by the investigating officer.

As for Commandant Morgan, it was presumed that he was 83-85 years of age. After undergoing a complete examination, he was found to be lacking in memory, and although he had been an officer of the Home since 1899, (he started as inspector) he failed to show much knowledge as to the function of the Home and how to coordinate the various department staffs. He displayed a lack of business and management ability as well as weakness in enforcing discipline in his staff, or showing empathy for members.

Minor complaints, such as the food being served cold or uncooked, were found, for the most part, to be the fault of the cook. This could easily have been resolved by closer supervision of the superintendent of the dining hall service. The barracks needed some improvements that would eliminate hazardous conditions. The fire escapes on the upper floors were three feet off the floor and the opening of the door was extremely difficult. Although a dangerous situation, it could easily have been corrected.

After the intense investigation, Mr. Walker listed his findings. He wrote that the commandant, the trustees, Dr. Hill and other employees attending the hearings made it extremely difficult for him to ascertain or uncover any clear evidence of harsh or cruel treatment. One incident used as an example was witnessed by Spencer Longwell, an artisan working on the roof of one of the wards, and his helper. It involved two demented patients. One was attacking the other with a small stick, causing blood to flow freely. Two attendants stood by watching until Longwell spoke up.

The evidence was taken in a hearing on December 31, 1919, in the Bath courthouse. The following day, Dr. Hill produced two witnesses who denied that any such incident occurred. On February 6, 1920, however, Dr. Hill admitted that such an event occurred but in a different ward than reported by Longwell.

Mr. Walker continued in his report that overall, the care provided in the hospital was inadequate; then he gave several suggestions to help rectify the situation. First, Mr. Walker recommended that all patients be admitted through a receiving ward under the charge of competent officials, and that all valuables being turned in be properly recorded. This would eradicate any temptations on the part of the staff.

The next recommendation was that patients be allowed to have credit at the store. Then, once a week, Mr. Balcom, who had been hired as cashier on August 5, 1905, could settle the accounts. This would eliminate the handling of money by the patients or staff. Balcom received a salary of $1,800 a year plus $20 per month for maintenance.

In conclusion, Mr. Walker recommended that Samuel Maurice Morgan, Commandant, and Doctor Raymond C. Hill, Surgeon-in-Chief, be removed.

Another recommendation made was to infuse "younger blood" into the Board of Trustees. The age of the present board was such that almost all members had served during the Civil War.

Curiously, Morgan would resign on September 1, 1920, but Dr. Hill would remain as surgeon until at least 1926.

SUPERINTENDENTS - DIRECTORS

1878-1880: Parkinson, Captain Edward Clements. Born in Ireland on July 5, 1842, Parkinson enlisted into B Company, 44th NY Infantry on September 9, 1861. He re-enlisted as a veteran in December 1863, and was commissioned into the 13th NY Heavy Artillery until June 28, 1865.

In 1880, Captain Parkinson moved to Seward, NE., where he was appointed Special Examiner, Bureau of Pensions. He served in this position in Portland, OR, Topeka, KS, Jefferson, MO, and Buffalo, NY. Parkinson moved to Rochester, NY in 1895; covering eight surrounding counties under his official supervision. He died on July 31, 1905.

1880-1887: Pitcher, General Thomas G. Born in Rockport, IN on October 23, 1824, Pitcher graduated from the United States Military Academy (USMA) in 1845, he served in defense of Harper's Ferry and in the Virginia Campaign. Pitcher, who rode into battle on his trusty steed "Proofreader." He was brevetted the rank of major for action at Cedar Mountain where he was severely wounded. Pitcher was mustered out of the volunteer service April 30, 1866 and was promoted to colonel and transferred to the 44th NY Infantry. He served as Superintendent of the United States Military Academy from August 1866 until 1871. He then became superintendent of the Home for Disabled Veterans in Washington, D.C. from 1871 to 1877. General Pitcher died at Fort Bayard, NM on October 21, 1895.

1887-1897: Rogers, General William Findlay. Born in Forks Township, PA on March 1, 1820, Rogers' military career began in 1846, serving as a member of D Company, Buffalo City Guard. In 1861, he accepted command of the 21st NYV organized in Elmira and was appointed colonel. He was brevetted brigadier-general for his faithful service in the Virginia and Maryland campaigns, before mustering out in 1863.

General Rogers served as department commander in 1878 and as commander of Bidwell-Wilkeson Post No. 9 and Chapin Post No. 2. He also served as post president of the New York Military Association. General Rogers died in Buffalo on December 16, 1899 and is interred in Forest Lawn Cemetery.

1897-1900: Shepard, Colonel Charles O. Colonel Shepard enlisted early in the war with the 121st NY Infantry. Wounded at Fair Oaks, he continued to serve with distinction. Declining political advancement, Colonel Shepard preferred promotion by his superiors in the fields. After the war, he served in official diplomatic positions for 16 years, first as consul in Yeddo, Japan and later at Leeds and Bradford, England. He also served as chief of the Charitable Bureau of the State's Comptroller's office in Albany.

Much controversy surrounded Colonel Shepard's tenure resulting in charges being brought against him. Although exonerated, he was relieved of duties in 1900.

1900-1902: Davidson, Colonel Andrew. Colonel Davidson was born on February 12, 1840 in Scotland. He enlisted as first lieutenant of Company H, 30th US Colored Troops (USCT) Davidson earned the Medal of Honor for actions at Petersburg, VA on July 30, 1864. It was not issued until October 17, 1892. The citation read "One of the first to enter the enemy's works, where, after his colonel, major, and one-third the company officers had fallen, he gallantly assisted in rallying and saving the remnant of the command."

Davidson served as superintendent until his untimely death on November 10, 1902. He is buried next to his wife, Altana, in Lakewood Cemetery in Cooperstown, NY.

1902-1916: Ewell, Colonel Joseph. In September, 1861 Ewell enlisted as first lieutenant in Company I, 52nd Regiment Illinois Volunteers. He served in Missouri, Kentucky and Tennessee under General U.S. Grant and served as captain in the 26th U.S.C.T. in South Carolina.

He was elected department commander, G.A.R. in June 1919 at the annual encampment held in Elmira. Colonel Ewell died at his home in Buffalo on June 19, 1924.

1916-1920: Morgan, Colonel Samuel M. Born in 1837, Morgan enlisted as a first lieutenant into Company F, 86th NY Infantry Regiment where he served with distinction. Amidst rumors regarding management of the Home, an investigation ensued and he was found mentally unfit to govern and was relieved of his duties. Morgan served as commander of Custer Post for many years and was an honorary member of the U.S.W.V.

On January 8, 1925, Morgan spoke at the Bath Rotary Club. In his speech, Morgan stated "we old men appreciate the courtesy of being invited to an occasion of this kind, for we are just waiting for the reveille to sound to call us home." In less than an hour, he was dead.

1920-1929: Tillson, Colonel John Charles Fremont. Colonel Tillson was born in Elmira on May 26, 1856. He graduated from the USMA in 1878 and spent the next 10 years at Ft. Keogh, Montana. He served in the Philippines and fought in the Spanish-American War. In 1900, his company held the Chien Mien gate at Peking during the Boxer Rebellion. After the rebellion, he was named Military Provost Marshall of Peking. In 1912, he commanded the US Expeditionary Forces in China. In 1915, he returned to the United States and was given command of the 22nd Infantry Regiment. He became commander of Fort Jay at Governors' Island, where his regiment was stationed. War was declared against Germany on April 6, 1917, and Colonel Tillson sent the 22nd Infantry to seize the 16 German ships then in the harbor.

Colonel Tillson retired in 1920 and was appointed superintendent of the Soldiers' Home. After 51 years of military service in state and federal government, Colonel Tillson retired at age 74 and moved back to his hometown of Elmira. He died on December 16, 1941 at the age of 85 and is buried in Arlington National Cemetery.

1929-1935: Bringham, Colonel Robert A. Bringham attended the USMA in the early 1910s, where he became a boxing champion. During the Great War, he was severely wounded in the Aisne-Marne offensive in 1918. Retired from the military, he became a professor of military science and tactics, as well as coached baseball and football at New York University. He later taught and coached at Staunton Military Academy in Virginia.

Colonel Bringham was mustered in as an honorary member of Wheeler Camp No. 103 on February 14, 1930. He was also president of the Bath Rotary Club in 1933.

On April 15, 1935, more than 200 people gathered at the Hotel Wagner in Bath to honor Colonel Bringham, who was being transferred to the Sawtelle Veterans Home in California. He received accolades from the NHDAV, American Legion, representatives of the VA at Washington; and members, officers and staff of the Bath Home for reviving the old Soldiers' Home with less than 200 members into a flourishing VA institution with nearly 1,500 members. Colonel Bringham retired in 1960. He died on November 19, 1974 and was laid to rest in Arlington National Cemetery with full military honors.

1935-1946: Hadley, Colonel John. Born in Marshfield, Maine, Colonel Hadley enlisted into Company D of the 46th Infantry in 1899. He served in the Philippines until 1901, when he returned to Maine. Here, he helped organize a company of the National Guard and was made captain when WWI broke out. As a major in command of the 1st Battalion, 103rd Infantry, he led his men in such major offensives as the Aisne-Marne, Champagne-Marne and Meuse-Argonne.

After the war, he became adjutant-general of Maine until 1922, when he resigned to accept an appointment as governor of the Eastern Branch in Augusta, Maine. He then transferred to the Illinois Branch and then to the Pacific Branch in November, 1926 before coming to Bath. Hadley was also president of the Bath Rotary Club in 1942.

1946-1954: Sprecklemeyer, John Ireland. A veteran of both World Wars, Mr. Sprecklemeyer was appointed Manager of Dayton, Ohio Soldiers' Home in 1954. He returned to the Washington area in 1955 to become an advisor to the Office of Defense Mobilization at the White House. He retired in 1959 and later served briefly as the first administrator of the hospital ship "Project Hope." He also served as president of the Bath Rotary Club in 1952.

1954-1966: Nichols, John M. Mr. Nichols once served as supply officer at the Bath VAC. He became manager with 30 years of government administrative service under his belt. He had served at Des Moines, IA, Sunmount, Northport and Manhatten Beach, NY, Chick Springs and Oteen, NC. He was administrative officer and assistant manager at the Lyons, New Jersey VA Hospital since October of 1947. Mr. Nichols led the fight to keep the Bath VAC open in 1965.

1966-1968: Byers, Harold W. Mr. Byers served as director until June 30, 1968 at which time he transferred to serve as director at the VA Hospital in Ann Arbor, Michigan. Considerable updating of buildings and equipment had been accomplished during his tenure. He also led the development of such newer programs as restoration, trial visit, Nursing Home Care and increased rehabilitation care in the domiciliary program. Upon his leaving, Mr. Byers spoke highly of the dedicated staff and volunteers and had high praise for the great community interest shown toward the VAC. It was with great reluctance that he and his family should leave here.

1968-1970: Michael, Milton Jr. US Navy Mr. Michael began his VA career in Richmond, VA in 1946, after a four year stint in the. He served as Chief of Personnel and Assistant Director Trainee at the Brooklyn VA Hospital in 1949. In 1952, he transferred to the Internal Revenue Service as Chief of Personnel in the New York Regional Office. He returned to the VA in 1956 as Chief, Personnel Division, Oteen, NC VA Hospital.

Mr. Michael later served as assistant director at Wilmington, DE and Whipple, AZ VA Hospitals until 1960. He later became assistant director of the Brooklyn Hospital and was appointed director at the Hot Springs, South Dakota VA Center in February, 1964.

1970- 1973: Tomasula, Albert. During his tenure at Bath, he was active in the Red Cross and was a member of the Traffic Safety Board. He was also involved in several health organizations. Mr. Tomasula is buried in the Bath National Cemetery.

1974-1978: Kelly, J.P. Mr. Kelly was director of the Philadelphia VA Hospital since 1972, when he was appointed director of the Bath VAC. He was educated at Miami University in Oxford, Ohio and worked in insurance and sales. He served as a major during WWII. In 1946, he was employed by the VA in its Central Office in Washington. He worked his way up through the ranks, serving in high level positions in Coatesville, PA., Poplar Bluff, MO., Knoxville, IA, and Hines, IL VA Hospitals.

1979-1983: Salmon, Milton. Mr. Salmon served as a master sergeant with the US Marine Corps during WWII. He entered the VA system in 1946 in Lyons, New Jersey. His service throughout the years in the VA included a variety of supervisory positions and ultimately led to his appointment as assistant director at VA Medical Centers in Alexandria, Louisiana, Charleston, South Carolina and Tampa, Florida. He also served as Hospital Administration Specialist in the VA Central Office in Washington D.C. as Chief of Activation Staff of the Department of Medicine and Surgery.

1983-1995: Gores, Mel A. During Mr. Gore's tenure, the mission of the Medical Center was expanded, resulting in an increased annual budget of 24 million in 1983 to 40 million in 1995. Over 21 million dollars of construction was completed during his term, including three major projects totaling over 15 million dollars. Among these accomplishments were the Ambulatory Entrance, Replacement of Section 1 in 1986, and complete renovation of the Nursing Home Care Unit in 1987.

1995-2000: Sullivan, Michael J. Mr. Sullivan served 32 months off the coast of Vietnam, earning eight combat medals. He brought with him to Bath 24 years of service within the VA. During his tenure, computer software and hardware was upgraded and educational opportunities were offered to ensure success in changing technologies. After transition from Regional to Network, Mr. Sullivan labeled the Bath VA as "the cash cow" of the Network.

2000-2004: Wood, David P. Mr. Wood led the medical transition from a Network-wide Care Line structure to a facility-based structure with line and budget authority and implemented Baldridge as the management framework. Efforts to improve and expand access to Veterans at Community Based Outpatient Clinics in Elmira and Wellsville were achieved. Mr. Wood championed full implementation of an electronic Medical Record and Bath VA Medical Center received the Hospital and Health Networks 2003 "Most Wired" Award for rural hospitals. Mr. Wood is presently the director at the VA Medical Center in Butler, Pa.

2006-Present: Howard, Craig S. Mr. Howard, a Certified Healthcare Executive with the American College of Healthcare Executives, earned his Bachelor of Business Administration degree from Marion College in Fond du Lac, WI. and a Master of Business Administration degree from Providence College, Providence, RI. He began his federal career at the VA Medical Center in Brocton, MA in 1978 and worked his way up through the ranks; serving at nine different VA Medical Centers. Mr. Howard assumed the position of director at the Canandaigua VA Medical Center on November 27, 2005. He and his wife Carla have two girls, Sara and Lily.

*NOTE: Throughout the years, there have been several interim directors. I decided not to include them because either their tenure was brief or adequate details could not be provided.

Profiles

Many interesting and influential individuals should be included on this list. However, time and space does not allow me to include all such notables. Here is but a handful; their backgrounds teeming with vibrant and colorful history that deserve recognition for their roles, not only in establishing and preserving our Home but their contributions to our Country.

Barnum, General Henry Alanson. In 1861, General Barnum helped organize the 12th Infantry Regiment, the first volunteer regiment to be mustered in the State of New York, in which he served as captain. Seriously wounded and captured at Malvern Hill, he was exchanged shortly thereafter. In September 1862, Barnum, now a colonel, served with the 149th NY. He was wounded at both Gettysburg and Lookout Mountain. During the Atlanta Campaign, Barnum commanded the 3rd Brigade in Sherman's March to the Sea. He was brevetted major-general of United States Volunteers (USV) on March 13, 1865. Barnum had earned the Medal of Honor which was issued in July of 1889. After the war, he served as New York Inspector of Prisons. He also served as department commander, G.A.R. in 1871 and 1872. Barnum initiated a second effort for a Soldiers' Home in NY State and served on the first Board of Trustees in 1872.

Beecher, Henry Ward. Henry Beecher, whose American roots extend back to 1637, belonged to one of the most influential abolitionist families in America. A very gifted preacher and reformer; he was the brother of author Harriet Beecher Stowe. He became pastor of Congregational Plymouth Church in Brooklyn in 1847. Known as the "Beecher Bible and Rifle Church" by some, his congregation provided guns, known as "Beecher's Bibles" to the "Free-Soilers" in the disputed Kansas territory. He was also a very staunch and powerful advocate for the New York State Soldiers' and Sailors' Home.

Cole, William Sterling. Mr. Cole was born in Painted Post, NY on April 18, 1904. He attended the public school and continued his education at Colgate University, Hamilton, NY in 1925; Albany Law School of Union University, Schenectady, NY, LL.B., graduating in 1929. He taught in the public schools and at Corning Free Academy in 1925 and 1926. Admitted to the New York Bar in 1929, he began his law practice in Bath, NY in 1930. He was elected as a Republican to the Seventy-fourth Congress and was reelected to eleven succeeding Congresses, serving from January 3, 1935, until his resignation December 1, 1957. Mr. Cole then became Director General of the International Atomic Energy Agency in Vienna, Austria, from 1957-1961 and later Chairman, Joint Committee on Atomic Energy. He resumed the practice of law in Washington, D.C. and was a resident of Arlington, VA, until his death on March 15, 1987. He is interred in Grove Cemetery in Bath, NY.

Davenport, Ira. Mr. Davenport was born in Hornellsville, NY on June 28, 1841 and moved to Bath in 1847. He attended Russell Collegiate School in New Haven, CT. Upon the death of his father in 1868, he assumed the management of the large estate and business affairs. Mr. Davenport made a large monetary contribution towards the Home and advanced thousands of his own money when the building funds were exhausted. He was elected to the State Senate in 1877 and served four years.

In 1881, he served 2 years as State Comptroller and was then elected to the House of Representative in 1884. He made an unsuccessful bid for governor of New York in 1885. He served two terms in congress from March 4, 1885 to March 3, 1889. He died on October 6, 1904, and is interred in the family cemetery on his estate "Riverside," in Bath.

Dolson, Joseph S. Dr. Dolson was born in Campbell, NY on February 6, 1825. He was schooled in Bath, Campbell, Elmira, and at Cazenovia Seminary. He taught school for several years before studying medicine; attending lectures at the Geneva Medical College. He graduated from the Albany Medical College in 1848. Opening a practice in Bath, Dr. Dolson treated the families of all those who enlisted during the "Great Rebellion" free of charge until their return. However, in 1862, he enlisted in the 161st Infantry Regiment and served in Baton Rogue as an assistant-surgeon. In 1864, he was elevated to full surgeon but shortly there-after contracted typhoid and was sent home. He served as the surgeon at the Soldiers' Home from March 1882 through September 30, 1887 when he resigned. He died in the second week of July, 1893.

Drummer, Henry L. As one of the most active and dedicated employees, Mr. Drummer gave 48 years of service to the Soldiers' Home. First appointed florist on November 27, 1884, he was later listed as Superintendent of Grounds until he resigned in August of 1932. Mr. Drummer was responsible for laying out walks and parks and supervised the landscaping. He was also responsible for surveying and developing the Home cemetery. Mr. Drummer had overseen the construction of the greenhouses and was responsible for propagating rare lines of ferns, palms, shrubs and flowers. Entertaining the veterans was another of his charges, which he did with great enthusiasm. He developed the moving picture service at the Home, installing the equipment and running the bi-weekly viewings. Mr. Drummer had also published the first souvenir photo album of the Soldiers' Home. These made for a very nice souvenir booklet and copies were made available to the public.

Mr. Drummer was also one of the first to recommend a study of nature in the curriculum as part of the school system. He had secured legislation by which the state offered premiums for vegetables and flowers grown by students. He also organized the nature study exhibits of schools and students which now grace the Steuben County Fair. For years, he superintended that department for the Steuben County Agricultural Society.

On his last day of service at the Home, a very touching tribute was given him. As he walked down the road leading away from the Home for the last time, nearly 1,000 veterans lined both sides of the road and rendered a salute. As he reached the limit of the grounds, Colonel Bringham offered appreciation on behalf of the institution and the members for his long years of faithful service. Mr. Drummer died on May 18, 1934, at the age of 67.

For his dedication to the veterans at the Soldiers' Home and his willingness to share his love of nature with the younger generation, Mr. Drummer was nominated and selected for the Steuben County Hall of Fame in 2006.

Gansevoort, Captain Robert H. Robert Gansevoort was born on December 7, 1834. As a young man, he studied medicine with Dr. Joseph S. Dolson. Gansevoort was attending medical college at Ann Arbor, MI when the Civil War broke out. He enlisted as a second lieutenant in the 1st NY Artillery in 1861 but resigned his commission in 1862 to re-enlist as a private in the 107th Regiment, NY Volunteers. He was soon promoted to captain of G Company. He served in nearly all the battles during Sherman's march to the sea.

Friends recalled that "In camp and march, in siege and fight," Captain Gansevoort was one of the foremost. After the war, he returned home, a broken man, the years of war having taken its toll. He moved to Georgia for health purposes. Soon after, he responded to a call for troops and headed for Fort Rice in the Dakota Territory. In 1874, Gansevoort had dislocated his shoulder falling from his horse. He returned to Bath and served as the first hospital steward of the Soldiers' Home. He resigned his position due to ill-health. Gansevoort died April 16, 1887; his funeral was attended by trustees and members of the Home. Delegates of Custer and Barry Posts acted as escort. He is buried in a family plot in Grove Cemetery, Bath.

Humphrey, Edward L. Mr. Humphrey entered the US Army as a second lieutenant in 1942 and served as a combat engineer. During the invasion of Normandy, he was seriously wounded in the leg, resulting in amputation. Upon return to civilian life, Mr. Humphrey operated an insurance and real estate firm in Bath. However, he was best known for his political and civic activities. In 1962, he was elected Town of Bath supervisor. He was also elected to the Steuben County Republican Committee. His untiring efforts to save the VA from closing in 1965 earned him the respect of, not only the people of Bath, but also such national figures as Robert F. Kennedy. Mr. Humphrey was head of the Baths Veterans and Civic Affairs Committee which he successfully led in the fight to preserve the VA Center. Mr. Humphrey died on September 4, 1968 at the VA Hospital at the age of 52.

Kellogg, Lynn W. Mr. Kellogg was born in Kanona, NY on August 20, 1893. In June, 1917, he enlisted in the United States Marine Corps. He was stationed first in Philadelphia, after which he was ordered to Camp Reed, Virginia, where he rounded out his twenty-one months of service. He returned to Bath and resumed work in insurance until the fall of 1919, when he was elected to the office of town clerk. Three years later, he was elected to the office of Sheriff.

Mr. Kellogg helped organized and became first commander of American Legion Post (Wescott), No. 173, of Bath. He was also a member in the "Forty and Eight," Local Voiture No. 95 and was a Free and Accepted Mason, in which he attained the thirty-second degree. Mr. Kellogg died prematurely on March 30, 1930 and was interred in Grove Cemetery, Bath.

King, General Horatio Collins. King was born on December 22, 1837 in Portland, Maine. In 1854, he began his education at Dickinson College where he earned his Bachelor's degree in 1858. Following graduation, he studied law with Edwin M. Stanton for two years. He moved to New York City in 1861 where he was admitted to the New York State Bar.

At the onset of the Civil War, King sought a commission in the Union Army and in 1862, was appointed Assistant-Quartermaster of Volunteers with the rank of captain. Soon after, King was given a more active duty assignment under the command of General Sheridan as Chief Quartermaster of the First Cavalry Division of the Army of the Shenandoah.

King took part in five battles and was brevetted Colonel of Volunteers for gallantry at the Battle of Five Forks. Discharged in October of 1866 with the brevets of major, lieutenant colonel and colonel, King returned to his law practice in New York City until 1871, when he assumed the associate editor's position at the *New York Star*. Soon after, King assumed the role of publisher of the *Christian Union* with his close friend, Reverend Henry Ward Beecher, as editor.

General King joined the National Guard of New York in 1876 and was elected major of the 13th Regiment. He was appointed Judge Advocate for the Eleventh Brigade in 1880 and, in 1883, was appointed Judge Advocate General, with the rank of brigadier-general by Governor Grover Cleveland.

King served as secretary of the Society of the Army of the Potomac from 1877 to 1904 and as president of the organization in 1904. He was a member of the Order of Elks, a Mason, and a charter member of the New York Commandery of the Military Order of the Loyal Legion. King was also an active member of the G.A.R., serving two years as post commander and one year as Department Judge Advocate General. He also served for ten years as a member of the Brooklyn Board of Education and a member of the New York Monuments' Commission. He was a trustee of Dickinson College from 1896 to 1918, and is perhaps best known by the college as the author of numerous school songs including Dickinson's Alma Mater, "Noble Dickinsonia."

On September 23, 1897, King was awarded the Medal of Honor for "conspicuous gallantry" while serving with the cavalry in March of 1865 near Dinwiddie Court House. His citation reads "While serving as a volunteer aide, carried orders to the reserve brigade and participated with it in the charge which repulsed the enemy." King died on November 15, 1918 in Brooklyn.

Lawrence, Captain Abram B. Lawrence was born in Warsaw, NY on May 18, 1834. He spent several years as a merchant's clerk in the village until 1862 when he was commissioned by Governor Edwin D. Morgan to serve as quartermaster of the 130th Regiment of Infantry which he helped muster. This unit later became known as the 1st NY Dragoons. He was noted for his meritorious service and was promoted to rank of captain by President Lincoln and assigned assistant-quartermaster.

He quickly rose to the rank of major and was made Chief Quartermaster of the 18th Corps. At General Lee's surrender at the Appomattox Court House, General Grant had specifically chosen Lawrence who, by then, had been brevetted lieutenant-colonel, to accept the arms and supplies of the confederate army. Colonel Lawrence provided thirty thousand rations to the defeated southern army.

Lawrence was mustered out of service in 1866 with his life brevets for "faithful and meritorious services during the war." He became active in the G.A.R. and was responsible for establishing no less than eight new posts in Wyoming County, NY. He served as commander of Gibbs Post No. 130 for several years. He also served as vice-department commander and was selected several times as the State delegate to the national encampment.

He was commissioned by Governor Samuel Tilden and appointed commanding officer of the Letchworth Rifles. Governor Johnson then gave Lawrence the official rank of Lieutenant-Colonel, National Guards. Lawrence died on March 30, 1912 and is buried in Warsaw, NY.

Leavens, Chas. C. Mr. Leavens was born in Montour Falls, NY on March 2, 1848. Too young to serve in the Civil War, he was perhaps the only officer on the staff to not have served at that time. He did however; serve the Home very admirably as quartermaster until his resignation on October 1, 1889. He became a traveling salesman but gave that up to serve as clerk at the famous Willard's Hotel in Washington, D.C. He returned to New York in 1922 and resided in Cameron until his death on May 13, 1938.

Letchworth, William Prior. Mr. Letchworth was a philanthropist, conservationist, businessman and humanitarian. He began amassing a modest fortune by the age of 22. Letchworth's dedication to the cause of the Civil War is documented by his paying another to serve in his place during the war. Even though he was a Quaker, in poor health and beyond the recommended enlistment age, he paid a substitute and supported his substitute's family until the war ended.

On January 1, 1874, he was appointed vice-president of

the State Board of Charities and on April 21, 1877, reappointed commissioner for the full term of 8 years. On March 14, 1878, he was elected president of the board which he held until he retired ten years later. In 1872, Letchworth became president of the Wyoming County Soldiers' Monument Association and made the first gift of a $1,000 towards the construction of the Soldiers' and Sailors' Monument in Warsaw.

One of Mr. Letchworth's greatest contributions was his gift of 1,000 acres to the State of New York, which is today known Letchworth State Park. Recognized as one of the finest arboretums in the east, Mr. Letchworth also encouraged scientific farming methods on three tenant farms located on the estate.

Logan, General John F. Logan studied law at Louisville University and his political career led him from county clerk to US Congressman. At the onset of the Civil War Logan fought at the Battle of Bull Run as a civilian. He later enlisted and rose to the rank of major-general. He fought in eight major campaigns and distinguished himself at Vicksburg. He commanded the entire Union forces at the Battle of Atlanta.

After the war, General Logan returned to Congress. He took part in Illinois' first veteran's memorial service in Woodlawn Cemetery in Carbondale in 1866. In 1868, General Logan was elected Commander in Chief of the G.A.R. He was again elected to the same position in 1869 and 1870. On May 5, 1868, he issued General Order No. 11 designating May 30 to be set aside in memoriam of fallen comrades. Originally known as Decorations Day it was later changed to Memorial Day.

Morgan, Edwin D. Morgan was an active member of New York State Senate. serving in the 6th District, 1850-53; NY State Commissioner of Immigration 1855-58; NY Republican State Chair, 1856-58 and 1874-75; Chairman of Republican National Committee 1856-64 and 1872-76; and Governor of

New York from 1859-62. He also served as US Senator from NY from 1863-69. He also sponsored the legislation that founded Central Park in New York City. During the Civil War, Lincoln commissioned him a major general of volunteers to run the military department of that state and improve the defenses of New York Harbor. He resigned commission in 1863 to serve in US Senate. After retiring, he became a philanthropist and patron of the arts, supporting medical and educational institutions in New York.

Palmer, Captain John. Born in Staten Island on March 22, 1842, Captain Palmer enlisted as a private or corporal in Company B, 91st NY Volunteers, his brother and his father had also enlisted. His father was killed on the battlefield at Petersburg. Palmer was promoted to captain on March 1, 1865 and at the Battle of Five Forks was severely wounded when a horse shot out from the adjutant of his outfit and landed on Palmer's back, nearly severing the spine. He was mustered out with the regiment on July 3rd, 1865 and returned to Albany.

He was a Charter Member of the Lew Benedict Post No. 5 and served as Department Commander, G.A.R. in 1875. In 1891, he was elected National Commander, G.A.R. and had the privilege of marching at the head of a column of 80,000 veterans for the 26th National Encampment in Washington, D.C. He is listed as one of the founders of the Soldiers' Home and is credited with raising $50,000 of the $100,000 needed to begin the project. He was elected Secretary of the State of New York in 1893 on the Republican ticket and held that office for four years. He was also President of the Board of Trustees in 1896 and 1897. Mr. Palmer died at his home on Madison Avenue in Albany, NY on April 15, 1905.

Robinson, General John C. General Robinson graduated from the United States Military Academy in 1839 and was commissioned second lieutenant, 5th Illinois Infantry. In 1861, he was appointed Colonel of the 1st Michigan Volunteers and later Brigadier General, USV, in 1863. He was brevetted three times for gallantry at the battle of Gettysburg, the Wilderness and Spotsylvania. While leading his division at Spotsylvania, he was seriously wounded in his left leg resulting in amputation. He served as Department Commander, G.A.R. in 1870 and as National Commander, G.A.R. in 1877 and 1878. General Robinson served as a trustee of the Soldiers' Home in 1872 and as Lieutenant-Governor of New York.

Rumsey, Colonel William. Colonel Rumsey was born in Salem, Washington County, NY, on December 25, 1810. He attended school at Auburn, NY, and Hobart College at Geneva, NY where he studied law. He was admitted to the bar in 1831 and commenced practice in Bath, NY, where he was Surrogate of Steuben County from 1840-1844. He held many local offices and was elected as a Whig to the Thirtieth and Thirty-first Congresses from 1847 to 1851. He enlisted in Battery E, 1st NY Light Artillery organized in Bath in 1861 and was severely wounded in the battle of Fair Oaks. Promoted to major by President Lincoln and later brevetted lieutenant colonel by President Johnson for "distinctive services for the campaign during May, June and July, 1864." After the war, he was appointed delegate to the State constitutional convention in 1867 and became a member of the commission to propose amendments to the State constitution in 1872. He was appointed in 1873 as an associate justice of the State Supreme Court to fill a vacancy in 1873 and was elected to that office in the fall of that year. Colonel Rumsey also served as commander of Post Custer No. 81. He died in Bath, NY in 1903 and is interred in a private cemetery on the Rumsey Estate.

Sickles, General Daniel E. Born in New York City, Sickles attended New York University where he studied law and apprenticed to a printer. He joined the Bar and served as a corporation attorney. He was also elected to the New York Assembly. After being appointed to the London Legation from 1853 to 1855, he served in the New York Senate before moving to the US Congress as a Democrat from 1857 to 1861.

Sickles met with trouble while in Congress when he shot a man, Francis Scott Key's son, across the street from the White House, for having an affair with his wife. His defense attorney, Edwin Stanton, had him plead temporary insanity and he was found innocent.

When the war broke out, Sickles helped raise a brigade of volunteers, the 70th NY Volunteer Infantry, in which he became colonel. He quickly rose to the rank of brigadier general which some argue was due to his contacts in Washington. During the battle of Gettysburg, General Sickles misunderstood or disobeyed orders, moving his men of the III Corps forward, off Cemetery Ridge, to ground more to his liking. This move exposed the II Corps' flank and almost cost him his III Corps. Nevertheless, he was awarded the Medal of Honor for his actions in Gettysburg in 1897. (Sickles lost his leg to a shell-burst; he donated the shattered appendage to a medical museum.)

Sickles was elected Department Commander, G.A.R. in 1868 and 1869. He also served as President of the Board of Trustees in 1897 and 1898. He resigned his appointment as Trustee in 1900 when he learned that Colonel Shepard, Superintendent of the Home was being replaced after a scandal involving the Officers of the Board and the trustees.

Slocum, General Henry W. Born in Delphi, Onondaga County, NY, September 24, 1827, Slocum attended Cazenovia Seminary in New York until he was admitted to West Point in 1848. Graduating 7th in his class he was commissioned second lieutenant, First Artillery on July 1, 1852. Slocum served in the Seminole War and was promoted to first lieutenant on March 3, 1855. After being transferred to Fort Moultrie, SC, he resigned his commission on October 31, 1856 to practice law in Syracuse, NY. When Fort Sumter fell, Slocum was appointed colonel of the 27th NY Infantry and fought at Bull Run, where he was severely wounded. After recuperating, he was promoted to major general and saw action in many major battles which included South Mountain, Antietam, Chancellorsville and Gettysburg. In September, 1865, Slocum again resigned from service and returned to settle in Brooklyn where he practiced law. He served three terms in the US House of Representatives, 1869-73 and 1883-85 and was a member of the board of the Gettysburg Monument Committee. He was appointed president of the department of city works in 1876 and elected as a Representative at Large from New York to the Forty-eighth Congress (March 4, 1883-March 3, 1885). Slocum became the first president of the Board of Trustees in 1879 and served in that position until his retirement in 1887. General Slocum died in Brooklyn, NY, April 14, 1894 and was mourned by all the members and Officers of the Home. He was interred in Greenwood Cemetery.

Tanner, Corporal James. Corporal Tanner had run away from home to join the Union cause. He enlisted into Company C, 87th NY Volunteer Infantry and had survived several battles until, on August 30, 1862, during the battle of Second Bull Run, a shell shattered one leg and tore the other nearly off. He was captured and held prisoner for ten days before being paroled. In 1863, he secured an appointment as Under-Doorkeeper of the New York State Legislature and then obtained a clerkship in the War Department in Washington. He was on hand that fateful night when Lincoln was assassinated, and recorded first-hand testimonies of the witnesses. He studied law in New York at the end of the war and in 1869 was admitted to the Bar. Tanner held a post in the New York Customs House from 1869 to 1877 and from 1877 to 1885 was Tax Collector in Brooklyn, NY.

He was also very active within the G.A.R. and was Department Commander in 1876 and National Commander in 1905-06. Tanner was probably the most colorful and instrumental force in establishing the Home. In 1876, he initiated a letter-writing campaign seeking funds for the Soldiers' Home. He also showed his compassion by ordering proper observances for Decoration Day and advised that confederate soldiers be invited to participate. He frequently lobbied Congress on behalf of veterans and in March of 1889, he was appointed Commissioner of Pensions. Although honest, his ineptitude and compassion for his comrades in this position caused his early resignation in September of 1889. From then until 1904 he became a private pension attorney, prosecuting various claims against the government. In April 1904, President Theodore Roosevelt appointed him a Register of Wills for the District of Columbia. James Tanner died in Washington D.C. and is buried in Arlington Cemetery. His wife Mero is buried with him.

Wylie, Farand Dr. Dr. Wylie was born August 20, 1819 in Covington, Wyoming County, NY He was a graduate of the Geneva Medical College. He practiced in Woodhull and Almond, NY until the War of Rebellion broke out and he responded to the call. He was commissioned as assistant surgeon in the 86th Regiment and served three and a half years before returning home to take up residence in Bath. He was the first surgeon of the Soldiers' Home until his retirement in 1883. He was a member of Custer Post 81, which turned out in full regalia for his funeral. His son Thomas was a member of the Home and died on June 12, 1899. He is buried in the National Cemetery.

Bath National Cemetery

The Bath National Cemetery contains over 30 acres of sparsely wooded hillside. Near the lower elevation stands the 40' obelisk monument. The plaque at the bottom reads "with a legacy bequeathed to the Home by Samuel Deitz, Esq., a patriotic citizen." The obverse reads "In Memory of the Soldiers and Sailors of the War for the Preservation of the Union who died in the New York State Soldiers and Sailors Home."

Initially part of the Soldiers' Home, the cemetery came under control of the Veteran Administration in 1930. It was maintained by the Engineering Service of the Bath facility until 1973, when it became part of the VA National Cemetery System, under the Department of Memorial Affairs.

The first interment at the Soldiers' Home was Private William O. Terrell, who died of consumption on February 14, 1879. Other notables interred here are George Beniski and Private Robert Knox Sneden. The former served in the stead of Grover Cleveland while the latter was noted for his drawings and painting of Civil War battles and leaders. His scrapbook is on display at the Virginia Historical Society.

Also included are five Medal of Honor recipients and 72 members from the famed 54th Massachusetts. In 1988, 28 Unknowns from the War of 1812 were discovered in Ontario and repatriated here with military honors.

Until around 1990, the Domiciliary Officer would attend all funerals. A funeral escort party was comprised of men from the companies. The party consisted of a firing squad, color guard, pall bearers and bugler, all in uniform.

Today, every branch of the military is represented by the approximate 14,200 military personnel interred here.

-July of 1976, the Bath American Legion placed 20 American flags along the avenue in front of the Historical Museum. Each flag represented the home state for a veteran buried in the National Cemetery.

-In 1977, during the Centennial Celebration, Building 42 was used as a museum to exhibit historic memorabilia.

-In 1983, a Historical Memorabilia Committee was established to collect and develop ideas for a VAMC Museum.

-In March of 1984, the museum became a station-level project under VAMC Director Mel Gores.

-Blueprints were drawn up by August of 1984 to renovate building 42 and by August 1985, enough money was available to begin the renovation. The tentative time of completion was the spring of 1986.

-In March of 1986, a policies and procedures program was initiated and the museum theme was changed to that of military and Bath VAMC history.

-On May 16, 1986, the museum opened and is currently one of approximately thirteen in the VA system.

-In December of 1986, the museum received a rare collection of G.A.R. National Encampment badges from John V. Willetts, a retired Brooklyn businessman.

-Manned by volunteers and open to the public, the museum contains artifacts which date back to 1776.

FARM AND GARDEN

Home Products Issued and Sold For 1907:

538 bushels of apples	$192.90
40 bunches asparagus	2.00
6,145 pounds beef	368.70
242 bushels beets	82.30
14 bushels beans, string	16.40
15,771 heads cabbage	315.42
149 bushels carrots	40.25
22 heads cauliflower	1.10
672 bunches celery	79.80
169 pounds chicken	23.55
200 bushels corn	60.00
1,072 dozen corn, green	81.60
14,260 cucumber	71.30
102 ½ dozen eggs	17.36
150 ton ensilage	600.00
400 bushels greens	120.00
63 tons hay	532.00
1,500 gallons kraut	225.00
5,010 pounds lard	501.00
4,645 heads lettuce	46.45
392 feet lumber, ash	11.76
240 feet lumber, maple	7.20
12,000 feet lumber, hemlock	180.00
27,599 gallons milk	3,035.00
1,385 bushels oats	497.90
828 onions	422.30
8,760 onions, green	87.60
172 bushels parsnips	148.75
167 bushels peas, green	83.50
96 peppers	1.92
6 bushels pie plant	3.00
15 barrels pickles	75.00
12,120 pounds pork, fresh	848.40

6,790 pounds pork, salt...475.30
1,618 bushels potatoes..880.20
11 loads pumpkins..11.45
2,116 bundles radishes...21.16
56 pounds sage...15.80
48 squash..0.96
25 tons straw...130.00
60 pounds summer savory..15.50
4,800 pounds tallow..204.00
75 pounds thyme...19.90
174 bushels tomatoes..174.00
438 bushels turnips...147.70
Value of calves and hides..151.00
        Total Value: $11,027

Bill of fare for year 1891

SUNDAY
Breakfast-Beef stew, bread, butter and coffee.
Dinner-Roast beef or mutton, potatoes, gravy, bread, butter, pudding, coffee and fruit in season.
Supper-Stewed fruit, cheese, bread, butter and coffee.

MONDAY
Breakfast-Mutton stew, bread, butter, coffee.
Dinner-Boiled beef, potatoes, soup, cold slaw, bread, coffee.
Supper-Hominy, bread, butter, syrup and tea.

TUESDAY
Breakfast-Bread, butter, toast, coffee and hash.
Dinner-Roast beef, mashed potatoes, gravy, bread, butter and coffee.
Supper-Prune pudding, bread, butter, tea.

WEDNSDAY
Breakfast-Bread, butter, hash and coffee.
Dinner-Boiled potatoes, chow-chow, bread, butter, coffee.
Supper-Milk toast, corn meal mush, syrup, bread, butter and tea.

THURSDAY
Breakfast-Ham or shoulder, potatoes, bread, butter, coffee.
Dinner-Pork and beans, bread and coffee.
Supper-Oat meal, syrup, cold corn beef, bread, butter and tea.

FRIDAY
Breakfast-Boiled mackerel, potatoes, bread, butter, coffee.
Dinner-Fresh fish, gravy, potatoes, cold slaw, bread, butter, coffee.
Supper-Ginger cakes, rice, cheese, bread, butter and tea.

SATURDAY
Breakfast- Beef stew or hash, toast, bread, butter and coffee.
Dinner-Corned beef, cabbage, bean soup, potatoes, bread, butter and coffee.
Supper-Rice pudding, cold corned beef, bread, butter and tea.

Menu for September, 1908

SUNDAY
Breakfast-Corned beef hash, bread, butter, coffee.
Dinner-Mutton stew, pie, bread, coffee.
Supper-Rice pudding and raisins, cheese, bread, butter, tea.

MONDAY
Breakfast-Beef stew, bread, butter, coffee.
Dinner-Roast beef, potatoes, green corn, bread pudding, bread, coffee.
Supper-Corn bread, peaches, bread, butter, tea.

TUESDAY
Breakfast-Beef stew, bread, butter, coffee.
Dinner-Roast beef, potatoes, beets, bread pudding, bread, coffee.
Supper-Tea biscuit, peaches, bread, butter, tea.

WEDNSDAY
Breakfast-Corned beef hash, bread, butter, coffee.
Dinner-Hamburger steak, potatoes, cucumbers, bread, coffee.
Supper-Hominy, prunes, bread, butter, tea.

THURSDAY
Breakfast-Beef stew, bread, butter, coffee.
Dinner-Barrel corned beef, potatoes, cucumbers, bread, butter, coffee.

Supper-Canned corned beef, potatoes, bread, butter, tea.

FRIDAY
Breakfast-Creamed codfish, potatoes, bread, butter, tea.
Dinner-Fresh fish stuffed, potatoes, tapioca pudding, bread, butter, coffee.
Supper-Oatmeal, cookies, apple sauce, bread, butter, tea.

SATURDAY
Breakfast-Bacon, potatoes, bread, butter, coffee.
Dinner-Vegetable soup, boiled beef, potatoes, bread, coffee.
Supper-Canned corn beef, potatoes, bread, butter, tea, tomatoes.

Glossary

American Red Cross: First introduced to the Swiss-inspired International Red Cross Movement while visiting Europe following the Civil War, Clara Barton returned home and with a circle of acquaintances founded the American Red Cross in Washington, D.C. on May 21, 1881. The first local chapter was organized in Dansville, NY on August 22, 1881. Barton had campaigned for an American Red Cross society and for ratification of the Geneva Convention protecting the war-injured, which the United States ratified in 1882.

Bath American Legion, Charles E. Wescott Post #173: Named after Private Charles E. Wescott, who was killed on July 15, 1918; becoming the first of ten Bath soldiers who paid the supreme sacrifice during WWI. The post received its charter on August 10, 1920 and remained a strong advocate for the Soldiers' Home in its many battles.

Compensated Work Therapy: The CWT program uses "work hardening skills" to prepare veterans for employment opportunities when they are ready to re-enter the community. About 120 veteran patients per year pass through the 8 week CWT course. While in the program, the veterans are trained in different skills and are employed in several area businesses to hone those skills. The participants in the CWT program are required to save 70% of their income for their discharge. The main goal of the program is to help the veteran patient gain successful employment when he leaves the VA.

Custer Post No. 81, G.A.R.: the post took its namesake from General George Custer, and received its charter on July 20, 1876. Custer Post enjoyed every holiday, celebration and ceremony at the Soldiers' Home during its existence. By 1931, the Post membership dropped to 8 members. On March 2,

1938, William Randolf, age 90, of Bath, died. He was the last surviving member of the post.

General Barry Post No. 248, G.A.R.: This post took its name from Major General William Farquhar Barry of NYC. Chartered on December 22, 1881; the camp consisted entirely of members of the Soldiers' Home which had a total of 634 names on its roster by the time they disbanded in March, 1936.

Grand Army of the Republic: Founded in Decatur, Illinois on April 6, 1866 by Benjamin F. Stephenson, only honorably discharged veterans of the Union Army, Navy, Marine Corps or the Revenue Cutter Service who served between April 12, 1861 and April 9, 1865 were eligible to join. The G.A.R. was broken down into State or Department levels. The departments were made up by camps stationed throughout the state. At one time, there were at least 672 posts in the Department of New York. Under the motto "Fraternity, Loyalty, and Charity," or "F, C, & L," the G.A.R. was active in relief work for veterans and in pension legislation. Its membership had at one time exceeded 400,000 members. The 83rd and final National Encampment of the G.A.R. was held in August, 1949 in Indianapolis, Indiana. Of the six members present, only one flew to the encampment. At 108 years old, James Hard flew out of Rochester, NY laden with 20 boxes of cigars given to him by well-wishers to hand out to his comrades. The last surviving member, Albert Woolston, died in 1956, at the age of 109.

Graphic Arts: The home of the Therapeutic Printing Program, Graphic Arts is a comprehensive program of the VA Healthcare Network Upstate New York. The program prepares veterans in recovery for employment in the printing industry. Patients enrolled through the Pre-Vocational Apprenticeship Program (PVAP) benefit from treatment services throughout their training. The goal of the program is to provide patients with entry-level skills to return to community employment. Combining educational presentations with hands-on training, this program utilizes state-of-the-art equipment to give veterans experience producing a wide range of print products.

Patients are trained for six to nine months by staff Print Management Specialists. Patients learn to prepare computerized print layouts, use darkroom equipment and offset presses to print, and finish jobs using a variety of bindery tools. Development of these skills enables veterans to compete in the job market and support their long-term recovery and health status.

Traditionally the Therapeutic Printing Program had focused on teaching students printing press operation. With the industry moving toward computerization in all stages of printing, an ambitious computer component has been added to the curriculum.

Gray Ladies: The Gray Lady began service in 1918 at the Walter Reed Army Hospital in Washington, D.C. Originally called the Hostess and Hospital Service and Recreation Corps of the American Red Cross, their name was shortened to Hospital and Recreation Corps in 1934. It was not officially changed to Gray Lady Service (a term coined by GIs due to the gray dresses and veils worn as uniforms) until 1947. These volunteers acted as hostesses and provided friendly, recreational and personal services of a non-medical nature to sick, injured, and disabled to patients, most of who had been injured during the First World War.

The service reached its greatest strength during World War II when almost 50,000 women served as Gray Ladies in military and other hospitals throughout the United States. Although their numbers declined after the war, Gray Ladies continued to maintain a distinctive presence in American hospitals until the late 1960s when the different volunteer branches of the Red Cross were discontinued in favor of a unified concept of the Red Cross Volunteer. The Gray Lady Service, as such, disappeared and volunteers who performed its traditional functions were simply called members of the Red Cross Volunteer Services.

In keeping with this new policy, a universal blue uniform replaced the distinctive ones that had identified Gray Ladies and volunteers in other Red Cross services for many years. Despite these changes, some former Gray Ladies continued to use the apparel they had worn so proudly for nearly 50 years and Red Cross leadership made no effort to ban this practice among the long-term volunteers. Even today, a few chapters continue to call some of their volunteers "Gray Ladies" who perform the traditional functions of the bygone service.

Clinical Informatics Section: CIS provides critical support to the successful integration of information technology and the delivery of health care in traditional facility-based clinical care settings, outreach activities to the home, personal health records and how computerized systems are configured to manage data. Clinical Informatics staff includes Clinical Application Coordinators, Bar Code/Medication Administration, medical records, and medical library staff.

Keeley League: Under the banner, "The Law Must Recognize a Leading Fact: Medical Not Penal Treatment Reforms the Drunkard," the Keeley League, a national patient mutual aid society that combined advocacy with support was founded in 1891 by former Civil War doctor Leslie E. Keeley. The "Keeley Cure" prescribed injections of a secret compound called "Double Chloride of Gold" four times a day and less powerful doses of the medicine every two hours. The patients were also treated with a several-week course of sympathy and understanding. It was hoped that the cure would break their addictions, restore their self-respect, and place their lives back on track.

Letchworth Rifles: Headquartered in Warsaw, the Rifles were known for their marksmanship and military training. They were designated as the 4th Separate Company of Infantry, 31st Brigade New York National Guard on May 18th, 1876. Mustered into service on July 26, 1876, it was called to service three times in 1877, the first duty guarding government property for two days in Portageville, NY. To what extent is uncertain. The second time was a call to put down the railroad riots in Attica and Buffalo, NY and the third, to suppress a riot on the Rochester and State Line Railroad in Gainesville, NY on October 18, 1877. The company disbanded on January 1, 1882 when membership fell below 46, the minimum required for state and county aid. The company was named in honor of William Pryor Letchworth.

Milton R. Wheeler Camp, No. 103: Wheeler Camp, No. 103 was formed on April 4, 1916. The members convened at the amusement hall or Annex C. The camp was named after a soldier of the Philippine Insurrection, the late son of Sheldon S. Wheeler, Civil War veteran and member of the G.A.R. Sheldon Wheeler was named an honorary member of the U.S.W.V. and resided at the Soldiers' Home.

The camp was chartered at the end of July or beginning of August, 1916. Initiation fee was $1.00 which included the first month dues, button and visiting card case. Their motto was "Friendship, Patriotism & Humanity." As the years progressed, membership grew. By December 10, 1930, 176 members were on record. An unknown number of these veterans also participated in the 75th Memorial Day parade in 1954.

Murphy Movement: Founded by Francis Murphy (1836-1907), an Irish immigrant who worked as a publican (innkeeper) in Maine, the Murphy Movement was designed to help fellow imbibers "see the light." Sympathy in the spirit of

Christian charity was showered upon those powerless to the evils of drink. After signing the following pledge *"With Malice toward none, with charity for all: I, the undersigned, do pledge my word and honor (God helping me) to abstain from all intoxicating liquors as a beverage, and that I will by all honorable means encourage others to abstain"* the undersigned then donned a blue ribbon, symbolizing his signing the pledge.

National Home for Disabled Volunteer Soldiers: One of the last acts signed by President Lincoln before his assassination in 1865, it originally incorporated the National Asylum. Because volunteer soldiers and sailors were not eligible for care in existing army and navy home facilities, the Asylum was designed to care for them. In 1866, a 12 member Board of Managers guided the Home and funding was provided by fines, forfeiture of pay and money due and unclaimed for three years. Pensions could also be forfeited if the member had no dependents. The Asylum was renamed the National Home for Disabled Volunteer Soldiers in 1873.

Between 1867 and 1929, the NHDVS expanded to 10 branches and one sanatorium, the oldest in Togus, Maine, established in 1867 and the last in Bath, New York in 1929.

Nutrition & Food Service: Manages the food service and food production activities and the diet therapy programs, nutritional assessments, resident and family education and employee training and development. The Food Service operates seven days a week, serving on a daily basis an average of 1032 meals. The average cost per meal is $8.12. Fifty-eight per cent of the meals are served cafeteria style while 42% are bedside trays.

Oxford Veterans' Home: Located in the Village of Oxford, NY, the Oxford Veterans' Home was formally opened in April 19, 1897 and immediately admitted 24 resident members. The

Woman's Relief Corps had persuaded New York State to establish and maintain a facility which allowed married veterans to be accompanied by their wives. By 1911, there were 172 resident members at the facility and the Home had expanded to five buildings, including four cottages and an infirmary (now known as the skilled nursing facility).

In 1972, the State legislature appropriated funds to develop plans for a new facility. In 1981, a new one-story building was formally opened. Each resident has a private room sharing an adjoining restroom shared with one other resident. There are no longer cottages identified as A, B, C, and D but were given distinctive names such as Apple, Spruce, Maple, Pine, Hawthorn, and Oak, each named after a tree.

Sons of Union Veterans of the Civil War: Because of its unique requirements for membership, the G.A.R. realized that their organization was destined to become non-existent. In an attempt to carry on their work, several groups were introduced by members of the G.A.R. Among them, the Sons of Veterans of the United States of America, formed on November 12, 1881 by Major A.P. Davis. They attended their first national encampment in 1883. They renamed themselves the Sons of Union Veterans of the G.A.R. and in 1904 they elected to be a civilian patriotic educational society.

In 1925, the name was changed to the Sons of Union Veterans of the Civil War (S.U.V.C.W.) to further identify their heritage. Prior to the death of its last member, the G.A.R. officially designated the S.U.V.C.W. as their legal heir. On August 20, 1954, the S.U.V.C.W. was officially incorporated by an Act of Congress.

As a part of their duty, the S.U.V.C.W. would send a Christmas and Mother's Day Committee to the Bath Soldiers' Home and the Oxford Home bearing gifts and visiting with the old soldiers and spouses. Gifts included tobacco, cigars, cigarettes and pipes, candy, oranges, peanuts, potted plants,

Mother's cards, cretonne and ribbon for bags, postage, printing, carting, express, telephone, radio, transportation and miscellaneous expenses.

Upholstery Program: The Upholstery Pre-Vocational Apprenticeship Program (PVAP) began in 1991. This six-month program teaches veterans to upholster furniture from a bare frame to a finished product; helping veterans to transition to working in small upholstery shops, larger factories, and operating their own businesses. Employers have been eager to hire these veterans because they have received valuable experience and are committed to their new trade. The program has reupholstered approximately 2,500 pieces on station since its inception.

VAMC Fire Department: In the beginning the fire company, which consisted of all able bodied members of the Home who were considered "volunteer firemen" and the Home Police were combined under Security until 1912.

In early June of 1929, the Home Fire Department was formed. It consisted of two forces, one active and the other the auxiliary. The active force was made up of all employees of the engineer's department and members of the Home who were physically able to perform the duty. Three men from this department were to be first, second and third assistant to the engineer. The auxiliary consisted of men on each floor of the barracks and hospital as designated by the surgeon and company commanders. Other men were designated by the quartermaster to have charge of the fire apparatus in the stables, shops, dairy, laundry and other buildings. The Bath Fire Department would be called only if deemed necessary by the chief engineer.

Around 1945, a General Fire Truck Company Pumper built in Michigan was acquired. In 1962, a second Pumper mounted on an International chassis was purchased with the capacity of 750 gallons per minutes. In 1979, this truck was replaced with a 1979 custom built Pumper, which had 1,250 gallons per minute capacity.

In 1964, a 7 ½ horse powered siren was installed on the roof of Section 4 to be used as an alarm signal in case of fire, disaster or other emergency.

Before 1972, the Fire Department and Police were housed in Building 14, which in the early days, was the site of the root or vegetable cellar. That same year the Fire Department and Police became separate departments.

In May of 1980, the Fire Department became the first in Steuben County to have a 5 inch diameter hose.

After September 11, 2001, the facility purchased a Hazardous Materials Response Trailer. All VA Firefighters are Hazardous Materials Technician certified and, because the county does not have a response team, they provide staffing and the trailer for community need. They are also qualified in Mass Decontamination training and have provided training at area hospitals as well as the International Emergency Management Symposium.

Today the Fire Department provides 24-hour, 7-day coverage in the area of fire prevention, protection and suppression, as well as emergency medical response and rescue to this facility which consists of 52 buildings, 2 to 7 stories high with 900,000 square feet of floor space located in 233 acres, including remote wooded areas and has a fire expectancy of moderate to high.

VA Police and Security: Since the Home Guard began in 1879 guardhouses had been placed in various sites upon the grounds. In the 1903 Annual Inventory there is listed a police headquarters, main guardhouse, river guardhouse and guardhouse-Longwell Lane. During the 40's, the guard force consisted of one chief, five civilian guards and three member guards. Violators of rules and regulations of the Home would find themselves in Manager's Court which was held each morning and, if found guilty, members could be sentenced to three days to six months exclusion from the Home, suspension of facility privileges, extra work or confinement. Confinement meant detention in the guardhouse, known as the vegetable cellar, where there were 12 beds and two cells.

In August of 1974, the Veterans Affairs Police and Security Section were activated at this facility. It replaced the Protective Security services provided by members of the Fire Department which was originally known as the Hospital Police Section.

In 1982, the VA police were placed under the office of the Director and the Under-secretary of the VA in Washington.

Due to his surroundings, the officer is required to exercise compassion and understanding. However, with the ever changing environment, the VA Police also changed. The officers must complete a training course in police skills and law enforcement at New Hospital Police Training Center at North Little Rock, Arkansas. CIP weapons were replaced with MACE and later, in 1994, traded in for batons. By October 2002, the VA police were armed with 9mm Baretta firearms. In 1993, they received their first cruiser.

Today, the VA Police provides enforcement of federal and applicable state criminal statutes and Department of Veterans Affairs regulations originating in federal statutes and codes in the physical protection of patients, visitors, and employees: the protection of property of the United States Government and personal property of those on the grounds; the protection of civil rights of all individuals while on federal property, and in the preservation the peaceful environment requisite to the operation of medical treatment programs.

VA Voluntary Services: The VAVS is accountable for the Voluntary Section Program, coordinating and integrating community volunteer resources into the appropriate aspects of the facility. It also develops programs, plans, and procedures for recruiting, selecting, interviewing, placing, training, and evaluating members of the fraternal, civic, local community, youth and veteran organizations into an organized unified group for service to the veteran patients and to gain support to meet the Medical Center's goals and mission.

With over 35 organizations supporting the VAVS, it is one of the largest centralized volunteer programs in the Federal government. Volunteers have provided over 676 million hours of service since 1946.

Veterans Bureau: Following World War I, the National Home was unable to absorb the excessive numbers of disabled veterans returning from overseas, thus the Veterans Bureau, under Charles R. Forbes, was created in 1921. However, the Bureau was plagued with scandals and the reputation of the Home had diminished so much Forbes offered his resignation on Feb. 15, 1923. An immediate Congressional investigation of operations followed. Congress authorized President Hoover to consolidate the National Home, Veterans Bureau and the Bureau of Pensions into the United States Veterans Administration in July of 1930.

ABOUT THE AUTHOR

Robert Yott is a student of the past. His non-fiction works uncovers local and military history; stories he feels need to be told. He served four years in the US Army and spent 35 years in the construction trade. Robert retired to a hobby beef farm in New York's southern tier. He lives there with his loving wife, Mona and their three cats.

Made in the USA
Middletown, DE
20 May 2024